WOODLAND STALKING

WOODLAND STALKING

PETER CARNE

SWAN·HILL
PRESS

Except where otherwise acknowledged, all
photographs reproduced in this book, including those
in colour, are by the author.

First published in the UK in 1999
by Swan Hill Press, an imprint of Airlife Publishing Ltd

British Library Cataloguing-in-Publication Data
A catalogue record for this book
is available from the British Library

ISBN 1 85310 856 1

Printed in Hong Kong

Swan Hill Press
an imprint of Airlife Publishing Ltd
101 Longden Road, Shrewsbury, SY3 9EB, England

Contents

Acknowledgments

T his book owes much to very many kind friends who have helped me in a variety of ways, not least those who tutored and guided me at the beginning of my own activities as a leisure-time woodland stalker, some thirty-five years ago. I am indebted in particular to those whose guest I have been at different times and places, and to property owners and others who have entrusted me to offer help with deer control and management, a privilege I have greatly valued and which has enabled me to broaden my experience and knowledge in a field which is endlessly challenging.

I owe a particular debt of gratitude to John Childs, who recently retired as Training Officer for the British Deer Society, for updating me on training facilities provided by that organisation and for patiently dealing with my queries, and to Peter Watson, Deer Officer for the British Association for Shooting and Conservation, and James Cordery of Sparsholt College, Hampshire, for supplying me with details of their respective stalking and training facilities. Others who have taken time and trouble to point me in appropriate directions on aspects in which they specialise include my long-time friend Fred Courtier, a former Game Warden to the Forestry Commission who now lives in retirement in the New Forest, Richard Prior, Dominic Griffith, Stuart Clark, Peter Robyns, Graham Stride, Roger Saunders of Jägersport, Armstrong's of Carlton, Fulton's of Bisley, Litt's of Newport in Gwent, and Chaplin's the gunsmiths of Winchester.

I am especially grateful to Guy Wallace, the professional dog trainer, for giving me the benefit of his expertise on dogs for deer, and to that doyen of deer men worldwide, G. Kenneth Whitehead, for allowing me access to published material of his own on trophy evaluation and for casting a critical eye over what I have written here about trophies. I warmly thank Christopher Borthen, Editor of *Stalking Magazine*, for allowing me to refer to articles by Kenneth Whitehead in that journal and to the accompanying graphics. I owe a very special debt of gratitude to Christopher for finding the time in his busy professional life to read the proofs of this book, a task performed with his customary editorial meticulousness and keen eye for detail.

Forest Enterprise has been helpful in supplying me with details of stalking facilities for clients on its various properties, and my special thanks are due to the Press Office of the Forestry Commission at Edinburgh, to Mrs J. Jones of the North and East England Forest Region headquarters office at York and the following Chief or Head Rangers: Jim Alexander, Trevor Banham, T.K. Bradbury, John Cubby, Peter Eccles and Derek Stocker, not forgetting C.J. Large, Forest District Manager at Rothbury in Northumberland. Where I live, in Hampshire, I have received much help from our local Forest Ranger, Eddie Moorhouse, as well as from the Forestry Commission at Lyndhurst, in particular New Forest Chief Keeper Martin Noble, Head Keeper Michael Clarke (now retired) and Keepers Jonathan Cook, Derek Thomson and Ian Young.

My old friend Chris Boulton, whose knowledge of matters rural has a breadth and depth unsurpassed by anyone else I know and who has helped me in a multitude of ways has given me sage advice on many matters dealt with in this book.

Colin McKelvie, in his role as Consultant Editor to the publishers, has given me much encouragement and guided me past potential pitfalls, but any errors of commission or omission which have slipped through the net unnoticed are of course my sole responsibility.

My wife, Gladys, has as always been supportive to a fault. Without her patience and forbearance in allowing part of our mutual living space to double as a writer's den this book could never have been written. In it I have not attempted to answer every possible query or to offer solutions to every problem, but what I have learned about woodland stalking, and some of the opinions I have expressed, will I hope be judged worth the reading.

Introduction

Much has been written about deerstalking but comparatively little about what, for the sake of convenience, is generally labelled 'woodland stalking', by no means all of which takes place in actual woodland although much of it does. Even less modern deer literature has attempted to deal in the round with all six species of deer which present opportunities for woodland stalking in Great Britain. This book endeavours to fill the gap.

No claim is made to be handing down tablets of stone upon which are engraved all the accumulated wisdom of woodland stalkers past and present. What is written here is offered in all humility as some of the fruits of the varied experience of one stalker, who does not pretend to know all the answers or assume that the views expressed are necessarily ones with which other stalkers of experience will universally agree. Upon learning that the book was in preparation, a much-respected long-time friend of mine brought me down to earth with a bump by telling me that if he, who happens to be a retired professional stalker of immense experience, had

been asked to write such a book, he would have turned down the invitation. Why? 'Because there are too many experts', ready to pounce and criticise, weighing in with contrary views of their own.

This I regard as no bad thing. If this book achieves little more than to stimulate critical thought and constructive discussion among my fellow woodland stalkers, thus enlarging our common pool of knowledge and leading to improved performance, it will have served a useful purpose. If there is one thing about woodland stalking upon which all of us are agreed, it is that learning never stops – or never should do. New developments constantly thrust themselves upon our attention. We can all learn from each other, which is one reason why this book is addressed alike to complete beginners and to dyed-in-the-wool practitioners who, having read it, will step forward and furnish us all with their own pearls of wisdom. Here, at least, is something to help wile away a few of those long and tedious winter evenings or to enjoy browsing through at bedtime.

CHAPTER 1
A Sport and a Service

Deerstalking used to be the sport of princes, peers, professional people of high standing, captains of industry and the like, and it still is. Now, though, it also attracts very many others from all walks of life, and their number is increasing. Yet it is still a minority sport, with a following which in no way compares with those for whom the shotgun is the sporting weapon of choice, and for whom winged game is the primary quarry. To this extent stalkers remain able to look upon their sport as the pastime, if not of a privileged elite in the old-fashioned sense, at least of those who are privileged in the sense of having a special responsibility for the well-being and good management of some of the largest wild land-mammals in the northern hemisphere.

Hunting, in the broadest meaning of the word, being innate in human nature, it is natural that the pursuit of relatively large quarry, 'big game' if you like to call it that, should have a particular appeal to those in whom the hunting instinct is still strong. Many have dreamt of hunting the traditional big game of Africa and elsewhere, and of following in the footsteps of great names like Selous and 'Karamojo' Bell, whose exploits are legendary, reading almost like a fairytale in the shrinking world of today. Some of us have had the good fortune of being able to enjoy, perhaps in our younger days, at least a brief spell in one of those parts of the world where big game, especially hoofed game, was still abundant and available. Having acquired a taste for hunting such game, many have looked around, perhaps without much hope at first, for possible alternatives nearer home.

Deer are obvious candidates. Until fairly recently, however, access to deer as a quarry for rifle sport was virtually restricted, in the case of Great Britain, to the Scottish Highlands and islands, with their deer forests where red deer have long been preserved and managed for stalking. Opportunities are nowadays very much more widely available, as are a number of other species besides red deer.

This change has taken place almost entirely since the Second World War, and is the legacy of a chain of events dating back to a much earlier time. A hundred years ago wild deer in Britain, outside of Scotland, were at one of the lowest ebbs in their history. The royal deer forests of earlier centuries had been progressively whittled down in size and number to a point where hardly any survived, and with the forests of the past had vanished their deer. South of the Scottish border the only significant herds of wild red deer remaining were in the Lake District and on Exmoor and the Quantock Hills in south-west England. Fallow still roamed wild in the New Forest, albeit in greatly reduced numbers, despite having been officially banished, and a remnant lived on in Epping Forest and in a very few other localities.

With roe deer the case was different. A century earlier they had become no more than a memory throughout almost the whole of England and Wales and much of Scotland. Then, in or around 1800, the species was reintroduced by private landowners to two estates in southern England. They quickly took root and began to colonise surrounding areas. By the end of the nineteenth century there were wild roe once more in Dorset, in parts of some adjoining counties, and in West Sussex. By then, further translocations had restored roe to parts of Scotland, where the indigenous population had almost certainly died out, and to one corner of East Anglia. The range of roe was still very restricted, but the seed had been sown for later expansion once circumstances were propitious.

As for the alien deer so familiar now in various parts of Britain and Ireland, these were virtually unknown when the twentieth century began, and would remain so for some time longer. A few were already present in deer parks, at that time a feature of almost every landed estate of consequence in England and of many others in Scotland, Wales and Ireland. The principal deer in these parks were fallow, always considered to be particularly decorative and suitable for being maintained in confinement, as indeed many had been throughout the centuries when this species was also a denizen of many royal forests as well as of numerous chases – un-enclosed areas of land, often under several different ownerships, reserved for deer and for hunting by specified non-royal individuals.

To remain 'leak-proof', deer park walls and fences need regular maintenance. Fences breached by fallen trees and park gates carelessly left open have been speedily taken advantage of by deer throughout the centuries. Deer in parks may be confined, but they are not domesticated, being more accurately defined as wild animals under restraint, such restraint being conditional upon barriers to their freedom remaining permanently in place. Accidents will happen, however, and once park deer, especially fallow, find themselves at liberty, they are apt to be very

An example of bark-stripping, which in this case eventually caused the death of the tree.

unwilling indeed to relinquish their new-found freedom.

In times past, though, this freedom was likely to be brief. Any deer which could not be coaxed or driven back into their park of origin were fairly quickly shot, estate staff being sufficiently numerous and owners more than anxious to ensure that this was done, and so, with some few exceptions, it was. All this changed in the twentieth century. The Lloyd George Budget of 1909 and subsequent measures imposed what many landed proprietors and others considered to be punitive taxation, ultimately sounding the death-knell of many an ancient family property.

With the break-up of large landed estates came the demise of many a deer park. In some cases the deer were left to roam free where this would never have been permitted by an earlier generation. In other instances deer park walls, left unrepaired through lack of money, began to crumble. Broken fences were not renewed, so deer escaped and remained at large. The upheavals of two world wars played an even more significant part in the same process. Deer parks were turned into military camps or transformed into agricultural units, the result in both cases being the same – the liberation of any deer which had not previously been exterminated.

With gamekeepers and other estate employees mostly having joined the armed services or having been otherwise redeployed into helping the national war effort, there was often nobody locally available to deal with escaped park deer. However, depredations to crops in those times of chronic food shortage provoked retaliatory measures, in which county war agricultural committees played their part, directed at killing these cervine plunderers by any and every means to hand.

Shotguns were universally employed to achieve this purpose, preferably, although not always, using SSG or other heavy-gauge shot to maximise the chance of a kill. In the New Forest and a few other places, deer drives to shotguns had been the norm for a fairly long period, strict rules of procedure having evolved to try to ensure that no deer wounded but not killed outright was left to suffer when the shoot was over. In the case of the New Forest, all the shooting was done by keepers working as a team of ten or a dozen. Beagles were always on hand to follow up any deer hit but not immediately recovered. All other shooting was suspended until the victim was found and humanely despatched if it was not already dead. I once attended one of these drives and was impressed by the effort made to ensure that everything went smoothly, according to a prearranged plan. On that occasion three dead deer were the net result of a hard day's work by four times that number of keepers.

At another time, in a large wood in Wiltshire, I found myself in the thick of a roe deer drive one February day when I was walking in the area. My abiding memory of that day was the substantial cull of roebucks, all with antlers still in velvet, many of which were of excellent quality. It seemed such a waste that they should have died in such a manner, at such a time, rather than being spared until antler growth was complete, two months or more later. They would have produced trophies any keen stalker would have given much to secure – or to pass up as first-rate breeding stock too good to be wantonly culled.

Both these events occurred in the mid-1950s, many years before the law of the land took any account of deer – what times of the year each sex might be shot, in what circumstances and with what weapons. This is not to say no one cared. Pressure was building in some quarters to find a much more acceptable way of controlling the numbers of Britain's wild deer, which by that time were very widespread and comprised half a

Unless adequately controlled, deer can cause unacceptable damage such as the bark-stripping to which this tree has been subjected.

dozen species. As well as fallow deer fugitives from parks and their descendants, and some red deer of similar origin, roe deer were becoming much more widespread. The reafforestation which began in Britain in earnest shortly after the First World War played an important part in this by greatly extending suitable habitat.

In addition, sika deer, at that time more generally known as Japanese deer from the country of origin of at least most of them, were making their presence apparent to foresters and others in various parts of England, Scotland and Ireland. Where they had become numerous they posed problems of their own. Another Asian deer species, muntjac, still had a limited distribution but was steadily increasing, although its potential for causing damage and needing any degree of control was as yet little apparent. As for Chinese water deer, these much more secretive Orientals still led lives that were largely a

When deer numbers become excessive, severe winter weather can cause heavy casualties. These fallow deer were victims of the exceptionally severe 1962-63 winter.

mystery to most of us who were doing our best to enlarge our knowledge of deer.

One thing we did understand all too well was that, whatever might be the case in a few special places like the New Forest, deer control methods in Britain in general left a great deal to be desired. Deer driven past lines of people armed with shotguns were killed quite unselectively. Drives mostly took place at the end of the season, when pheasant shooting was over and 'vermin' could be dealt with by the gamekeeper and his friends. These latter tended to be a mixed bunch, ranging from those who had helped out as beaters and pickers-up on driven game shoots to farmers, country neighbours in general and almost anyone who was willing to tote a gun for such occasions.

Preliminary briefings did not always cover every likely contingency or make due allowance for varying levels of competence by the shoot participants, such as stressing the importance of shooting only at very short range – at best, not more than 25 yards – to minimise the risk of wounding rather than killing the deer outright. One had only to relate the number of shots fired to the total bag at the day's end to be aware just how random much of the shooting often was and how many deer were almost certainly 'walking wounded' as a result, or perhaps had crawled away, to die slowly, unseen and in great pain and distress.

The sheer scale of these annual deer drives throughout the length and breadth of Britain reflected a horrifying volume of potential cruelty. Even worse, it was demonstrably the case that they were not achieving their purpose of reducing deer numbers sufficiently in relation to the damage they caused to farm and forest crops. In an effort to make up the shortfall, recourse was often had to snaring, even by Forestry Commission staff on land owned by the State. I well recall being told that in one southern England forest with a large deer population, up to 90% of the annual cull was at one time achieved by snaring.

All this went on out of public view, otherwise there would surely have been an outcry which would have made protests against conventional field sports by abolitionists seem feeble by comparison. Those in the know who were concerned about these matters aired their views in the sporting press and pressed for change via bodies such as the Deer Group, set up in 1953 to promote the study and proper conservation of these animals.

Moves were afoot behind the scenes to bring about radical changes within the Forestry Commission. In 1956 the Commission appointed its first Game Warden, who set about training a staff of wildlife rangers in the essentials of modern deer management as practised in Germany and elsewhere on the Continent. The basic control tool was the rifle. Widespread prejudice against rifles on grounds of safety had hitherto made it seem unlikely that they would ever be acceptable for controlling deer in Britain

Young broadleaved trees in particular need protection by plastic tree shelters in areas of high deer density.

except in sparsely populated areas such as the deer forests of the Highlands. I can remember being forthrightly assured by a New Forest keeper that, whatever might happen elsewhere, it would never be deemed safe to use rifles for deer control in a public access area such as that where he was employed. Born to a family whose male members had been forest keepers for generations, he was a man for whose detailed knowledge of local conditions and circumstances I had always had great respect, but on this matter of rifles and their supposed unsuitability for replacing shotguns against deer in the New Forest, time was to prove him – and others – wrong.

One of the new Game Warden's first tasks was

to demonstrate how, with proper precautions, rifles could safely be used for deer culling in almost any situation. Once this view gained wider acceptance the way became clearer for legislation aimed at the improvement of methods for managing deer. Scotland was the first beneficiary, with an Act in 1959 embodying various protective measures for red deer in that country, although in this case problems other than shotguns were the main driving force for change. In 1963, the year which saw the founding of the British Deer Society, another new era was inaugurated with the passing of a Deer Act for England and Wales which, among other important provisions, gave particular impetus to the general adoption of rifles for deer control, on public land and otherwise.

It was while attending a House of Commons celebration of the passing of the 1963 Deer Bill into law that I was invited by one of its sponsors, the late John Cordle, M.P. to introduce deer control with the rifle to a shoot with which he was involved, in a corner of southern England where shotgun drives had been the rule up to then. Being able to instigate such a change was both a privilege and a great responsibility which made me all the more aware of the likely consequences of failure, but the happy outcome was that shotguns were never used again there to keep the deer population in check.

As the 1960s progressed and deer control by rifle, reinforced now by the law, became the rule, woodland stalking came into its own not just as a sport but as a necessary service performed by a steadily growing number of people. In the early days many were self-taught, but as experience was gained wild deer in Britain were able to benefit from being elevated at long last from the status of mere vermin, to which they had sunk over the centuries from the royal game they had once been.

CHAPTER 2
Two Kinds of Stalking

Deerstalking is not an ancient sport. Its first beginnings in Britain were in the early nineteenth century, when the development of firearms reached a stage which made possible an alternative way of culling deer to methods employed in the Scottish Highlands, in particular, up to that time. These earlier methods were minor variants of what, in Gaelic, was called a *tainchell* – a drive organised perhaps once a year in which all the members of the clan would play their part and in which hundreds of deer might be slain.

In preparation for one of these hunts, men with dogs would spread themselves around the chosen area. This would be sufficiently large to contain a substantial number of deer, and for the manoeuvre of surrounding it to be accomplished without disturbing them. At a given signal the ring of humans and dogs would close in from the sides and rear, leaving a narrow open neck at the front where the principal slaughter would take place, originally with cold steel or its equivalent in pre-firearm times, and later with powder and shot.

Some of these *tainchells* were major spectacles to which distinguished guests were invited. One such was arranged in the sixteenth century by the Earl of Atholl to entertain Mary Queen of Scots, and the kill was prodigious, accounting for fallow deer, roe and some wolves as well as the red deer which, as one would anticipate, were the principal quarry.

In some parts of the Highlands, the Isle of Rhum being one, drystone walls were constructed to surround selected areas of deer ground to facilitate these drives. With men and dogs behind them, any deer thus enclosed were then funnelled, on the appointed day for a drive, towards the killing-ground in the narrow neck left open for this purpose.

Deerhounds had an important part to play in these operations, their particular role being to pursue and pull down animals that might otherwise have escaped. In the very early days of stalking, and for quite a long time afterwards, it was customary to have hounds on the leash to run down and secure any beast that was wounded but not killed by the vital shot. In the days before magazine rifles this was particularly important, as early single-shot weapons and even some double-barrelled rifles were much less predictably accurate than their modern counterparts.

Two particular individuals may be said to have been primarily responsible for putting deerstalking firmly on the map as a sporting activity. The first was William Scrope, whose book, *The Art of Deer-Stalking*, published in 1839, uniquely evoked the joys as well as the trials and the trauma of pitting one's energies, determination and wits against the 'monarchs of the glen', as Edwin Landseer was later to laud them in his famous painting. By taking up the new field sport during sojourns at Balmoral, Prince Albert set the stamp of royal endorsement on it, which did more than almost anything else to give deerstalking the seal of approval it needed to be generally accepted as the premier

Woodland stalking is a relatively new field sport in Britain and Ireland.

Ancient deer forests once again came into their own and new ones joined them, many on land which had scarcely seen a deer for generations. Minor mansions posing as shooting lodges sprang up in unlikely places, miles of new access roads were constructed and Highland people found new employment as professional stalkers, ponymen, and in a range of other capacities to provide for the needs of the incomers when they came north every autumn for a few weeks' escape from the dark, satanic mills of Victorian industry. As more and more land was required for deer, sheep were removed to make room for them and the whole of Highland life was refocused upon what had now become an element of unsurpassed importance in the local scheme of things.

Surveying the red deer for the stalking of which they were paying out so much money, many newcomers concluded that deer of Highland stock were undersized, puny and generally of poor quality value compared with their deer park cousins in kindlier latitudes. More money was therefore laid out on the purchase and transport to the Highlands of some of these heavy-antlered prodigies, quite often a largely fruitless exercise because the qualities thus imported endured for no more than a generation before the deer reverted to type, at a level of quality determined less by good breeding than by an environment exceptionally harsh and unforgiving.

As with any new field sport, conventional practices and modes of operation soon evolved to meet the needs of the situation. Stalking tenants could not be expected to cope single-handed with the varied demands of unfamiliar topography, stamina-testing terrain and climate, a notably unpredictable quarry and the ultimate logistics of conveying shot beasts from hill to larder.

The lynch-pin of it all was the full-time professional stalker. His job being an all-year-round one, he could be looked upon to know every inch of the ground in his care, every nuance of changing weather and how this might affect the day's stalking and, above all, how best to conduct his employer or perhaps a guest 'rifle' undetected to within range of a shootable stag. The ponyman with his garrons, as these animals were called, would wait at a distance for a signal

With the long distances usually involved, spying for deer on the open hill makes the use of a telescope, in this case a two-draw one, almost essential. In the very different conditions of woodland stalking, binoculars are more appropriate.

Highland sport and a pillar of the Highland economy.

This process was aided by several factors. The early to mid-nineteenth century was a time of unprecedented economic expansion, with England 'the workshop of the world' and many newly-rich manufacturers and others looking around for ways of enjoying some of their wealth. For any who looked to the Scottish Highlands, previous problems of access were greatly eased by those new inventions, the steamboat and, later, the railway. Impoverished lairds were only too pleased at the appearance on their scene of this new breed of seasonal Highlanders, people with plenty of money to spend and the will to do it in ways that would benefit landowners as well as themselves. Leases were readily agreed, and red deer gained enhanced esteem as the *raison d'être* for this new prosperity.

to come and collect any fallen stags. In more recent times, on many forests, mechanical transport has replaced equine assistance.

Right up to the point of squeezing the trigger, the 'rifle' of the day is in the hands of the professional stalker, who will spy out the ground with his 'glass' or telescope, locate a shootable stag and then work out how best to approach it. He will also carry the rifle until the person who is to use it has been brought to a position from which he can take the hoped-for shot. All this is normally done in the open, 'on the hill' as the usually mountainous ground is invariably referred to with characteristic understatement. To anyone wholly unfamiliar with the Scottish Highland scene, the term 'deer forest' must seem an excessively imaginative description for country quite often devoid of trees.

With open hill stalking, the established practice is for the deer forest owner or lessee and his guests to address their attention exclusively to stags, of which a predetermined number will have been earmarked for culling during the relatively short open season, between August and mid-October. Most of the stalking will be done during the last six weeks of the season, working up to a peak in the final fortnight, when the annual rut will be in progress. In August many younger stags will still have their antlers encased in the hairy coating of skin and blood vessels called velvet, which will not be rubbed off until antler growth is complete, although this may not prevent such animals of particularly poor quality from being singled out for shooting.

The culling of hinds is traditionally left to the professional stalker and his assistants and is carried out during the winter, when the days are short and weather conditions most extreme. Hind control in these circumstances is very hard work. It is also vitally important for the management of the herd that sufficient females are shot each year to minimise mortality from shortage of food and seasonal stresses as well as to keep the overall deer population at a level which can be sustained without unacceptable damage to the environment – a golden rule for deer management, on the hill or anywhere else.

Many professional stalkers prefer to do this work themselves. Others invite friends, and on some deer forests client stalkers are nowadays accepted as participants in the hind cull. This much more modestly priced alternative to stalking stags, which is also now fairly widely available on a daily basis through sporting agencies and a number of hotels, provides an annual Highland holiday for some stalkers from the south who may never have any other opportunity for the sport.

In the course of successive visits, such guest stalkers acquire the special skills demanded by Highland conditions and so become useful team members for hind-culling operations rather than time-consuming amateurs requiring constant ghillying. Those who have yet to try it may become tempted, in the process, to suppose that low-ground stalking requires no different skills and is surely far easier as well as infinitely less demanding physically. The truth could hardly be more different, as many have had cause to discover.

For low-ground stalking read 'woodland stalking', a term now generally accepted as applying to all types of deerstalking other than that on the hill in Scotland, the North of England or elsewhere – there are a few estates in Cumbria and some properties in Ireland where high-ground stalking is conducted along similar lines to its Highland counterpart. Within this all-embracing definition, woodland stalking includes stalking on farmland or anywhere else away from cover. It also includes still-hunting – shooting from a set position rather than moving around – so that in this connection 'stalking', strictly speaking, is a misnomer, unless it takes account of the crucial need for a silent and stealthy approach to whatever point of vantage has been chosen for an ambush!

The dim dawn of woodland stalking broke in the closing decades of the nineteenth century, when a few individual sportsmen perceived the merits of this method of getting on terms with roe in particular. Fallow deer in the New Forest also furnished sport of this nature for the then Deputy Surveyor or Chief Forest Officer, the Hon. Gerald Lascelles who, in his book *Thirty-Five Years in the New Forest*, published soon after his retirement at the beginning of the First World War, recorded the delight he obtained from 'creeping the rides' for this purpose on a summer's evening. Roe in Ireland had a brief history as a species introduced to one area, the Lissadell estate of the Gore-Booth family in

County Sligo, where they are on record as having been stalked with a rook rifle when they emerged from cover towards sundown. These immigrants were later sacrificed to the need to protect a forest nursery against deer damage, with the result that stalkers in Ireland who wish to try their luck with roe now have to cross the water to do so – as quite a number in fact do.

The early twentieth century saw a few pioneering spirits like the late Frank Wallace and Henry Tegner stalking roe deer with the rifle and telling the rest of us, through their writings, just what fine sport we were all missing. Then woodland stalking in Great Britain was given a very decided fillip by a number of Continental *émigrés* seeking asylum here from the Nazis, who taught us how this sport played an important part in deer management in Germany, Poland and several other mid-European countries, where it was firmly rooted in the life of the countryside.

A further boost came after the Second World War when many servicemen learned for themselves what woodland stalking as practised in Germany and elsewhere was all about, and brought their new knowledge back to Britain.

This perhaps was the most important individual influence in eventually bringing about a root-and-branch reappraisal of how deer ought to be managed in woodland conditions in Great Britain. The Forestry Commission's first Game Warden, the late H.A. ('Herbie') Fooks, was himself a man well grounded in Continental deer management methods, having earlier been in overall charge of forest game management in the British Zone of Occupation in Germany. His manual summarising methods of deer control in woodland areas, published in the 1960s by the British Deer Society, was one of the first guides of its kind to be available in English.

Woodland stalking now has as secure a place as any among established British field sports. We have learned much from our overseas neighbours and, having tested what we have learned against British conditions, have adapted some points of detail in the light of experience gained and thereby developed our own approach to what many have come to recognise as a particularly challenging and rewarding outdoor activity which has a vital contribution to make in the sphere of sound countryside management.

CHAPTER 3

Six Species of Deer

Whereas stalking on the hill is almost exclusively concerned with one species, woodland stalking can involve up to six different kinds of deer – the whole range of species present in the wild state in Britain – or, in the case of Ireland, three species. This potentially wide variety of possible quarry is part of the sport's appeal. There is no one woodland or other low-ground area where all six kinds of deer in Britain are to be found, although there are quite a number of places where two or even three species share the same ground and consequently need to be controlled. While there are basic rules and guidelines for stalking which are applicable to all, each species poses challenges and problems of its own. The first priority for anyone new to stalking is not to worry too much about these at this early stage but to familiarise oneself with the deer themselves, their differing characteristics and their individual status as wild animals in these islands.

Red deer (*Cervus elaphus*)

As Britain's and Ireland's largest wild land mammal, red deer stand up to about 1.2 metres (4 ft) high at the shoulder and may weigh as much as 150 kg (330 lb) in the case of stags, although size and weight can vary considerably, dependent upon the quality of the habitat and the condition of the individual beast. Red deer in southern deer parks, in the south-west of England, East Anglia and in woodland conditions generally, are on average considerably heavier in both body and antler development than those living in the harsher climatic and environmental conditions of the open hill in northern England and Scotland. In Ireland similar variations occur between those in the south and the north of the island. Female red deer (hinds) are usually about 15 cm (6 in) shorter in stature than adult males and weigh about one-third less. Stags are altogether bulkier than hinds, and with the approach of the rut in autumn a stag's neck thickens and grows a mane. Hinds are of much more graceful build and their necks are characteristically slender.

Coat colour is the same in both sexes: reddish-brown in summer on the back and flanks, changing in autumn to a much thicker and coarser grey-brown winter coat, which grows through the summer pelage. When the heavy winter coats are shed in spring, coming out in great tufts as their owners brush against vegetation or barbed-wire fences or merely lie down, the deer look scruffy and moth-eaten until the change is complete. Buffish-coloured all the year round, the rump patch or speculum is surmounted by a shortish, wedge-shaped tail.

The stags grow antlers which, at first, may consist of no more than a single spike on each side, becoming progressively bigger and branchier with each succeeding year's regrowth until the animal reaches its prime, after which antlers will tend to become blunt at the tips, have fewer points or tines and generally decline. Antlers grow from bony projections from the skull known as pedicles. The ridge at the base of each antler is called the coronet. In a typical mature, good quality 'head' each antler will consist of the main stem or beam with a brow tine near the base, a second (bez or bay) tine and a third (trez or tray) tine a few inches farther up the beam, and then a varying number of points on top, ideally forming a crown or cup. Linear indentations along the beam and tines are known as gutters.

Most red deer antlers are cast in March or April, older beasts dropping theirs first. A few young stags, especially yearlings (called brockets) with their first modest growth of headgear, may still be antlered in May or even June. Within its covering of skin, blood vessels and nerve tissue known as velvet, new antler growth begins almost at once and progresses rapidly. By late August or early September regrowth is complete except in the case of the youngest stags. Having served its purpose of nourishing and protecting the new antlers as they grow, the velvet dies and is rubbed off against trees, ground vegetation or anything else to hand. Stag groups start to break up as the older animals begin to make their way to traditional rutting areas in readiness for taking up their individual rutting stands or to challenge master stags for dominance of the hind harems claimed as their own.

Well before the end of September the rut is usually in full swing. As it progresses harems tend to become smaller, and as master stags tire or are ousted younger males have their chance to take over, although many may never manage to reproduce their kind at all. Around mid-October the rut begins to wane, although some activity is likely to continue into November. Hinds are served as they individually come into season, whether during the main rut or otherwise. At the height of the rut stags utter their characteristic challenging roar and often make themselves black and fearsome-looking by rolling in peat or mud wallows. Roaring tends to be less evident in woodland conditions, and harems tend to be smaller than those on the open hill.

With the rut over, exhausted stags regroup with their own kind in loosely organised assemblages to spend some time recovering condition before winter sets in. Hinds with their followers live in matriarchal groups with a well-defined 'pecking order' determining status within the group. Calves, as infant red deer are called, are mostly born around midsummer, are almost invariably single and, like most new-born deer, are white-spotted on the flanks for the first few weeks of life. Within a very short time they are on their feet and able to follow adult deer on their normal day-to-day movements. They remain dependent upon their mothers for both milk and education until autumn is well advanced.

In woodland conditions red deer are crepuscular in the main, emerging from cover towards dusk, often continuing to feed through much of the night and retreating into the trees soon after dawn, there to remain hidden until evening but with their presence made all too obvious by their large, oval hoofmarks or slots. Such large animals cannot move around without leaving much other tell-tale evidence over a period of time. In woodland they browse as well

as graze, and on neighbouring farmland can cause much damage among root crops in particular, while in summer they may flatten growing corn simply by lying in it instead of making their way back to cover in the woods as the sun comes up.

The Scottish Highlands contain the largest coherent population of red deer anywhere in Europe. Most lead an open-hill existence throughout the year, but where wooded wintering grounds at lower altitudes are available these, of course, are made full use of, and an increasing number live more or less permanently in the forestry plantations from which they were originally excluded by deerproof fencing.

Nearly all the larger Western Isles of Scotland have red deer and they are well established as woodland-dwellers in Galloway, in southern Scotland. In the Lake District there are separate open-hill and woodland populations, while in south-west England the wild red deer of Exmoor and the Quantock Hills live partly in woodland and partly on high moorland and other open land including farmland, moving freely between the two. By far the highest densities of red deer in the West Country are in the areas hunted by the three packs of staghounds – the Devon and Somerset (basically Exmoor and its surrounding coverts), the Quantock and the Tiverton (moorland, marginal farmland and woodland south of the former Taunton to Barnstaple railway). Red deer also occur at much lighter densities in woodland areas of west Devon and east Cornwall.

Elsewhere in England there are a number of small, isolated feral populations of red deer, mostly descended from park escapes or, in some cases, deliberate releases, all of which are highly vulnerable to indiscriminate shooting and survive in the wild through enjoying some measure of protection. Two of the largest individual populations of this type are in the New Forest and in the Thetford Forest area of south-west Norfolk and north-west Suffolk. Individual red deer have a relatively large home range which can often bring them into conflict with farmers and others to whom their incursions are decidedly unwelcome, which is one of the reasons why there are not more of them in the wild. Odd ones, especially stags, sometimes stray many miles from the regular haunts of their species, and will not uncommonly team up with domestic livestock or even, occasionally, with other deer species in the absence of their own kind – a trait by no means confined to red deer.

The main areas in Britain where woodland red deer are stalked with the rifle are Dumfries and Galloway, and Grizedale Forest in southern Lakeland. An increasing number of red deer are nowadays culled by stalkers around the fringes of stag-hunting country in south-west England, but stag-hunting enthusiasts are reluctant to encourage this. Wild red deer in Ireland almost all live on the open hill, in and around Killarney, Wicklow and Donegal's Glenveagh National Parks, so they offer little opportunity on that island for woodland stalking.

Roe deer (*Capreolus capreolus*)

Like red deer, roe are a native British species, although some present-day populations are of Continental origin or have been influenced to some extent by introductions from the Continent. Roe are not native to Ireland, and although some were introduced to an estate in County Sligo in the nineteenth century the survival of this stock was fairly short-lived.

Of the half-dozen deer species which now occur in the wild state in Britain, roe come fourth in order of size, standing from about 60 to 75 cm (2 ft to 2 ft 6 in) or slightly higher at the shoulder. There is only a small difference in size and body weight between the two sexes, the males (bucks) weighing up to about 30 kg (66 lb) while the females (does) scale around 5 kg (11 lb) lighter. The upright or slightly lyrate, typically three-pointed, antlers of the bucks are rarely more than 25 to 30 cm (10 to 12 in) long in mature animals living in optimum conditions of food and habitat. Three-antlered specimens sometimes occur, the third antler usually being vestigial and growing from what in effect is a double pedicle on one side. Does with vestigial antlers, almost always in velvet, are not uncommon. Coat colour changes from a warm foxy-red with a buffish rear end in summer to greyish-brown on the head, back and flanks, with black markings around the muzzle and a prominent buffish-white rump patch, expandable

under the impetus of alarm, during the winter half of the year. The very short tail is invisible in the field, being hidden among the hair at the base of the spine.

The annual cycle in roe is different from that of other deer species. Bucks cast their antlers in November or early December, growing new ones during the winter, which are complete and clean of velvet by April or early May, older animals being first to complete the process. While in velvet several bucks may consort together, but once antler growth is complete a strong territorial instinct asserts itself. As mature bucks lay claim to individual territories from which they aim to exclude all others, a great deal of chivvying and chasing goes on in spring while disputes are resolved, immature and inferior bucks being relegated to fringe areas.

Things settle down somewhat by June, with a relatively quiet spell then prevailing for a few weeks until the rut begins in the second half of July, or sometimes earlier. With roe this inspires no distinctive vocal activity, though the rhythmic 'bough-bough-bough' bark of alarm uttered by both sexes when disturbed at any season is perhaps more readily aroused at the time of the rut than otherwise. A roe buck being seen off by another will utter panting, hoarse gasps as if of protest or perhaps of fear for its life while being pursued. Fights at this time can be vicious and sometimes fatal if a participant briefly presents an unguarded flank to its adversary.

Contrary to what is sometimes thought, roe are not monogamous. Bucks will opportunistically serve any available doe which comes into season, and a doe which has not conceived from one mating will accept a second attempt by a different partner, should one materialise. A buck paying court to a doe in season will quite often chase her in circles or figures of eight before she submits to his advances. That such a doe has no intention of not being 'caught' becomes all too clear if something happens to prevent the intended outcome of these antics. I once shot a buck in the act of mating, and the frustration of the doe on seeing her swain collapse in mid-action was made apparent as she stood there, staring and barking in perplexity before making her departure.

Bucks give vent to their own frustrations by thrashing saplings with their antlers, thereby advertising their presence not just to does and to other bucks but also to foresters and others reluctant to tolerate any damage they may cause to young plantations. Two or three months previously they will have left their mark on other young trees while removing velvet from their antlers and delineating the limits of their respective territories.

Bucks remain continually active and on the move through the height of the rut, which continues into August, dying away around the middle of that month. A short secondary or 'false' rut is sometimes noticed in October, probably spurred by very young does or others coming very late into season. Precocious doe kids (fawns) of the year sometimes produce kids of their own a year later as the result of a late conception.

Roe are one of those mammal species, badgers being another example, in which conception is followed by delayed implantation of the ovum. After lying dormant until late December, the fertilised egg then implants and development rapidly proceeds. Twin births are more common than singles and triplets are not rare, especially where food and habitat are of the best. Most kids are born around the end of the third week in May, but births have also been recorded both a good deal earlier and later. Kids remain dependent upon maternal support for some months, not just for milk but, as in the case of other deer, for education. A doe will continue to be accompanied by her young of the previous year until quite late in the following spring when, with new arrivals imminent, the yearlings are obliged to make their own way in the world.

Does are not truly territorial but will occupy individual home ranges which may overlap to some extent, quite often with those of grown-up daughters. In winter and early spring small random assemblages of does and their followers suggest some measure of herding activity, and roe will congregate where appropriate to enjoy the 'early bite' of fresh spring greenery on farmland. In no sense however can roe be considered truly gregarious. It is the mutual intolerance of these deer at too high densities – bucks of other bucks for much of the year, and does of does – which is the driving force in the expansion of the species into new areas, a process which accounts for their presence in much of their present-day range in Britain.

Where disturbance is minimal, roe will move and feed intermittently throughout the hours of daylight, especially in winter, with activity peaks in the early and late hours of the day. There is also a good deal of nocturnal activity. Roe are essentially woodland animals, frequenting ancient hardwood areas and plantations of conifers with virtual impartiality, dependent upon whichever type of cover is available. They thrive in young conifer plantations with an abundant and varied ground flora, where they will graze and browse a very wide range of species, being highly selective and delicate feeders. Plantations of young hardwoods are highly vulnerable to browsing and need protection by plastic tree-shelters or deerproof fencing where roe are present. 'Dead hedging' with piled-up brash from forestry thinnings is sometimes employed to help safeguard re-established coppice growth, which is also extremely vulnerable.

As well as those living in woodland proper, many roe lie up by day in thick hedgerows, tall field crops or any other reasonably sheltering and secluded scrap of cover. They dislike cold winds much more than rain, but heavy downpours will keep them in cover, waiting to re-emerge and feed when the weather improves.

Although roe are now more widely distributed in Britain than at any time since the Middle Ages, there are still extensive areas where they remain absent, although roe-free countryside is diminishing all the time. They were originally present throughout the British mainland wherever the habitat was suitable, but from Norman times onwards they suffered a period of decline. The precise cause of this is not clearly understood, but the fact that roe were less highly esteemed and therefore less stringently protected than other game in the royal forests of the past must undoubtedly have had something to do with it.

By the closing years of the eighteenth century roe had long since vanished from Wales and were all but extinct in England. In Scotland north of the Highland line the indigenous stock survived and was fairly widespread at lower altitudes. The old Caledonian pine forest, or what still remained of it in Strathspey, Morayshire and elsewhere, was the main stronghold of these animals, whereas in southern Scotland woodland clearance had eradicated the species from wide areas.

Recovery began in or around 1800 when a Dorset landowner, the Earl of Dorchester, introduced roe to his estate at Milton Abbas, near Blandford Forum. At about the same time roe were introduced to Petworth Park, West Sussex, by its owner, the Earl of Egremont, and from these two releases are descended most, if not all, of the present-day roe of southern England. The Dorset roe spread in course of time throughout that county and into neighbouring ones. For most of the nineteenth century the Petworth roe remained more or less securely enclosed within the very large park there, but eventually some got free to colonise the surrounding countryside, extending their range until they linked up with the Dorset roe somewhere in Hampshire.

Roe now occur continuously from east Cornwall to west Kent, and north to the valleys of the Thames and the Bristol Avon and beyond. Fairly recent introductions have re-established them in north Gloucestershire, Warwickshire, Oxfordshire and parts of Shropshire, and from the latter county they are now pushing into Wales. Roe in Thetford Forest and elsewhere in East Anglia are descended from animals of German origin introduced in the nineteenth century.

Some Austrian roe were at one stage released in the Windermere area of Cumbria but most of the northern English roe of today are thought to be of native stock, which was helped to return from near-extinction by large-scale reafforestation during the twentieth century. This lavish provision of new habitat has likewise benefited roe in southern Scotland, where at one stage the species had all but disappeared, although re-introduction has played a part here too. Most of the Scottish islands lack roe, exceptions being Skye, Islay, Bute, Seil and possibly one or two others. Mainland areas of Britain where roe are still absent include nearly all of Wales, most of Cornwall and Kent and much of the Midlands, but all of these are almost certain to be colonised in time, as the outward spread which has been in progress for almost two centuries fills in the remaining gaps. It is this dramatic resurgence by roe which, more than any other one factor, has provided the wherewithal and the motivation for the sport of woodland stalking.

Fallow deer (*Dama dama*)

This is the common deer species of parks, for which purpose, more than any other, it was probably introduced in the first place to many countries in northern Europe. Fallow first reached Britain at some time prior to the Norman conquest, after which they became widespread, not only in deer parks but as wild animals in royal forests and unenclosed chases. They originated from lands bordering the Mediterranean, but having been moved around by man more than any other species of deer, few if any wild fallow in any country today are of stock native to where they now live.

Fallow are medium-sized deer. The males (bucks) stand up to about 90 cm (3 ft) at the shoulder, with a body weight when mature of around 80 kg (175 lb). The females (does) are smaller, in about the same proportion to bucks of average size and weight as hinds to stags in red deer. Fallow occur in four main colour varieties, the so-called black, common, menil and white, and there are intergradations between these. 'Black' fallow are smoky-grey on the back and flanks in winter and darker in summer, with no white rump patch. 'Common' fallow are reddish-brown dappled with white spots on the upper flanks in summer, with a lighter shade of fawn below a white mid-flank dividing line, and white underneath. Patterns of flank dappling are as individual to specific deer as fingerprints are to individual humans. In autumn this dappled pelage is replaced by a winter coat of mulberry brown, which in certain conditions of light can look almost black, with the white spots still showing faintly through. The underside remains white, as does the shield-shaped rump patch with its surmounting 'horseshoe' of black tapering centrally down along the dorsal side of a rather long and conspicuous tail. Whereas roe will expand their rump patch when alarmed and in retreat, fallow will lift their tail to maximise the visual impact of the white rump (except in black fallow!) on any deer which might be following. Equally characteristic of fallow is their rectangular body profile when seen sideways on, from a little distance. They will sometimes utter a brief, crisp bark of alarm before running away on being disturbed.

Menil fallow differ from the common variety

by being white-spotted on the flanks throughout the year, usually with a brown 'horseshoe' and dorsal tail surface surmounting the white rump patch. In the half-light of dawn and dusk menil fallow can look almost white. 'White' fallow proper are seen at close quarters to be more buffish than pure white in colour, while deer of this type in their first year of life look decidedly buff-coloured. There are a few herds of all-white fallow, but deer of this type also crop up as individuals among herds mainly of other colours, and many herds of fallow present an assortment of different colours, although usually with one of the four main varieties predominant over others.

Antlers range in size and shape from short single spikes in the case of yearlings (prickets) to the very handsome broad-palmed trophies of top-quality bucks in their prime. Degrees of palmation vary with age and condition. Royal forest keepers of old, and some of their counterparts today, have claimed to be able to identify the age of any individual buck by its antler development, categorising them as prickets, sorels, sores, bare bucks, bucks and great bucks in yearly order of supposed age. Modern research, however, suggests that there is no such simple way of assessing age with accuracy.

A typical antler of a mature fallow buck has a brow tine just above the coronet, no bez tine but a trez tine about 15 cm (6 in) farther along the beam, and finally the area of flattened horn known as the palm from which a varying number of points or spellers project to the rear. Atypical antlers are not rare. A Hampshire trophy of my own has neither a bez nor a trez tine on the right antler but both on the left one. Split palms are also quite common. At one time these were supposed to be a particular characteristic of New Forest fallow, but modern management based upon selective culling has made it clear that bucks with this type of antler were simply poor specimens or immature animals that would later produce more impressive trophies with good palmation. Judged by the quality of antlers, some of the very best fallow in Britain are those in Petworth Park, West Sussex.

Like red deer, fallow are gregarious, with the sexes usually herding separately. Very large aggregations of a hundred or more animals may sometimes assemble at favourite feeding areas, but these will normally represent a number of social groupings which will go their separate ways if they are disturbed or otherwise ready to depart.

The yearly cycle of fallow also has close parallels with that of the larger species, although bucks cast their antlers a little later, from mid to late April extending into May. As with other species, older bucks are the first to cast and also the first to clean off velvet, a process completed, in their case, by early September. Bucks then begin to disperse, the older ones to take up stands in readiness for the rut. At this season the prominent Adam's apple which is characteristic of male fallow is complemented by a thickening of the neck which enhances the intimidating appearance of the bigger beasts in particular.

The rut begins towards mid-October and lasts from ten days to a fortnight before activity declines. Whereas red stags seek out the hinds, 'master' fallow bucks resort to traditional stands where they advertise their presence by a combination of scent and sound: urinating and rubbing their antlers in the result, thrashing shrubs and saplings with their antlers, and 'groaning' their rhythmic, belch-like rutting challenge call to potential rivals, which are always likely to be waiting in the wings. All this draws in the local does, which are served as they individually come into season, either by the original stand buck or by a successor should he be ousted by a rival. Fights between bucks are fast and noisy but rarely cause any serious injury.

As the rut subsides older bucks retire to recoup their energies. The males drift back to their normal haunts to regroup in loose assemblages, separate once more from the socially more coherent doe assemblages, although these latter are often made up of different individual deer from one occasion to another.

Doe herds briefly break up as their members disperse to give birth to their young (fawns), an event which takes place mainly in June. Single births are by far the most usual, although twins do sometimes occur and in some fallow populations there appears to be a higher than average incidence of twin births. As with other deer species, fallow fawns need education a good deal longer than they need milk, and will often remain in their mothers' company, in the case of female offspring in particular, until they are long past the stage of being physically or otherwise directly dependent upon their dam.

Fallow favour relatively large woodlands, especially deciduous woods and mixed deciduous and conifer plantations, although they are not averse to plantations of pure conifer where no other woodland cover is available. Like red deer and roe they will readily emerge at dawn and dusk to feed in the open, and will sometimes lie out well away from cover by day where they are sufficiently free from disturbance. Away from woods they will feed on a wide variety of items including heather, young grass and cereals, root crops and apples in season. Their woodland diet is equally varied – bramble leaves, ivy, tree foliage, acorns, beech-mast, wild fruits and ground herbage all being exploited in their turn.

Forestry damage by fallow takes two main forms: bark-stripping, usually in winter – a habit they share with red deer and which can cause severe economic loss – and browsing the leading shoots of saplings, thereby seriously retarding their growth. Individual plastic tree-shelters are now widely used to protect young trees, especially oak, beech and other broadleaved species, against this latter form of damage, and where fallow are present these tree-shelters need to be higher than is necessary where roe are the sole potential culprits. Whereas roe are apt to cause more damage to forestry than to agricultural interests, the reverse is true of fallow, with the sheer numbers of this gregarious species making their impact all the greater. Over and above what they may actually consume, fallow are prone to flattening extensive areas of field crops by couching in them, and almost never lying down in the same place twice!

Sika deer (*Cervus nippon*)

Introduced in 1860, sika deer from Japan joined red and fallow deer already present in Powerscourt Park, on the edge of the Wicklow Mountains not far from Dublin, and were later redistributed to various other parks and estates in Ireland. Scotland and England were not far behind in acquiring these deer, some initially from Ireland and others directly from their country of origin. Many deer park owners experimented with sika, which also became established in some areas in the wild state, as a result either of escapes or of deliberate releases.

Sika are native not only to Japan but to the island of Taiwan, the Ryukyu Islands between Japan and Taiwan, and the eastern Asiatic mainland from Manchuria to Vietnam. Within this extensive range there are a number of subspecies, those from Japan being among the smallest. Mature male Japanese sika deer (stags) are slightly smaller than fallow and considerably larger than roe, standing about 80 cm (2 ft 6 in) at the shoulder and typically scaling from 70 to 90 kg (160 to 200 lb). Female sika (hinds) are slightly smaller and much lighter in weight. The rump patch is brilliantly white throughout the year and can be prominently expanded under the impetus of fear to provide a conspicuous 'target' for other deer in the group to follow when in flight. The tail, quite short and either all white or with a thin black line on the dorsal surface, is normally held flat against the rump patch and is fairly inconspicuous except in warm weather when it is likely to be in constant agitation as a fly-deterrent.

Flank coloration is a warm chestnut dappled with white or buffish-white in summer, changing in autumn to mostly unspotted black or blackish in stags and light grey in hinds for the winter months. With the approach of the rut, spread over a period from late August to November or even December and peaking in the first half of October, the necks of the stags thicken and a mane develops. Viewed head-on, sika are seen to have a light-coloured eyebrow stripe which, with their characteristically short ears, gives them a teddybear-like appearance. A light-coloured patch on the site of the scent gland on the hock is also peculiar to sika.

The antlers of sika are simple in structure and show relatively little variation between stags of equal maturity. The first head normally consists of a single spike on each side, and the second may be of either four or six points. A stag in its prime will rarely produce a head of more than eight points, and where feeding conditions are poor, mature heads of no more than six or seven points are quite common. A full eight-point trophy will have a brow point, a trez point, a higher inward-pointing tine and then the tip of the main beam as the components of each antler, while seven-pointers usually lack one of the two inward-pointing tines. In the New Forest, and occasionally elsewhere, stags with trophies of nine, ten, eleven or even twelve points are not unknown, the additional points usually being located between the third tine and the tip of the main beam. Mis-shaped or seriously malformed antlers are surprisingly rare in this species.

Antler casting begins in March in the case of older animals and continues through April into early May. Regrowth is completed in August except among the younger stags, and the approaching rut is announced by the characteristic triple whistles with which mature stags advertise their presence in traditional rutting locations. These whistles are mostly uttered in sequences of three, as I have suggested, but may also be heard in any number from two to five, though rarely more. Each individual whistle begins on a high note and declines down the scale to a terminal moan. Although these calls sound like whistles and are commonly described as such, they are of course vocal utterances, one of a fairly wide range of calls made by these deer in differing circumstances. Another quite common call during the rut is a single long and declining querulous moan, uttered at fairly frequent intervals, whereas the triple whistles tend to be punctuated by fairly long periods of silence. The alarm call of sika of either sex is a characteristic short, sharp squeak.

Mature stags take up stands where they can intercept hinds in the course of their daily movements, or to which they hope to attract hinds by their unmistakeable presence broadcast by sound, scent and sight. Sika stags, like red deer, resort to wallowing during the rut, and fights between rival stags can be vicious and prolonged.

Except during their rather prolonged rut, sika stags and hinds mostly live in sexually separate groups. Larger assemblages, sometimes of twenty or more animals, are not unusual, especially in winter, but quite small groups, for example of a mature hind, a yearling and a calf, are also seen. Calves are almost invariably single, most being born in late May or June, although April-born calves are by no means unknown. Late births are also quite common, as might be expected of a

species with so extended a rutting season.

Sika are grazers rather than browsers, although in some places this appears to be reversed. Although basically woodland-dwellers, they will emerge to feed in the open during the early and late hours of the day and during the night, and can cause quite serious agricultural damage where their numbers are excessive. As well as browsing the leading shoots of saplings and doing some bark-stripping, an additional type of forestry damage to which these deer are prone is scoring the boles with the brow tines of their antlers, thereby disfiguring otherwise sound timber and exposing it to attack by disease.

In England the largest wild population of sika is in Dorset, where these animals were introduced towards the end of the nineteenth century to Brownsea Island in Poole Harbour. They began swimming away to the mainland almost at once, and are present today throughout almost the whole of the Poole Basin and beyond, from Dorchester in the west to Wareham Forest and the Isle of Purbeck in the east. There are also a few wild sika in west Dorset. In Hampshire the species is restricted to the south side of the New Forest and private land between there and the coast. There are also a very few sika at large in parts of West and East Sussex and Kent. The only other significant English population is to be found in the Bowland area of east Lancashire, near the Yorkshire border, where the species was introduced in the early years of the twentieth century to provide a quarry for hunting with hounds. The pack concerned, the Ribblesdale Buckhounds, has long since ceased to operate, but the deer remain in moderate numbers, thanks largely to a degree of toleration by local farmers.

Releases and escapes have led to sika deer being present in a number of Scottish localities, among them Peeblesshire, Argyllshire, Inverness-shire, Ross-shire and parts of Sutherland. Most of these separate populations have been expanding over the years and several are now on the point of linking up to create what is likely to be a continuous belt of sika-colonised country from the Mull of Kintyre all the way up the west coast, along the Great Glen and across central and Eastern Ross into Sutherland. In Ireland wild sika are well established in the Wicklow Mountains area, alongside the native red deer in Killarney

National Park, and in the northern counties of Fermanagh and Tyrone.

All this may sound like good news for stalkers, but there is another side to the coin: the ever-present menace of hybridisation by sika with red deer. This has already occurred on so massive a scale in Ireland that all the deer on the Wicklow hills may now have some element of hybrid blood in their veins. Many still look like one species or the other, but a not inconsiderable number are so obviously hybrids that they could not easily be mistaken for anything else.

In the Furness Fells area of south Lakeland, a good many years ago now, a wandering sika stag made its way into red deer country. It was fairly quickly shot, but not before it had sired hybrid calves on a few of the red hinds. Despite all efforts to eliminate these, the hybrid strain persisted, re-erupting all too visibly in the shape of 'red' deer calves with dappled flanks and sika-type white rear ends. This experience served to warn how easy it is to pollute an otherwise pure blood line with a hybrid element, and how difficult it can be to undo the damage that has been done.

There has also been hybridisation of sika and red deer in Argyllshire, where the two species were once separate but now share common ground as a result of range expansion. The same is true of Inverness-shire. The likelihood of such cross-breeding has been shown by the Lakeland experience, among others of a similar nature, to be very greatly increased when a stag strays away from its own kind and finds itself in the company of the other during the rut.

Eggs cannot be unscrambled and it is probably too late to disentangle red deer and sika where they already co-exist in significant numbers. The best that can now be done is to make every possible effort to keep the two species apart where they do not at present overlap, to cull sika especially hard where they do, to eliminate stags of either species which seek the company of the other and to cull all obvious hybrids as a top priority measure. These things are already being done by many deer managers in the areas affected, and there is scope for leisure-time stalkers to make their own useful contribution when opportunities present themselves.

Reeves's muntjac (*Muntiacus reevesi*)

In 1893 the eleventh Duke of Bedford was looking around for wildlife species not commonly kept in British deer parks to add to those he already kept in his park at Woburn, in Bedfordshire. During that year he obtained a number of muntjac: miniature forest-dwelling deer, native to India and to various countries in tropical and sub-tropical south-east Asia.

There are a number of species of muntjac, and new ones have continued to be discovered and identified until very recently. The duke received specimens of two of these: the relatively large Indian muntjac (*Muntiacus muntjac*) and the smaller Reeves's muntjac (*Muntiacus reevesi*) from south China. These were placed in an enclosure, and eight years later both were given their freedom, some to roam the whole park and others, apparently, to take their chance in the surrounding countryside.

What happened subsequently is not entirely clear. Perhaps it was a mistake to try to keep two presumably competing species of muntjac on the same ground, but in any ensuing rivalry for territory or food the bigger and stronger species might have been expected to prevail. The exact opposite happened, and after a time it became apparent that all the surviving muntjac were either pure Reeves's or perhaps hybrids between Indian and Reeves's, though with Reeves's characteristics predominating.

Later studies revealed that Indian and Reeves's muntjac have different chromosome counts and are incapable of producing fertile offspring. Since the muntjac of later years therefore could not possibly be hybrids and were certainly not Indian, what can have happened to have caused these to disappear entirely? A story at one time current maintained that the Indian muntjac proved unduly pugnacious, and that after one of them had savaged a park-keeper's dog, orders were given for the entire extermination of this species in favour of the milder-mannered Reeves's. The twelfth Duke of Bedford once told me that he thought this was unlikely, and that Reeves's muntjac were ultimately preferred as being a rarer and more interesting species. This of course does not invalidate the version of events which claimed that the Indian muntjac were intentionally destroyed, whatever the reason for this may have been. If, as seems possible, all the Indian muntjac were within the park itself and only the Reeves's had completely free range, this should not have been unduly difficult.

One way or another, Reeves's muntjac not only survived but flourished. During the lifetime of the twelfth duke, who died in 1953, they were given sanctuary in the Woburn estate woodlands, and evidence has emerged that they were covertly released in a number of other locations, some of them a long way from Woburn. This helped to accelerate the dispersal of a deer species from warm climates now firmly established over wide areas of central and southern England and becoming increasingly familiar to those who stalk in their leisure time.

Muntjac are roughly the size of a spaniel. A mature individual of the Reeves's species stands about 45 cm (18 in) at the shoulder and weighs from 13 to 15 kg (about 30 to 35 lb). In live weight, females (does) are often heavier than males (bucks) as a result of almost always being pregnant. The summer coat of a warm chestnut bay on the flanks with a thin, dark dorsal stripe changes in autumn to a darker, greyer, thicker winter pelage, the lighter-coloured underside merges with white on the belly, on the inner surface of the thighs and on the underside of the gingerish tail, which is about 15 cm (6 in) long and is raised vertically to reveal a whitish stern when its owner takes flight from disturbance.

Dark brown streaks on the upper surface of the head often contract with a yellow stripe across the forehead just above the eyes. The antlers of mature bucks rarely measure more than from 7.5 to 10 cm (3 to 4 in) from the coronet to the tip of the beam, and may often be much shorter. Sometimes there is a vestigial brow tine, but quite often not. The antlers emerge from disproportionately long pedicles, which extend along the face as bony ridges. Most bucks cast their antlers in late spring and regrow them during the summer. Does, on the other hand, have no annual breeding cycle. Fawns are almost always single and are born at any season after a seven-month pregnancy, within days of the end of which a doe will again come into season and the whole cycle will be repeated. This sequence is made possible by the bucks remaining fertile even when their antlers are in velvet.

Muntjac are lovers of very thick cover, woods with a dense growth of bramble being particularly favoured since this provides both food and shelter. They feed on a wide variety of woodland fruits, foliage, flowers and other available vegetation. In spring they will briefly emerge from cover to feed on fresh young grass on adjacent fields and on forest rides, but they are otherwise rarely seen in the open except sometimes as raiders of market gardens, where brassicas and carrots receive their unwelcome attentions. In suburban areas, large gardens with sheltering shrubberies and the like are also favoured by these small deer, which will often acquit themselves well when confronted by the household dog.

A certain amount remains to be learned about the social habits of muntjac. They are a territorial species, each buck claiming its own small realm and being ready to fight to defend it against others of his sex. Such fights can be quite extraordinarily vicious for so small a beast, which can attack not only with antlers but with its elongated canine teeth which project in the form of tusks. Fatalities sometimes occur, and I once inspected the victim of a fight to the death which had stab wounds all over its body.

Does also spread themselves as thinly as local circumstances permit except when drawn to some common food source such as a heavy fall of acorns. Except in the case of a doe with a fawn at heel, of a buck on the trail of a doe which has come into season, or of two bucks in the act of settling a territorial dispute, muntjac are otherwise rarely seen except singly. In the course of their normal movements they carry their heads low, their backs are slightly arched, and their pottering gait and furtive demeanour mark them out as animals which prefer to stay well hidden within their customary thick cover. They communicate with each other by a characteristic short, sharp bark, uttered every few seconds and often continued for many minutes at a time. Another means of announcing their presence to others of their kind is by anointing saplings and other prominent objects around their individual territories with scent from their head glands.

Muntjac are now well distributed throughout most of the rural Midlands and over a large part of East Anglia. They are resident now in

Lincolnshire and some have already reached Wales, while south of the Thames they have colonised Berkshire and are increasing in most other counties. Formerly isolated pockets of muntjac in Warwickshire, west Wiltshire, central Hampshire and elsewhere are now in the process of linking up with the core population based on Woburn.

Severe winter weather can bring about heavy mortality, but the mainly very mild winters of recent decades have presented muntjac with few problems. For a species of sub-tropical origin, indeed, they have done remarkably well in Britain, where they have proved themselves tough and adaptable to all but the very worst of our weather. There is probably some predation by foxes, and dogs running out of control in public access areas are an undoubted cause of casualties, but motor traffic almost certainly kills more muntjac than anything else. Whatever the law now says on the subject, shotgun drives still seem likely to account for some, and unascertainable numbers fall unintended victims to foxhounds, which encounter them by chance and 'chop' them before they can be whipped off.

As the need for the systematic management of muntjac becomes more evident, stalkers have an increasingly important part to play in getting on terms with these challenging aliens. If muntjac stalking as a sport as well as a vital countryside service was slow to take off, it is now attracting enthusiasts not only in Britain itself but from the Continent, where such opportunities are lacking.

Chinese water deer (*Hydropotes inermis*)

The sixth and final species of deer to be found living wild in Britain, Chinese water deer are, as their name suggests, native to riverside reedbeds and similar wetlands in eastern Asia. In the early years of the twentieth century the eleventh Duke of Bedford obtained some to add to the varied assortment of exotic wildlife species in his park at Woburn in Bedfordshire, where they adapted themselves well to the very different conditions of life afforded by open grassland areas.

Park gates carelessly left open during the wartime occupation of Woburn Abbey by government departments with their staff were blamed by the twelfth Duke of Bedford for the escape of some of these deer into the surrounding countryside, where they have maintained themselves ever since within a fairly limited radius of their place of origin. Life in the wild in rural Bedfordshire is not greatly different for them from that of those which remain in the park. Most of them live on open farmland, lying up among tall field crops, in the shelter of hedgerows or well away from cover of any kind. Limited use is made of woodland, including some plantations owned by the Forestry Commission, but these deer are not woodland animals in the true sense and do better on open pasture, which is where those in Woburn Park spend most of their time. They can also be seen in numbers at Whipsnade in very similar conditions, having been introduced there from Woburn.

Elsewhere in England, Chinese water deer are at home in the wetland conditions offered by Woodwalton Fen in Cambridgeshire and in a fairly wide area in and around the Norfolk Broads region of East Anglia. These stem from local releases or escapes, which have also accounted in the past for these deer turning up in other localities where they are not now present.

Although quite often confused with muntjac, Chinese water deer are larger, being about midway in size between muntjac and roe deer. Adults of both sexes stand about 50 cm (20 in) high at the shoulder and slightly higher at the haunches, the hind legs being longer than the front ones. Mature animals weigh between about 12 and 15 kg (33 to 35 lb). Their most distinctive feature is that the males (bucks) are antlerless but grow elongated canines, the exposed portions of which may be well over 5 cm (2 in) in length and are used for fighting. The very short tail is almost invisible when buried in the very thick, typically pale grey winter coat, which changes in spring to reddish for the summer half of the year. Seen head-on, with their rounded ears these deer look even more teddybear-like than the much larger sika. They have a graceful, bounding gait when in flight. In parkland conditions they will flop down and couch again on short greensward after running a short distance, but in open countryside they are likely to run much farther.

Chinese water deer are not a herding species.

For much of the year they are mutually tolerant as they lead their individual lives, which may draw them in numbers to graze quite close together, but around the time of the rut they become aggressively territorial, with paired bucks and does each occupying their own chosen patch of ground from which the bucks will fight off intruders of their own sex. The rut takes place mostly in December, the young being born between May and July. Multiple births are usual, as many as seven foetuses having been found in a doe when eviscerated, although two or three are more frequent. There is a correspondingly high rate of infant mortality. Most adult deaths occur in winter, perhaps more through seasonal stresses than from any clearly definable physical cause.

Chinese water deer are opportunistic grazers, harmless to forestry and scarcely more than a very minor nuisance to farming interests. In Bedfordshire, in the past, they have offered a tempting quarry to farm workers carrying shotguns on their tractors. Except where numbers build up locally to an unacceptable level there is little call for concerted culling, although some stalkers are attracted to these deer by the novelty factor of shooting an unfamiliar species.

Chinese water deer are a popular exhibit in wildlife parks, and it is by future escapes from such places rather than natural spread from their present restricted range as wild animals that they are likely to colonise new ground as time goes by.

CHAPTER 4
Starting Stalking

Before plunging into the practicalities of becoming a woodland stalker, take time to reflect upon your motives. Perhaps these are primarily to strike a balance between having a few deer on land you own or occupy and allowing them to increase to pest proportions, in which case the issue will be straightforward. You want to shoot some deer, and you want to know how to do it properly and how to tool yourself up for the task. Deerstalking as a sport will be a secondary consideration, although there is no reason why this should not be part of the picture.

For those with no personal stake of this kind involved, motivation will be different. They will suffer no pecuniary loss from not becoming stalkers, so why do they want to do it? The hunting instinct is innate in man, having once been crucial for human survival. As human society evolved, the instinct endured but not the same need, and hunting became a luxury perquisite of the privileged.

Generations of urban living have dulled the hunting instinct for many, although in most people it is still there, just below the surface. For proof of this one need only attend a live-capture exercise of the kind occasionally organised for scientific purposes, under licence from English Nature, by the Forestry Commission and observe the excitement of participants, many of whom might profess to find field sports as such repugnant.

So we have this hunting instinct. Whether it is right to indulge it for sport in today's world is a matter for individual judgment on the basis of what conscience dictates. Where deer are concerned, however, there is the further consideration that hunting, or at any rate stalking, is essential for their ultimate well-being as well as for that of the countryside at large. Primordial predators such as the wolf, brown bear and lynx being no longer available to relieve us of the responsibility for keeping wild deer populations at a level the environment can

sustain – would we want them to do so anyway? – man has no option but to predate on deer himself.

Hard though it is to convince some starry-eyed members of the public of this inescapable fact, even organisations opposed to all forms of sport which involve the taking of life accept that some deer have to be shot as a practical necessity, albeit not as a form of sport.

The many whose love of stalking takes second place to their love of deer do not fall far short of this ideal, yet stalking can never be a cold, calculating, unemotional activity. With adrenalin flowing freely, one's heartbeat rate accelerates

Before you first go out stalking in earnest there are many preparations to be made.

A clean kill is every stalker's prime aim. This sika hind fell instantly to a neck shot.

when a shootable deer emerges at shootable range. Success or failure now hangs in the balance. It all depends on you, the stalker, to place a shot in exactly the right part of the deer's anatomy to achieve the desired result. You squeeze the trigger, the deer falls, gives a few convulsive kicks with its back legs and then lies still. No matter how many times this happens, there is a moment of exultation tinged with regret at ending the life of a beautiful wild creature. On the other hand, if something goes wrong and is not quickly rectified, self-doubt assails you as you sink into near-despair, cursing yourself for being the very worst kind of incompetent idiot while vowing somehow to be sure of doing a better job next time.

Such challenges lie far in the future if you have yet to acquire a rifle and deal with all the other preliminaries to becoming a woodland stalker. First of all, then, the rifle, which must conform to many criteria, not least the law of the land as regards what is legal to use to shoot deer. If you wish to stalk in England and Wales, your rifle must have a minimum calibre of .240 in (6 mm), this being the interior diameter of the barrel, corresponding to the diameter of the projectiles to be fired. A muzzle energy of at least 1,700 ft lb (2,305.2 joules) is another requirement as defined by The Deer (England and Wales) Act 1963, now consolidated with subsequent legislation in The Deer (England and Wales) Act 1991.

Deer law in Scotland is based on The Deer

(Scotland) Act 1959 and subsequent amending legislation, all now embodied in The Deer (Scotland) Act 1996, another consolidating measure. As originally laid down by The Deer (Firearms etc.) (Scotland) Order 1985, restrictions in Scotland are on ammunition rather than rifles. Bullets must expand on impact and, if roe are the target, must weigh not less than 50 grains (3.243 g), have a muzzle velocity of at least 2,450 feet per second (746.76 metres per second) and a muzzle energy of not less than 1,000 ft lb (1,356 joules). For all other deer, that is to say red, sika, red/sika hybrids and fallow, bullet weight must be at least 100 grains (6.5 g), muzzle energy at least 1,750 ft lb (2,372.7 joules) and, as with roe, have a muzzle velocity of at least 2,450 feet per second (746.76 metres per second). Ballistics details are printed on every box of ammunition. In Scotland, therefore, but not in England and Wales, rifles in the .222 and .22/250 (5.6 mm) calibre range and using appropriate centrefire ammunition are legal for shooting roe, and indeed many stalkers regard them as ideal for this purpose.

The Wildlife (Northern Ireland) Order 1985 governs the position in that province, where .236 (6 mm) is the minimum permissible rifle calibre for deer of all species and a minimum muzzle energy of 1,700 ft lb (2,305.2 joules) is stipulated for what again must be soft-nosed or hollow-pointed ammunition. In the Republic of Ireland rifles for deer must be of a calibre not exceeding .270 (6.8 mm) and have a minimum muzzle energy of 1,650 ft lb (2,246.9 joules) firing a soft-nosed or hollow-pointed bullet of not less than 55 grains (3.6 g). The use of rifles of heavier bore than .22 (5.6 mm) was banned in the Republic for security reasons between 1972 and 1993, during which time .22/250, .220 (5.6 mm) Swift and 5.6 x 57 mm RWS were mainly resorted to by stalkers. Shooting deer with rifles firing rimfire ammunition was, and is, prohibited by law in the Republic, as is also the case throughout the United Kingdom.

While it remains illegal to use anything other than expanding ammunition for shooting deer, Sections 9 and 10 of The Firearms (Amendment) Act 1997 impose further restrictions by banning the possession or use of such ammunition except for shooting deer and vermin. For this purpose firearm certificate holders must have obtained from their local constabulary specific authorisation to hold and purchase this ammunition. Stalkers who held firearm certificates prior to 1 October 1997, when this provision came into force, were required to obtain written authorisation before that date to hold and purchase expanding ammunition.

An additional complicating factor is a requirement under the same Act for stockists and vendors of expanding ammunition to hold a grade 1 firearms dealer's licence, which means additional expense for many dealers. Stalkers should also note that target centrefire expanding ammunition, with its centre of gravity at the rear to give rapid expansion on striking the target, is both illegal and unsuitable for shooting deer. The correct ammunition to use should be of approved design for deerstalking, giving controlled expansion on impact, thus achieving maximum knock-down effect.

Popular deer rifle calibres include .243 (6.1 mm), 6.5 x 54 mm (.256) Mannlicher-Schonauer, .270 (6.8 mm), 7 x 57 mm (.284) Mauser, .30–06 (7.62 mm) and .308 (7.62 mm), the last-named in particular being a good, all-round calibre for the deer species present in Britain and Ireland. In the case of the 6.5 x 54 mm Mannlicher-Schonauer, it should be pointed out that factory-loaded ammunition with 156 grain (10.109 g) and 159 grain (10.303 g) bullets fails to produce the minimum muzzle velocity – 2,450 feet per second (746.76 metres per second) – required by law in Scotland. However, hand-loaded ammunition, which is increasingly used by United Kingdom stalkers, of 140 grain (9.072 g) and 120 grain (7.776 g) bullets falls well within the legal limit.

Rifles of .243 (6.1 mm) calibre are a popular choice for roe and muntjac, although many think .222 (5.6 mm) would be even better if legalised for use for this purpose in England and Wales. As a comparatively lightweight weapon the .243 (6.1 mm) rifle is a favourite with lady stalkers. Some stalkers of both sexes use it for the larger species, but most prefer a larger calibre and, hence, a heavier rifle. In other respects the question as to which is the 'best' rifle is one that is endlessly debated. Those who are deer men first and rifle enthusiasts second, among whom I include myself, tend to be guided in their choice by those who are more technically qualified, or

perhaps by whatever stalker of more than minimal experience offers opinions on the subject.

I started out with a borrowed Mannlicher-Schonauer 6.5 x 54 mm (.256). This I found perfectly satisfactory for roe, fallow and sika, but when the time came to return it to its owner I took advice from friends in the Forestry Commission as to what they considered was a suitable all-round calibre for use against all deer species in Britain, since I had neither the means nor the wish to amass an armoury of weapons. My final choice fell on .270 (6.8 mm) as a happy medium with what seemed to be just the right potentiality for my purpose. It also happened to be the rifle calibre favoured by the Forestry Commission's wildlife rangers for deer control, so it was perhaps not surprising that I received the advice I did! Some dislike the .270 (6.8 mm) as being excessively noisy, but I stuck with my Sako Finnbear, which did everything I wanted, coping satisfactorily with every British deer species from red to muntjac. Had I acquired a quieter weapon I might have become a trifle less gun-deaf, or I might have escaped this common affliction altogether by using ear-muffs from the outset, although few people seemed to do this in my early days as a stalker. So be warned, and take proper precautions if you hope to be able not only to hear but also to understand pub conversation when you reach your seniority!

My Sako came complete with a riflescope of reputable German manufacture for just over £100, which I saved up as the proceeds from a course of evening lectures at an adult education centre one winter. Today the equivalent could be expected to cost at least ten times that sum.

Apart from some de luxe models at the upper end of the price range, the deerstalking rifle market is dominated by foreign manufacturers, with prices dependent upon the prevailing rate of exchange. As a general indication, Brno and Remington rifles in a range of deerstalking calibres have been available recently from around £500, Tikka from around £500, Sako for around £900, the Mannlicher Model L .243 (6.1 mm) for £1,150 and the Sauer 90 range from just over £1,500.

For a secondhand rifle in serviceable condition you may need to part with no more than a couple of hundred pounds or so, but beware of buying a weapon which has not been well maintained, perhaps with a barrel all but shot out. Reputable gunsmiths will be likely to have one or two good secondhand rifles in stock which they will support with a guarantee. If in any doubt, seek expert opinion from a qualified riflesmith.

Modern stalking rifles have many refinements of design which have as much to do with appearance and with satisfying the individual tastes of prospective purchasers as with enhanced reliability. At the end of the day any rifle which is not a total write-off, or at any rate in need of drastic mechanical attention, will shoot as accurately and effectively, within its ballistic limitations, as its handler can make possible. One thing to bear in mind, however, is that the stocks of cheaper rifles – the wooden parts which support the action elements – are sometimes made of inferior wood, which can warp when subjected to humidity or dampness, and this will affect the weapon's accuracy.

My first rifle came without a telescopic sight, which did not strike me at the time as being particularly unusual, as indeed it was not until comparatively recently. They were once considered by some to be unsporting because they made accurate shooting 'too easy' or offered too great a temptation to shoot deer at excessive ranges, thus increasing the possibility of losing an animal injured but not killed by a badly placed shot, but riflescopes are now universally employed. Indeed, many present-day stalkers would consider it less than sporting *not* to use one and thereby sacrifice the great benefits available to the sport as a result of the many developments since the last war by the optical industry in advancing product quality and versatility. In a word then, a 'scope is now as essential a tool for stalking as the rifle to which it is fitted, and selection of a suitable one is a matter of the very first importance to every stalker. If economy is a governing factor, it is better applied to the cost of the rifle than of the 'scope.

Riflescopes, like binoculars, have two identifying numerals. Taking a 6 x 42 'scope as a purely random example, the first figure means that the image seen is magnified six times, while the second figure gives the diameter in millimetres of the front or object lens. The wider the object lens, the greater is its capacity to give a clear image in poor light, although beyond a certain size the type of optical distortion known as parallax can become a significant problem.

Six is generally considered to be the optimum magnification for a fixed-power 'scope; any magnification much larger is apt to induce inaccurate shooting by unduly magnifying hand-shake, which can undermine a stalker's confidence in placing an accurate shot. 'Scopes combining variable magnification with superb optical quality are nowadays available. My son has one of these, a 'scope of American manufacture with a range of magnification of from three and a half to ten, and he would not use any other.

For a riflescope of this calibre, a Leupold one in this case, you must be prepared to invest between £400 and £500. Fixed-power 'scopes are obtainable for as little as around £60, and for a couple of hundred pounds or so you can buy a top-quality optic. Those for which the mounts designed to fix the 'scope securely to the rifle come in one piece are an ideal choice for extra reliability. If at any time your 'scope, perhaps a cheaper one, plays you up, have the problem rectified promptly or give up stalking until you can afford a better optic.

At the eyepiece end of the 'scope is a reticle in which horizontal and vertical wires intersect at a central point of aim. These can be manually adjusted to correct elevation and windage when you are sighting in your rifle and bullets are hitting the target consistently off-centre. Patterns of cross-wires vary. In some the wires are of even thickness throughout their length, while in others the cross-wires are thinner at their point of intersection. In yet others the horizontal wire tops, at its centre, a thicker vertical one with either a flat or a pointed apex – I strongly recommend the former because in poor light a pointed apex can result in shots going high. In other respects the choice of reticle is largely a matter of personal preference, depending on which you find easiest to align with a chosen target.

All these facts about rifles and 'scopes will avail you nothing, however, until you face up to the most important fact of all, which is that in the United Kingdom it is a privilege to be allowed to own and use firearms and not a constitutional right, as in the United States of America. Furthermore, it is a privilege subject to ever tighter constraints with every headline-grabbing incident of gross firearm misuse. Apart from a few very special categories of people such as Crown servants in pursuance of their duties, possession or use of a rifled weapon requires, as already indicated, the preliminary grant of a firearm certificate (F.A.C.) by the police in the area where the certificate holder resides. This F.A.C. must be specific to the weapon or weapons involved and to any related ammunition.

The police are required to satisfy themselves that every applicant for an F.A.C. has a legitimate need and purpose for acquiring the items for which a certificate is requested, is of sound mind and stable temperament and is not otherwise ineligible for use or ownership of firearms. Anyone who has been sentenced to imprisonment or youth custody for a term of between three months and three years must wait five years after completion of the sentence before an F.A.C. can be granted, while a prison sentence of more than three years disqualifies the person concerned for life from access to firearms. There is also an age restriction. An F.A.C. will not be granted to anyone younger than fourteen, and young people between the ages of fourteen and seventeen may not buy or hire firearms or ammunition.

For others there should be no insurmountable obstacle to obtaining the necessary authorisation to buy or borrow a suitable rifle and ammunition. In the case of shared use or ownership, details of the weaponry will appear on the certificates of all parties involved. My son's first F.A.C. allowed for shared use of my old Sako .270 (6.8 mm). He now has his own rifle – another Sako .270.

Ask at your local police station for the official form of application for a firearm certificate. As well as supplying the more obvious personal details you will need to give particulars of the calibre and type of rifle required, the maximum amount of ammunition you will need to possess at any one time and how much you anticipate purchasing on any one occasion. You will also need to say why you want the rifle, where you intend to use it and what measures you have in mind to ensure its security and that of the ammunition when not in use.

Taking these in the order mentioned, give as your reason for needing the rifle 'deer control and shooting under controlled conditions on approved ranges', inserting 'vermin destruction' after 'deer control' if you also expect to shoot foxes and the like, perhaps at your stalking landlord's request. There could, however, be a snag here. Some police forces are reluctant to grant certificates for full-bore rifles for any purpose other than shooting deer and target shooting on ranges, so try to ascertain the position locally on this, bearing in mind that unless your F.A.C. specifically allows for vermin destruction you will be technically in breach of the law if you use your rifle for that purpose.

When stating where you intend to use your weaponry, name the property or properties and give the names and addresses of the owners, who can then expect a visit from the police to check public safety implications such as possible danger to users of footpaths and other rights of way, proximity of residential properties and the like. Your local chief officer of police is empowered by law to add whatever conditions he sees fit to the permitted legal use of any weaponry covered by an F.A.C. In one case known to me, permission to use a rifle on one named property where there were a number of public footpaths stipulated that shooting there should be from a high seat only. In addition to properties where you intend to stalk, no harm will be done by repeated reference to 'approved rifle ranges' to allow for the obvious need to satisfy others, as well as yourself, that your rifle and 'scope combination can, in your hands, consistently place bullets in a predetermined target area. Many F.A.C.s provide automatically for range shooting, but it is as well to make sure of this.

The ultimate aim of most stalkers is to be granted an open certificate, bearing some such wording as being for 'deer control and vermin destruction in areas where the holder has satisfied himself that the public safety will not be endangered and for target shooting on approved ranges'. Such a request is likely to be looked upon with favour once you can demonstrate to your local police that you need extended permission to stalk in a number of new areas.

In a very different position are those who

want to stalk but have nowhere to do so. The police may well be reluctant to grant an F.A.C. to such people, so what should they do to strengthen their claim? Many newcomers to stalking already have friends who are active stalkers and who may well be willing to take them under their wing in the early stages. If such mentors are able to give their pupils practical training on ground they stalk themselves, and their stalking landlord is agreeable, written confirmation of this should help to swing a decision by the police in the novice's favour.

Another approach is to supply evidence of having attended a course such as those run by the British Deer Society, which cover basic training on deerstalking rifles and their handling and include the opportunity to shoot on an approved range with a rifle provided for the purpose. Full stalker training courses as such are a follow-on from this for those who already have their own rifles, and evidence of advance arrangements to attend such a course ought to prove helpful in obtaining the essential F.A.C. Details of stalker training facilities will be found in chapter 9.

On the question of safe storage for your weaponry when not in use, anything less than a steel security cabinet of approved design, bolted to a wall, is unlikely to be regarded as adequate. The cabinet will need to have a separate locked compartment for ammunition. Gun security cabinets are of various capacities, so when ordering think ahead and anticipate possible future needs, including shotguns. Regularly advertised in the sporting press, gun cabinets are obtainable by mail order at prices which start at little more than £100.

Details of any firearms you already own and of any previous F.A.C. or shotgun certificate you hold will also be asked for. For a very small extra charge you can now obtain a combined firearm and shotgun certificate, co-terminous and renewable after a period of five years.

Your application must be countersigned by someone of professional standing such as a member of parliament, justice of the peace, minister of religion, doctor, lawyer, established civil servant or bank official who is not related to you and who has known you for at least two years. The countersignatory will also be required to certify one of the four passport-type photographs 45 x 35 mm which must accompany your F.A.C. application as being a current likeness of you.

Before a decision on your application can be made the police will want to visit you at your home address to satisfy themselves that arrangements for secure storage of your rifle and ammunition will meet their requirements, and to check other relevant details.

The Firearm (Variation of Fees and Period of Certification) Order 1994 set charges at £56 for an initial F.A.C. £46 for a renewal and £26 for a variation. A variation is required if you should wish to change your rifle, purchase a new one or otherwise alter anything specified on your original certificate. Other statutory measures governing these matters are The Firearms Act 1968, the Firearms Rules 1969 (for England and Wales), The Firearms (Scotland) Rules 1969, The Firearms Act 1982 and The Firearms (Amendment) Acts 1988 and 1997. The 1988 Act prohibits ownership or use in the United Kingdom of all automatic, semi-automatic, self-loading and pump-action full-bore rifles except under special licence, .22LR rifles being excluded from this prohibition.

Recommendations by Lord Cullen following his judicial inquiry into the Dunblane shootings of March 1996 have resulted in further tightening-up of U.K. firearms legislation. The Firearms Rules 1998 require applicants for the grant, variation or renewal of an F.A.C. to furnish details not only of why they consider they should be permitted to own firearms and on whose property they propose to use them but of their medical practitioner, who must be authorised to supply any information the police may require about the applicant's medical history. Applicants must also nominate two referees able and willing to authenticate information supplied by the applicant about himself and to complete a confidential questionnaire about the applicant based on their personal knowledge of him. Referees must be honest and reliable and may not include a police officer, a civilian employee of the police, a registered firearms dealer or a member of the applicant's family. They must have known the applicant for at least two years on a professional or business basis or socially. The Rules also make provision for combining in one document

Visitor's Firearms and Shotgun Permits. An overseas visitor using one of these Permits may bring his or her own rifle and ammunition and may purchase ammunition but not firearms while in the U.K.

Once your certificate has been granted and you are safely home and dry, remember to have it with you on every outing with the rifle. The police may ask to see it at any time and, if you fail to produce it on request, may impound any firearms and ammunition you may be carrying.

All F.A.C.s carry four statutory conditions: the F.A.C. must be signed for on receipt, rifles and ammunition must be kept in a secure place, no unauthorised person may have access to them, and the police must be notified of any change of address by the holder and if the rifle is lost, stolen or transferred to different ownership.

With regard to further conditions which may be imposed at the discretion of your local chief officer of police, it is important to bear in mind that different chief officers and, through them, their firearms licensing officers, implement the complexities of firearms law in different ways. Should the grant of an F.A.C. be refused on what you consider unjust grounds, action is open to you in the civil courts.

Non-F.A.C. holders who are not otherwise barred from having access to firearms are entitled to benefit from another provision of The Firearms (Amendment) Act 1988, the so-called 'estate rifle facility'. This enables a person over the age of seventeen to stalk under the personal supervision of the owner of the property concerned, or his servant, who must himself hold an F.A.C. valid for shooting deer on that property. The non-certificate-holding stalker may buy ammunition for the rifle but may not be charged for using the weapon. This exemption is clearly advantageous to anyone who may be anxious to 'test the water' before deciding whether to take up woodland stalking in earnest.

The Home Office has advised that game licences are likely to be discontinued in the near future, but until that happens a game licence is required for shooting deer other than on enclosed land, which has been interpreted to mean any land which is not physically enclosed by a fence, hedge or wall which may not necessarily be intended to restrict the free movement of deer.

If you are not already insured against third party risks through the terms of your membership of an organisation such as the British Association for Shooting and Conservation (B.A.S.C.), take out a policy for this purpose, giving cover against claims up to the value of £2 million or whatever maximum value is appropriate at the time in question. Should you be shooting deer for reward, either as an employee or on contract, your employer will be subject to the provisions of health and safety at work legislation, and should also be adequately insured.

CHAPTER 5
Rifle Lore

Having acquired a suitable rifle, a novice stalker's first need is to acquaint himself thoroughly with it, how it works and how it should be looked after, all of which we will now deal with.

As a major evolutionary advance from smooth-bore guns for the purpose of firing a single solid projectile at any one time, rifled weapons have a history dating back about 500 years. Rifles first made their mark as weapons of war against the British when those developed for sporting purposes were used in the eighteenth century by Americans fighting for independence. It was during the following century that substantial improvements of design, not only of rifles but also of ammunition, prepared the way for later refinements which have provided us with the superb stalking weaponry of today.

A stalking rifle's working parts are centred upon its action element, in which, with standard bolt-action weapons, a detachable bolt feeds cartridges from a spring-loaded magazine into a chamber ready for firing. The trigger, also spring-loaded when cocked for firing, is protected by a trigger-guard and secured against accidental firing by the application of a safety-catch which is in many ways the most important part of the rifle.

As well as bolt-action magazine rifles, the Firearms (Amendment) Act 1988 permits the use of centrefire lever-action and single-shot-action weapons for stalking, the latter being quite popular, with the Ruger No. 1 a good example of the genre.

Triggers are single-stage, two-stage, single-set or double-set. A single-stage trigger responds to a single moderate pressure from the firer's trigger finger, while a two-stage trigger requires a second moderate pressure to activate the firing mechanism. Set triggers give hair-trigger action. A single-set trigger is pushed forward to engage trigger action, which can be cancelled by applying the safety-catch before squeezing the trigger. Double-set trigger action involves two

A good all-round calibre is .270/6.8mm, as pictured here and used successfully by the author against everything from red deer to muntjac without causing excessive damage to the venison. Some stalkers consider .308/7.62mm to be even better. Stalkers endlessly argue the merits and demerits of different rifle calibres and bullet weights.

triggers positioned one behind the other, the front one being pushed forward to engage the rear one for hair-trigger action, requiring only the very lightest finger pressure on the trigger.

When the safety-catch is released, a squeeze on the trigger causes the firing-pin attached to it to strike the percussion-cap at the rear end of the round of ammunition in the chamber, igniting a primer which in turn ignites the explosive charge within the metal-jacketed cartridge. This creates high pressure from gases which propel the bullet into and through the rifled barrel towards its target. The purpose of the rifling, visible as a groove spiralling along the length of the barrel, is to make the bullet spin and thus give stability in flight to help maximise accuracy of shooting, the bullet itself being streamlined in shape to minimise air resistance.

When a round has been expended, taking less than half a second from the moment of trigger action to the arrival of the bullet at a target 100 metres away, the explosion causes the rifle to recoil against the firer's shoulder, a kick of varying severity with different calibres and cartridges. The recoil's impact is cushioned by a pad of rubber or other suitable material at the butt end of the stock – the wooden or possibly synthetic (e.g. fibreglass or other man-made substitute material) component into which the metal parts are slotted. The firer prepares for possible further action by quickly opening the bolt or activating the lever, making sure as he does so that the spent cartridge case is extracted from the chamber and expelled from the action area ready for another round to be pushed into the breech.

As I said in the last chapter, to be lawful for use against deer rifle ammunition must be soft-nosed or hollow-pointed and designed for stalking as opposed to target shooting. Bullets of these types are designed to achieve maximum knock-down effect by controlled expansion on impact rather than passing straight through the target animal's hard and soft tissues, causing little damage as they do so and emerging largely undeformed by their contact with flesh and bone *en route*. These bullets are of lead, coated usually with copper or with an alloy of copper and nickel, the cartridge cases of pure or nickel-

plated brass to provide a degree of elasticity combined with the necessary strength to withstand lateral and rearward pressure from the gases which drive the bullet forward. the elasticity of brass allows for expansion to fill the chamber and so prevent the escape of gases except in the appropriate direction.

The ideal rifle would be one which fired a bullet in a dead straight line from weapon to target under all possible conditions. The force of gravity ensures that such an ideal is unattainable, but manufacturers have striven to approach it as closely as the laws of physics make feasible – which is very close indeed, when one comes to consider the problems involved.

If you throw a stone at a distant object, the resultant tug-of-war between the declining impetus of its forward movement and the constant pull of gravity can have only one ultimate outcome. However energetic your throw, the stone will fall to the ground in the end, and at no stage during its flight from your hand will its direction of movement be wholly

Table 5:1   Relative ballistic performance of specimen rifle ammunition of identical calibres but different specifications and bullet weights.

| | Velocity in feet and metres per second | | | |
	Muzzle	100 yd 91.44 m	200 yd 182.88 m	300 yd 274.32 m
.243/6.1 mm 80 grains/5.18 g hollow point	3,350 fps 1,021 m/s	2,995 fps 913 m/s	2,593 fps 790 m/s	2,259 fps 689 m/s
.243/6.1 mm 100 grains/6.48 g boat-tail soft point	2,960 fps 902 m/s	2,760 fps 841 m/s	2,570 fps 783 m/s	2,380 fps 725 m/s

| | Energy in foot pounds and joules | | | |
	Muzzle	100 yd 91.44m	200 yd 182.88 m	300 yd 274.32 m
.243/6.1 mm 80 grains/5.18 g hollow point	1,993 ft lb 2,703 joules	1,551 ft lb 2,103 joules	1,194 ft lb 1,619 joules	906 ft lb 1,229 joules
.243/6.1 mm 100 grains/6.48 g boat-tail soft point	2,080 ft lb 2,820 joules	1,770 ft lb 2,400 joules	1,510 ft lb 2,048 joules	1,280 ft lb 1,136 joules

| | Trajectory in inches and millimetres | | | | |
	100 yd 91.44 m	150 yd 137.16 m	200 yd 182.88 m	250 yd 228.6 m	300 yd 274.32 m
.243/6.1 mm 80 grains/5.18 g hollow point	+1 in +25.4 mm	+1.1 in +27.94 mm	0.0	-2.4 in -60.96 mm	-6.2 in -157.48 mm
.243/6.1 mm 100 grains/6.48 g boat-tail soft point	+1.4 in +35.56 mm	+1.2 in +30.48 mm	0.0	-2.3 in -58.42 mm	-5.8 in -147.32 mm

Table 5:2   Relative ballistic performance of specimen rifle ammunition of identical calibres and specifications but different bullet weights.

| | Velocity in feet and metres per second | | | |
	Muzzle	100 yd 91.44 m	200 yd 182.88 m	300 yd 274.32 m
.270/6.18 mm 130 grains/8.42 g boat-tail soft point	3,060 fps 932.69m/s	2,830 fps 862.58 m/s	2,620 fps 798.58 m/s	2,410 fps 734.57 m/s
.270/6.8 mm 150 grains 9.72 g boat-tail soft point	2,850 fps 868.68 m/s	2,660 fps 810.77 m/s	2,480 fps 755.90 m/s	2,300 fps 701.04 m/s

| | Energy in foot pounds and joules | | | |
	Muzzle	100 yd 91.44m	200 yd 182.88 m	300 yd 274.32 m
.270/6.8 mm 130 grains/8.42 g boat-tail soft point	2,700 ft lb 3,661 joules	2,320 ft lb 3,146 joules	1,980 ft lb 2,685 joules	1,680 ft lb 2,278 joules
.270/6.8 mm 150 grains/9.72 g boat-tail soft point	2,705 ft lb 3,668 joules	2,355 ft lb 3,193 joules	2,040 ft lb 2,766 joules	1,760 ft lb 2,387 joules

| | Trajectory in inches and millimetres | | | | |
	100 yd 91.44 m	150 yd 137.16 m	200 yd 182.88 m	250 yd 228.6 m	300 yd 274.32 m
.270/6.8 mm 130 grains/8.42 g boat-tail soft point	+1.7 in +43.18 mm	+1.4 in +35.56 mm	0.0 0.0	-2.7 in -68.58 mm	-6.8 in -172.72 mm
.270/6.8 mm 150 grains/9.72 g boat-tail soft point	+2 in +50.8 mm	+1.7 in +43.18 mm	0.0 0.0	-3.1 in -78.74 mm	-7.7 in -195.58 mm

| | Velocity in feet and metres per second | | | |
	Muzzle	100 yd 91.44 m	200 yd 182.88 m	300 yd 274.32 m
.308/7.62 mm 125 grains/8.10 g soft point	3,028 fps 922.93m/s	2,717 fps 828.14 m/s	2,442 fps 744.32 m/s	2,184 fps 665.68 m/s
.308/7.62 mm 150 grains/9.72 g soft point	2,820 fps 859.54 m/s	2,488 fps 758.34 m/s	2,179 fps 664.16 m/s	1,893 fps 576.99 m/s

| | Energy in foot pounds and joules | | | |
	Muzzle	100 yd 91.44m	200 yd 182.88 m	300 yd 274.32 m
.308/7.62 mm 125 grains/8.10 g soft point	2,546 ft lb 3,452 joules	2,050 ft lb 2,780 joules	1,656 ft lb 2,246 joules	1,324 ft lb 1,795 joules
.308/7.62 mm 150 grains/9.72 g soft point	2,648 ft lb 3,591 joules	2,061 ft lb 2,795 joules	1,581 ft lb 2,144 joules	1,193 ft lb 1,618 joules

unaffected by gravity. You will therefore have to aim above the object you wish to hit – if indeed you are going to hit it at all.

The same basic laws apply to ballistics – the technical term for the interaction between guns, projectiles and natural forces which governs the performance of projectiles. For a bullet to hit a target horizontal to the rifle from which it is to be discharged, the rifle must be aimed fractionally above the horizontal to allow for the pull of gravity. The resultant curved route of transit of the projectile is its trajectory, and the heavier the projectile the more pronounced will be the curve, requiring proportionately greater

Table 5:2 (continued)

| | Trajectory in inches and millimetres | | | | |
	100 yd 91.44 m	150 yd 137.16 m	200 yd 182.88 m	250 yd 228.6 m	300 yd 274.32 m
.308/7.62 mm 125 grains/8.10 g soft point	+1.4 in +35.56 mm	+1.3 in +33.02 mm	0.0 0.0	-2.8 in -71.12 mm	-7.2 in -182.88 mm
.308/7.62 mm 150 grains/9.72 g soft point	+2.4 in +60.96 mm	+2.0 in +50.80 mm	0.0 0.0	-3.8 in -96.52 mm	-9.9 in -251.46 mm

elevation of aim by the rifle to hit the target.

The shorter the distance between rifle and target, the flatter will be the trajectory, and vice versa. The varying ballistic performance of different categories and weights of ammunition is very precisely calculated and details are given by manufacturers with every box which leaves the factory. Bullet weights are detailed in grains or grams. Other essential information includes the velocity of the bullet at the muzzle (M.V.) and at various distances from the rifle, measured in feet or metres per second; bullet energy at the muzzle (M.E.) and at various distances from the rifle, measured in foot pounds or joules (a foot pound being the amount of energy required to lift one pound in weight to a height of one foot); and the rise and fall of bullet trajectory above and below the line of sight (LoS) of a riflescope at different stages of its transit to reach targets at different ranges.

Except when shooting roe deer in Scotland, where variants of the .22 centrefire rifle and bullets of not less than 50 grains (3.24 g) and a muzzle velocity of at least 2,450 feet per second (746.76 metres per second) are legal for the purpose, bullet weights of at least 100 grains (6.48 g) are advised for shooting deer in general. For many years my own choice of bullet weight was 130 grains (8.42 g) which I found suitable for everything from red deer to muntjac, but some stalkers opt for a lighter bullet for the smaller species on the grounds that it causes less damage to the meat. I am bound to say, however, that the weightier bullets I used never caused excessive damage to meat, even of muntjac. So long as deerstalking is practised, stalkers will differ in their views as to which rifles and ammunition are the best for specific purposes – of this at least there can be no doubt!

A clear understanding of basic ballistics is essential to consistently successful rifle shooting. When you know how the bullet of your choice is designed to perform at various distances you can zero your weapon accordingly, aligning the cross-hairs in the reticle of your telescopic sight to correspond with the point on a target where the bullet is meant to strike. As I have said, this will depend upon the range, or in other words the distance from rifle to target, you have selected as appropriate (see figure 5.1). Should you decide to zero your rifle so as to hit a target spot-on at, say, 150 metres, it will fire slightly high at 100 metres, but rather less so at 50 metres, due to the rise and fall of the bullet during its flight over those distances. If your zeroing range is 100 metres, the rifle will shoot low at any range in excess of this – just how low varies considerably with different weights of bullet. On the other hand, if 100 metres is your selected zeroing range, some ammunition will register accurately not only at this distance but also at 50, while others will strike marginally low at the shorter distance. Ask your firearms dealer for an ammunition catalogue – a study of the ballistics tables (see pages 41–4) will clarify these points.

So much for theoretical zeroing. On the practical side, book yourself in if possible to take part in a stalkers' shoot at a Home Office-approved rifle range. Range days are periodically organised by British Deer Society (B.D.S.) branches for their members, and sometimes by other organisations. On a proper range you will have not only all the necessary facilities to zero your rifle correctly and safely, but also the benefit of advice and help from other participants. Most shooting will be from the prone position, with a sandbag or perhaps your rucksack or a rolled-up jacket to help steady your aim when firing, but there may also be opportunities for shooting from a sitting position or while standing and

Table 5:3   Relative ballistic performance of specimen rifle ammunition of identical calibres and specifications but different bullet weights, including short-range and long-range trajectories.

	Velocity in metres and feet per second			
	Muzzle	100 m 109.36 yd	200 m 218.72 yd	300 m 328.08 yd
.270/6.8 mm 130 grains/8.42 g Winchester Power Point	933 m/s 3,061 fps	847 m/s 2,779 fps	765 m/s 2,510 fps	690 m/s 2,264 fps
.270/6.8 mm 150 grains/9.72 g Winchester Power Point	869 m/s 2,851 fps	780 m/s 2,559 fps	698 m/s 2,290 fps	623 m/s 2,044 fps

	Energy in joules and foot pounds			
	Muzzle	100 m 109.36 yd	200 m 218.72 yd	300 m 328.08 yd
.207/6.8 mm 130 grains/8.42 g Winchester Power Point	3,667 joules 2,704 ft lb	3,022 joules 2,229 ft lb	2,465 joules 1,818 ft lb	2,006 joules 1,479 ft lb
.270/6.8 mm 150 grains/9.72 g Winchester Power Point	3,671 joules 2,707 ft lb	2,957 joules 2,181 ft lb	2,368 joules 1,746 ft lb	1,887 joules 1,392 ft lb

	Short-range Trajectory in millimetres and inches					
	50 m 54.68 yd	100 m 109.36 yd	150 m 164.04 yd	200 m 218.72 yd	250 m 273.4 yd	300 m 328.08 yd
.270/6.8 mm 130 grains/8.42 g Winchester Power Point	+5 m +.20 in	+18 m +71 in	0.00 0.00	−59 mm −2.32 in	−157 mm −6.18 in	−310 mm −12.2 in
.270/6.8 mm 150 grains/9.72 g Winchester Power Point	+11 m +43 in	+28 m +1.10 in	0.00 0.00	−68 mm −2.68 in	−189 mm −7.44 in	−370 mm −14.57 in

	Long-range Trajectory in inches and millimetres				
	100 m 109.36 yd	150 m 164.04 yd	200 m 218.72 yd	250 m 273.4 yd	300 m 328.08 yd
.270/6.8 mm 130 grains/8.42 g Winchester Power Point	+48 mm +1.89 in	+44 mm +1.73 in	0.0 0.0	−84 mm −3.31 in	−220 mm −8.66 in
.270/6.8 mm 150 grains/9.72 g Winchester Power Point	+62 mm +2.44 in	+51 mm +2.01 in	0.0 0.0	−104 mm −4.09 in	−267 mm −10.51 in

aiming free-hand or with a stalking-stick as a hand-steadier. Bear in mind also that when shooting prone, on a rifle range or otherwise, a bipod support for your rifle is an invaluable aid to straight shooting.

If you do not have access to range facilities, find a suitable place of your own where you can not only do your initial zeroing but also check out your rifle and 'scope for accuracy whenever the need arises or when there has been a lengthy time lapse since you last did any shooting. Such a place will need to be far from dwellings, be reasonably level and afford a solid backdrop behind the target for spent bullets.

If possible use targets of the type supplied for members by the National Rifle Association (N.R.A.) for match shooting on ranges. Your firearms dealer may stock what you need, or you could adapt ordinary air-rifle targets with a 2.5 cm (1 in) diameter bull's eye surrounded by an inner ring, a 'magpie' and an outer ring at 2.5 cm (1 in) intervals, pasted onto a piece of stiff card or plywood about 1 metre (3 ft) square and covered in turn by a sheet of white paper. Use split canes or something similar as vertical supports for the target, anchoring these securely to prevent them moving in the wind. If a really strong wind is blowing, wait until quieter

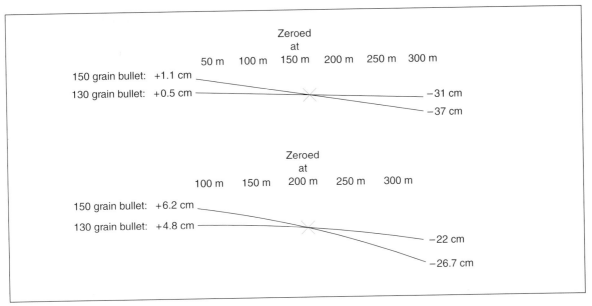

Zeroed
at
	50 m	100 m	150 m	200 m	250 m	300 m

150 grain bullet: +1.1 cm
130 grain bullet: +0.5 cm
−31 cm
−37 cm

Zeroed
at
	100 m	150 m	200 m	250 m	300 m

150 grain bullet: +6.2 cm
130 grain bullet: +4.8 cm
−22 cm
−26.7 cm

weather for this important operation or bullets may be blown slightly off course and so give inaccurate target placement.

Before you shoot, much waste of expensive ammunition can be avoided by first bore-sighting your rifle, at quite short range if necessary, perhaps in your garden if it is secluded and not overlooked by neighbours. Make sure that the 'scope mount screws are tight and the rifle is otherwise ready for use. Then remove the bolt and clamp your weapon or otherwise firmly support it to stop it moving, with the barrel trained on a target, making sure the point of aim is exactly central to the bore as you look along the barrel from the breech. Now move your eye to the 'scope and see if the reticle cross-hairs intersect at the same point of aim as the one on which the bore is focused. If not, adjust the reticle as necessary by correcting into the true point of aim as indicated through the bore.

To make these adjustments, check the instructions you received with your 'scope. Many 'scopes have 'click' adjustment dials, each 'click' representing a measured correction of, say, 1.25 cm (½ in) at 100 metres to the LoS through the 'scope, either horizontally or vertically, depending which cross-hair is being adjusted.

Corrections can be made more easily by the use of a collimator, a pocket-sized optical accessory which slots into the muzzle to give a reading through your 'scope, showing the collimator's cross-hairs against a grid.

Adjustments are then made as with the bore-sighting method previously described.

For the actual sighting-in process, make sure you have plenty of ammunition, all of identical specification. Other essentials include a pen, adhesive tape, opaque masking paper or some other means of marking bullet-strikes on the target, unless you intend to use a fresh target for each test firing. Binoculars or, better still, a telescope for observing bullet placements without the need to walk to and from the target between each firing will help save much time and effort. Unless you are very cramped for space, it is also a good idea to take along an observer to stand well to the side of the target during firings and to report results after each firing, using a steel tape to measure the tightness of groups and the distance and direction of bullet placements from the bull's eye, more commonly referred to in shooting circles as the bull. The direction in which bullets have struck in relation to the bull can be indicated by calling out where they are in terms of the hour hand of a clock together with how far they are from the intended point of impact – 'nine o'clock, four inches', 'ten o'clock, five inches', etc.

First shoot from a prone position if possible, just as you would on a rifle range, preferably with a groundsheet between yourself and damp vegetation or earth. Remember not to lean too far into the 'scope or you will risk becoming a member of the 'cut eyebrow club', in which you

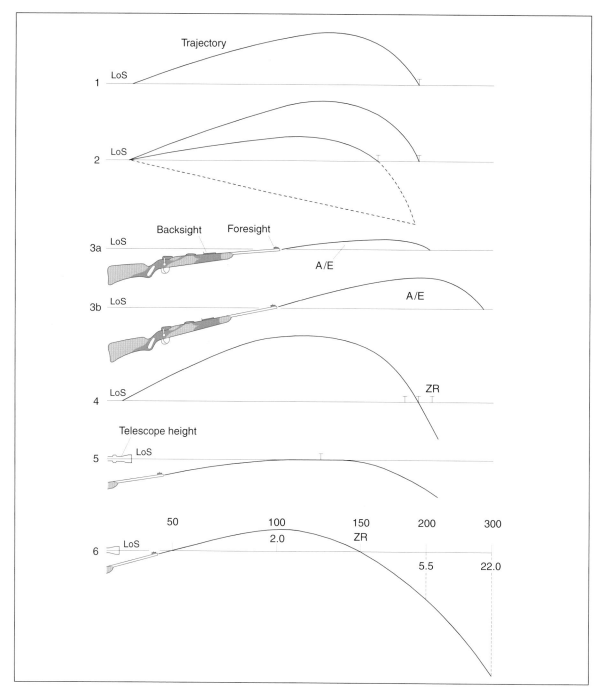

Fig. 5.2 Performance of rifle ammunition at different distances in relation to varying angles of elevation (A/E) of the rifle.

would find yourself in the company of many distinguished fellow stalkers!

If you have a high seat at a location where rifle zeroing will not cause unacceptable disturbance, by all means use it for the purpose; you will have the advantage of having the handrail to help provide a rock-steady aim. Another method I have employed is to place a folded coat or a bag on the roof of a car parked sideways-on to the target, using the coat or bag as a hand-steadier while shooting across the top of the car. The important thing is to feel satisfied that any

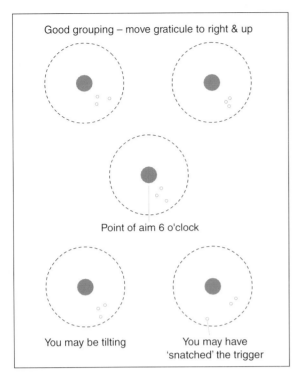

Good grouping – move graticule to right & up

Point of aim 6 o'clock

You may be tilting

You may have 'snatched' the trigger

Figure 5.3 Good grouping

misplaced shots are not off course because of unnecessary hand-shake on your part.

Shooting in groups of three and checking the results after each group, take your first shots from fairly close range – 50 or even 25 metres, carefully paced so you know exactly how far from the target you are while shooting. If your 'scope is widely off target, shots at longer range might not register at all, and so be wasted. Having made such preliminary adjustments as may then prove necessary, increase the distance between the firing point and target to 100 metres and use this range as your baseline for definitive zeroing. Now fire three further rounds and have their mean point of impact (M.P.I.) checked by drawing straight lines linking the resultant bullet-holes in the target. From halfway along the length of each line, draw another line at right angles to the opposite corner of the triangle formed by the first three lines. Where the second three lines intersect is the M.P.I. Measure the distance from this to the bull and make appropriate adjustments to the reticle of the 'scope. If you have assessed these adjustments correctly, your next three shots should be truly 'on target'. A tight group of three in the bull is

.243/6mm is a popular rifle calibre for roe in all parts of Britain and some stalkers use it against the larger species with consistent success.

the ideal for which you are aiming, a 10 cm (4 in) group or less being the standard required for passing the National Stalkers Competence Certificate (N.S.C.C.) shooting test.

If you inadvertently 'pull' a shot, disregard it and start a fresh group. Flinching can be a more serious problem, perhaps brought about by the effects of having joined the 'cut eyebrow club'. I cured myself of this more than minor inconvenience by temporarily fitting a short rubber sleeve to the eyepiece end of the 'scope which had caused the problem.

What rifle is best for muntjac? .222/5.6mm would be ideal if legal for deer in England but as the law stands we are obliged to use heavier calibres. As it happens, this buck was cleanly shot by the author with his .270/6.8mm Sako Finnbear, which has served him equally well with red, fallow, roe and sika, not forgetting wild goats!`

If, despite all your efforts, your bullet placement proves erratic, recheck your rifle and 'scope for loose screws or other obvious causes of trouble. A hot barrel can alter bullet performance, so allow the rifle to cool before you fire a fresh group of three. Consistently misplaced shots will completely shatter your self-confidence, so if the problem persists unduly, stop shooting for the day and seek the advice of a qualified riflesmith before using your weapon again.

Once your rifle is properly zeroed, keep it as free as possible from the screw-loosening vibration which may perhaps be caused by a bumpy ride in a 4WD across rough terrain, for example. When you are travelling, carry it in either a wooden rifle case or a well-padded rifle slip of the kind now widely marketed. Should you accidentally drop your rifle or knock the 'scope, check zero before you go stalking again – never take chances by using a doubtful weapon against live quarry.

For optimum performance, handle your rifle with the care a precision instrument deserves. The degree of care bestowed on rifles by different owners varies dramatically. Many stalkers own more than one rifle, using, say, a .243 (6.1 mm) for roe and a .30–06 or a .308 (7.62 mm) for the larger species. Some possess among their armoury a treasured Rolls-Royce of a weapon which is used only for very special occasions and then with a measure of reluctance for fear of irretrievably tarnishing a much-loved rifle's pristine perfection.

At the other extreme are some who rarely take so much as an oily rag to their rifles between outings. A friend who is something of a rifle buff once cheered me up momentarily by suggesting that too much cleaning is as bad for a rifle as too little. I then realised, however, that what he meant by 'too much cleaning' was a too vigorous and too frequent application of a wire brush to the barrel between outings. Rifles are robust tools and can undoubtedly stand up to some very un-sympathetic treatment but, like any other tool, they repay being properly looked after. If you want to ensure the best from your weaponry, giving it adequate care and maintenance is therefore a commonsense course of action.

Never neglect the cleaning of your rifle after use. The basic accessory for this is a cleaning rod, preferably of steel which may or may not be plastic-coated, onto which are screwed jags or brushes of the correct size for the calibre of the weapon being dealt with. A jag, for the uninitiated, is a threaded metal attachment around which cleaning patches are wrapped to penetrate the full length of the bore, with the cleaning rod swivelling during each traverse to follow the corkscrew twist of the rifling.

This cleaning method has long superseded the boiling-out process well remembered by the older generation as routine for removing corrosive fouling from the barrels of service rifles after firing. This fouling came from the cartridge primers then in use, and boiling out was always followed by a vigorous, much-repeated application of a pull-through – a length of cord with a cylindrical weight at one end and a loop or loops at the other end for the standard 4 in x 2 in cleaning patches. Woe betide any hapless squaddie who failed to produce a rifle barrel of sparkling clarity for subsequent inspection!

Modern primers are non-corrosive, which helps to make rifle cleaning much less laborious and messy, and if for some reason you have to postpone cleaning for a day or two until a more convenient time, your rifle will not be ruined as a result. One thing better not delayed, however, is drying off your rifle should you get caught out with it in wet weather. Keep an old towel in the boot of your car for a preliminary wiping off before you return the rifle to its slip. If it has a floating barrel, that is to say a barrel which has no contact with the woodwork of the stock, run a piece of 'four-by-two' or other absorbent material between the barrel and the stock along the full length of the gap between the two so as to soak up and remove any moisture. Another safeguard is a light application of oil by aerosol spray, or of grease, to the barrel's underside as part of a thorough annual servicing, but take care not to allow mineral oil or grease to come into contact with the adjacent woodwork, which can become spongy, shifting the bedding of the barrel and action with resultant loss of zero.

The blueing of modern rifle metalwork is designed to make it rust-resistant, but blueing can sometimes get scratched or damaged, enabling moisture to find a way through. Drying out is best done by exposing the rifle to warm, dry air, but on no account place it in contact with anything hot or the stock may warp, which could result in inaccurate shooting.

Begin cleaning by inserting a bore guide into the chamber of the rifle. Bore guides are made of plastic and are available in different sizes for different calibres. Their purpose is to keep solvent and dirt from getting into the action when the rifle is being cleaned.

Now screw a jag to the cleaning rod and wrap around it a piece of 'four-by-two' soaked in one of the nickel and lead solvents which are specially supplied for cleaning rifles, then push it through the bore guide and along the full length of the barrel to remove the worst of any fouling. Discard the 'four-by-two' at the end of each traverse and replace it with another after withdrawing the cleaning rod and jag. Should fouling be particularly bad for any reason, then before you do this, screw the phosphor bronze brush which should also be part of your cleaning kit onto the rod, dip it into a non-copper solvent and give the barrel a gentle scrubbing. Push the brush all the way through the bore from the breech end until it emerges from the muzzle before withdrawing it completely from the breech between each forward and backward traverse, thus allowing the bristles to regain their normal position before re-entering the bore. The bristles will otherwise suffer damage from reverse flexing within the bore, and use with a copper solvent will quickly destroy the brush's texture. Go easy with phosphor bronze brush treatment, which should not be repeated too often because its harsh abrasive action, if overdone, can damage the bore. It is nowadays recommended that brushes as well as cleaning patches should always enter the bore from the breech end and be removed after emerging from the muzzle, and the rod should be withdrawn before the process is repeated.

After pushing through one solvent-soaked patch and repeating the process several times with a second one before finally discarding it, lay the rifle aside for a short while so that the residual solvent in the barrel remains in contact with the bore. After a brief break for this purpose, run a number of dry patches through until one emerges free from soiling. Should there be any copper fouling, follow the same procedure using a special copper solvent, unless you have a general-purpose solvent for tackling copper as well as other types of fouling. If the rifle is to be stored for a lengthy period, it will do not harm to leave the bore lightly coated with solvent or rifle oil, but do not forget to remove this before the rifle is used again. Lightly wipe over all metal parts with rifle oil. Use a light oil spray to protect working parts not otherwise easy to get to, being careful as you do so not to bring this oil into contact with woodwork, and wrap the bolt in an oily cloth before storing it separately from the rifle.

From time to time lightly wipe a wooden stock with linseed oil to keep it in good condition. Prolonged exposure to damp as well as to fluctuating temperatures and other extreme conditions can cause warping of the woodwork, with disastrous effects on your shooting.

If you have any doubts at all about your technical competence, do not attempt to dismantle the action, least of all the trigger mechanism. Set triggers are particularly dangerous for non-experts to meddle with. If you are one of those unfortunates with five thumbs instead of fingers, you will be wise to confine your mechanical attentions to keeping screws tight, but take care not to over-tighten them and remember always to use a screwdriver of the correct size for each screw and so avoid burring the screw-heads. Where rifle maintenance is concerned, the best advice is 'If in doubt, don't.' In any case, have your rifle given a thorough annual servicing by a qualified riflesmith.

Riflescopes also need careful attention. Wipe them over periodically with optical cleaning tissues. Protect them with 'scope-caps against damp and dirt, and should they be accidentally damaged have them checked over by an optical specialist.

Take care of your ammunition. If it gets wet, be sure to dry it before you use it. Carry what you need in a pouch for better protection when you go stalking. If you accidentally drop a round the soft point may be deformed, but if the deformity is not serious it should not affect its ballistic performance.

Your stalking weaponry should last you a lifetime if it is properly looked after.

CHAPTER 6
Safety First

Most of us were taught early in life never, under any circumstances, to point a gun at another person. Where deerstalking is concerned there are other safety considerations which are equally important and which should be observed at all times.

Secure storage of weaponry when not in use may once have meant no more than hiding it from prying eyes in a padlocked loft or broom cupboard. You might possibly live in an area where the police still find this acceptable, but you would be wise to plan more in terms of a locked gun cabinet of approved design, screwed to a wall, as discussed in chapter 4. The rifle bolt and ammunition should be locked away in the separate compartment provided for the purpose in modern gun cabinets so that if, in spite of all your precautions, the rifle should somehow fall into unauthorised hands, it could not be used.

Never shoot deer against a skyline and always ensure a solid back-stop to receive the spent bullet in the interests of safety. Even against a solid back-stop, never shoot deer when they are bunched one behind another like the red deer hinds on the right of this picture or you may unintentionally wound a deer other than your target animal. These Quantock deer were photographed in the heart of stag hunting country and were ineligible for stalking in any case!

Whenever you have to leave your rifle in an unattended vehicle, lock it in the boot or, at the very least, conceal it, making sure to take the bolt and ammunition, and your firearm certificate, with you.

Before every outing with the rifle remember to remove oil from the barrel. Neglect to do this can cause, at best, a misplaced shot. In one instance I recall, an oil-fouled barrel caused a bullet aimed at a vital spot on a roe doe to be deflected and make a hole in one of its ears. A flick of the ear was the deer's only immediate reaction; it was not until a second shot achieved what the first one was meant to do that the wound was discovered. But had the rifle been of a smaller calibre a burst barrel might have been the result.

This highlights another important safety measure. Always – and I mean always – check that the barrel is unobstructed before loading up at the start of a stalk or for target shooting. Whenever there is a possibility of mud, snow, a twig or any other foreign object having entered the barrel, check and clear it after first unloading the rifle. Ordinary sticky tape stuck over the barrel end is a simple safeguard against obstruction. It need not even be removed before firing, since the bullet will pass straight through it.

Always keep your rifle unloaded, with the magazine empty, except when it is being made ready for use. It may seem safe to remove a cartridge from the breech while retaining a full magazine, ready for quick action, when driving along estate roads from one stalking venue to another, but this is emphatically not recommended and would lose you essential points in any examination on safety.

When the actual stalk begins, unslip your rifle and then load up, with a full magazine, a round in the breech and the rifle's safety catch on 'safe'. From time to time check that it remains on 'safe'. Unload before crossing a fence or other obstacle, passing the rifle, bolt open, to a companion, if you have one, while you negotiate the obstacle and, of course, doing the same for him if he has a rifle. The same rule about having your rifle unloaded applies when climbing into or out of a high seat as when travelling in a vehicle.

Deer should be spied for through binoculars, not through the 'scope sight of your rifle, which would necessitate pointing the weapon otherwise than at a pre-selected quarry. Should you find yourself in the company of a stalker who treats binoculars as a superfluous encumbrance you would be wise to watch out for other ways in which he might be inclined to cut corners – in safety and in other respects.

Never shoot at a target which does not have a solid background. A bullet will normally pass through a deer, expanding or breaking up as it does so but remaining potentially lethal. A solid background means earth, preferably not rock which can cause a ricochet. Trees and bushes are far from solid and may conceal a courting couple seeking a spot to enjoy some privacy. If a skyline shot seems very tempting, with a target you could hardly miss presenting itself broadside-on at incredibly close quarters, remember the wide open space beyond, in which your bullet could end up anywhere.

Make sure your rifle is kept in good order. A maladjusted safety-catch or firing-pin is an obvious source of danger which should be put right without delay. The services of a qualified riflesmith are called for here, and it is also a good idea for a riflesmith to check and service your weapon every so often, say once a year.

Damaged ammunition is another potential cause of barrel-burst. If you own rifles of different calibres, take particular care not to mix up the ammunition. Some rifles will accept ammunition designed for larger calibres, and you could squeeze the trigger on one of these with disastrous consequences.

There are other hazards, apart from those connected with your weapon. A gralloching (disembowelling) knife with a folding blade and an unreliable blade-lock can all too easily close on your fingers. Having used both folding- and fixed-blade knives, I have always felt happier with the latter. If you are obliged to gralloch a deer in poor light, take extra care how you handle the knife, remembering always to point the cutting edge of the blade away from yourself – especially from that most vulnerable part, the hand which is not holding the knife but engaged in gripping some part of the carcase. And in case of a slip of the knife or other mishap it is best to keep a small first-aid kit in your car.

A health hazard not to be disregarded is the risk of contracting Lyme disease as a result of bites from ticks, which are vectors for the infective agent and often parasitise deer heavily. First identified in America and now known to be much more widespread, with increasing incidence in Britain, Lyme disease can cause symptoms varying from flu-like ones, with general malaise and sometimes prolonged physical weakness, to arthritis if left untreated, but if dealt with in good time it is completely curable. Always wear plastic gloves when handling tick-infested carcases and take care not to pick up ticks, or the nymphs of ticks, on your clothing. If in spite of all precautions a tick or nymph fastens onto you, a dab of nicotine will make it release its hold. Tweezers will also do the trick, but beware of removing the tick minus its mouth-parts. Ticks can also be picked up while walking through bracken or long grass, so protect your nether regions adequately, particularly in summer.

When stalking alone, especially in remote areas or on difficult terrain, always let someone know where you will be and approximately when you expect to return. And do not push yourself beyond your physical capacity. Seek help if need be to haul out a heavy carcase or one that requires an uphill drag; you are likely to suffer a slipped disc or worse if you attempt it single-handed.

To sum up, never take risks which might endanger yourself or others.

CHAPTER 7
Stalking Equipment

When I first took up woodland stalking, the sport was so new in most parts of Britain, and the number of those taking part in it so small, that hardly anyone had given serious though to 'tools of the trade'. So far as what to wear was concerned, it was largely a matter of 'anything goes'. I wore my oldest and boldest, happily justifying my choice by telling the curious that my kind of stalking was one countryside pursuit which was free from the dictates of fashion.

That was a fairly long time ago, however. Now there are more than enough woodland stalkers for a flourishing trade in appropriate clothing and accessories to have developed, with fashion making a certain impact. So let us look at what is needed, starting with the basic essentials and then considering just a few of the many refinements of apparel and equipment now on offer.

You could spend a sizeable sum on clothing alone, although you need not do so – unless perhaps to impress your friends. For nether wear, a reasonably robust pair of green or brown cords, thick woollen boot socks or stockings and green wellington boots are perfectly adequate, exchanging the wellingtons for light, soft footwear in warm, dry summer weather. Wellingtons of any sort used to be frowned upon as unacceptably noisy, but with the pliable, close-fitting green ones, especially those which strap at the top, one can walk quietly and comfortably, with dry feet, for many a mile.

A reasonably weather-resistant green jacket of soft, non-rustling material, with plenty of pockets, will serve you well. Nowadays most stalkers wear camouflage jackets of suitably light material to be comfortable in summer as well as giving reasonable protection against the weather. Next in order of importance is a hat or cap, not so much to keep your head dry and warm as to conceal it from your quarry; this is particularly important if you are going thin on top or, at the other extreme, have an unruly shock of white or

A many-pocketed 'winter warm' affords maximum weather protection and comfort for woodland stalking in the cold months. This Swedish-made garment is worn in this picture by its British importing agent, Peter Robyns of Hayling Island in Hampshire.

greyish-white hair, either of which is likely to give your presence away very quickly, nullifying all your other efforts to make an unobtrusive approach.

What kind of hat or cap, though? In the early days I made the mistake of wearing a deerstalker *a la* Sherlock Holmes. Excellent though this is for braving the elements on the open hill, with the flaps tied down under one's chin to hold it on in the fiercest wind, in woodland, when tied across the crown of the headgear, the flaps are apt to get caught up in every overhanging shrub, as I very soon discovered. My next choice was a battered felt hat of a type whose shape could be altered to suit the mood of the moment, and I stuck with this for years. On one occasion I left it behind at the home of a friend, and was overjoyed some days later when it came back through the post with a note attached to tell me it was being returned promptly as it was clearly a very old and treasured possession. Saturation with hair-grease added an extra dimension of waterproofing and I wore it for many more years. Indeed, I believe I still have it somewhere.

A hat with a brim helps deflect the weather, and there are plenty of suitable ones from which to choose at shops which equip the shooting man. A camouflage hat to go with a similar jacket is your best bet. Another important aid to self-concealment is a face-mask, which need be no more elaborate than a simple piece of camouflage netting tied round the back of the neck and covering all of the face below the eyes. Many stalkers neglect this, and I sometimes wonder how many deer are 'spooked' in consequence of not disguising that most unmistakable of all warnings to deer – the human face.

Uncovered human hands are also conspicuous. Mittens or gloves serve the dual purpose of providing further camouflage while also keeping your hands warm, especially on a cold winter's day in a high seat. Of the two, shooting mittens have the advantage of leaving your finger-ends free for action. A gloved forefinger is less than ideal for squeezing a trigger with the appropriate sensitivity to pressure, but there is a type of shooting glove which exposes the forefinger alone. On balance, however, I favour mittens, not least because they can be worn for camouflage in summer without making one's hands unduly hot.

What to wear underneath in winter depends on what you plan to do – keep on the move or still-hunt. If you intend to be physically active throughout the stalk, your normal outdoor underwear should provide all the warmth you need. But a high-seat session in really cold weather can be a major feat of endurance unless you are adequately clad. Beneath something a good deal warmer than a lightweight camouflage jacket, a polo-neck sweater and thermal underwear come very much into their own here, and this is one of those situations where 'long johns' have much to commend them, as does headgear which covers the ears. For many years my own practice was to wear two of practically everything – jackets, trousers, pullovers, socks – and if the general effect was to make me look like Michelin Man this was a small price to pay for the comfort I was able to enjoy. If the weather is windy as well as cold, remember that deer dislike such conditions as much as you and I do and you will probably be wasting your time anyway, as well as risking catching pneumonia.

In all circumstances, protect your hearing with muffs or ear-plugs every time you squeeze the trigger. Many who started stalking decades ago, myself among them, neglected this sensible precaution and now suffer some degree of deafness.

When choosing binoculars remember that, as with riflescopes, their individual capability is defined by two numerals. The first of these gives the power of magnification and the second the diameter in millimetres of the object lens. Thus, an 8 x 30 binocular, which is much favoured by birdwatchers, magnifies the view eight times and has a front or object lens 30 mm in diameter. The wider the differential between the first and second numerals, the greater is the light-gathering potential of the optic: an important consideration when assessing the shootability of a deer viewed in the half-light of dawn or dusk. This means that an 8 x 30 optic does not give quite so clear a view in poor light as, say, a 7 x 50 or 10 x 50, which are two other popular sizes. On the other hand, binoculars of these two sizes are necessarily bigger and therefore heavier and more cumbersome than their 8 x 30 counterpart, which can be slipped into a large pocket if you get tired of its dangling from your neck. Other binocular specifications which are suitable for deerstalking include 8 x 56, 7 x 42 and 10 x 42.

Binocular prices vary greatly. In general you can expect to get what you pay for but, again as with 'scopes, you just may strike lucky with a cheap product which is adequate for the purpose – my son still uses a binocular for which I paid a modest £12 at a well-known multiple store many years ago, although I had to examine several before I found one that was suitable. Optics which cannot be sharply and speedily focused or which cause eye-strain after a minute

A rifle accessory box with Zeiss 8 x 56 B/GAT binocular with leather pouch and wide neck strap, leather ammunition wallet which can fit on belt or be carried in pocket, dog collar with flashing strobe light, ammunition carriage/storage box, protective bolt bag, Butler Creek flip-up riflescope lens covers and diary/notebook. Accessory box lid also contains small items.

or so are to be avoided. Rubber-armoured binoculars have the inestimable advantage of not making a noise at the worst possible moment should you knock them against something solid but, as at least one expert has warned us, rubber can hide a multitude of sins. Obviously, however, if you make a three-figure investment in a binocular which bears a world-famous brand name, you can expect a quality optic, whether rubber-sheathed or otherwise.

Next to your rifle and 'scope, a good binocular is by far your most important stalking accessory and well repays being looked after. Always keep it in its case when it is not in use and protect the lenses against damp and dirt with lens-caps while you are stalking. If moisture should find a way in the lenses will become fogged and useless. If they do not dry out of their own accord they will need professional attention, as also of course they will if you knock them out of alignment by dropping the optic on to a hard surface.

Although the conventional deerstalking optic for the open hill is a telescope, the all-important high magnifications these offer for viewing deer at great distances are inappropriate for stalking in woodland conditions. Binoculars giving very

high magnifications are also unsuitable because of the shaky image they are bound to give when hand-held.

As I said in the last chapter, your cleaning and maintenance kit should include, at the very minimum, a cleaning rod with jag, a phosphor bronze brush and a nylon brush of appropriate calibre, lead-and-nickel and copper solvents, rifle oil for the metal parts, linseed oil or similar for wooden stocks, cleaning felts and rags, lens-cleaning tissues, 'four-by-two' cleaning patches and screwdrivers to fit all screws.

Some stalkers claim consistent success in shooting accurately while standing, without having anything against which to steady their aim, but if there are ways to be more certain of placing a bullet exactly where it is needed, it clearly makes sense to use them. When a tree or something equally solid is not available as a hand-rest, a stalking-stick comes into its own. For many years I have used a thumbstick with a screw-on extension fashioned for me by a friend who is a retired plumber. Without the extension, which lengthens the stick to head height, it is short enough to be stowed in the boot of the car as well as to double as a walking-stick. A stalking-stick should be long enough for you to use it while standing erect. The rifle should not come into direct contact with the stick, but should be rested on the thumb of your non-shooting hand while you grip the stick with the fingers of that hand. This will enable you to steady your aim in the vertical dimension while also supporting the weight of the rifle. There will still be some sideways instability, but one way of overcoming this is to go one stage further. With an old bicycle tube or something similar, lash two long canes together a few centimetres below their apex. This will provide you with an easy-to-carry lightweight bipod ready to be quickly and effectively deployed by spreading the two canes scissors-fashion, with their upper ends just above eye-level and their lower ends on the ground.

High seats will be dealt with in chapter 14 but, by way of a handy, portable 'low seat' I have long used a conventional shooting-stick with a leather bootlace attached so that I can sling it diagonally across my back while I am walking, thus keeping my hands free for other purposes. With a 'low seat' you can place yourself at whatever point of vantage best suits the need of

This Jägersport aluminium high seat weighs only 27lb (12.5kg), gives a height to seat pan of 10ft (3m) and is shown complete and ready to put up against any suitable tree. Additional height extensions are available.

Jägersport's Woodland Mk II high seat, either lean-to or free-standing, also has a foam-padded shooting rail to obviate the accidental clatter when taking aim in a hurry.

the moment and remain there, alert but relaxed and unobtrusive, until your quarry presents itself.

For hard-to-find carcases shot at dusk, a long-beam battery lamp or, at the very least, a torch will help avoid wasted time, frustration and possible failure, so remember to carry one in your vehicle.

Having shot your deer and located it, you will need a suitable knife to gralloch it, immediately if possible. A sheath-knife with an upward curve to the blade tip will serve you best, not only for gralloching but also for skinning. A good selection of knives designed specifically for these purposes are nowadays available, with blades of sufficiently soft steel to be easily sharpened after each using – and you will need a grindstone to do this.

Unless you prefer to leave the offal in the carcase until you get home, carry some fairly large freezer food bags in your rucksack or your pocket, and when you gralloch have one or two ready in which to place heart, liver and kidneys. The spoils of the gralloch itself should be disposed of in such a way as to leave no visible trace of your post-mortem surgery, preferably by burying them, for which purpose a spade will be needed as one of your in-car stalking accessories.

Depending upon the size of the carcase, a roe-sack or equivalent or perhaps a drag-rope will be needed. A purpose-made roe-sack is worn as a valise and has a washable lining. It can also double as a rucksack until it is needed for its prime purpose, when it has the advantage of leaving your hands and arms free to cope with your rifle and stalking-stick without having to make a double journey. With its four legs tied or strapped together, a roe can be carried over your shoulder, albeit at some risk of splashing blood over your jacket. Muntjac, on the other hand, are small and light enough to be carried in one hand with the legs thus tied. If there is no alternative

Jägersport twin stalking stick shown at maximum elevation of 66in (158cm) and minimum of 31in (79cm) with adjustment for use standing or as a bipod when sitting, also as a lightweight universal walking stick.

This home-made alternative to a straightforward stalking stick, with two sticks held together by Velcro, helps give added stability for shooting from the standing position. The sticks are lightweight canes which when closed can serve as a walking stick.

but to drag a shot deer back to your car, tow it head foremost, underparts upwards, taking the greatest possible care not to contaminate the carcase.

To transport it home, either leave the carcase in the roe-sack or perhaps stow it in some other temporary container such as a large agricultural feed bag or a plastic dustbin liner – remembering however that the latter are easily punctured. Plastic container trays of a suitable size to hold a roe carcase are also available. Alternatively, lay each carcase belly upwards on protective plastic sheeting, allowing the cooling process to start without further delay as you head home. Whatever your chosen method of portage, keep dogs and carcases safely separate.

If you are stalking single-handed and you have a pick-up truck, Land Rover or other suitable

A loading winch for heavier carcases, powered by the battery of the vehicle used for loading and extraction, has helped save many a 'bad back'.

vehicle, a battery-operated winch can be fitted to it for loading carcases too heavy for you to haul aboard unaided. A block-and-tackle is another answer to heavy lifting problems, especially with

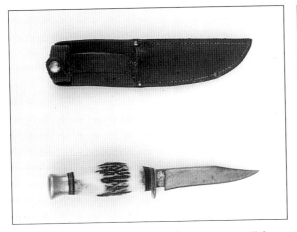

A sharp-bladed sheath knife will serve you well for gralloching and skinning carcases.

A versatile carcase and forage transporter is this Daihatsu Conversion.

Ideal for long hauls over rough terrain, the Trammic Occid carcase transporter at the 1997 Oxfordshire Deer Fair.

This pocket-size carcase carrier is the Honda Power Barrow.

Manual hoist fitted to ball hitch on pickup for loading carcases into pickup made by David Stretton, agricultural engineer, of Castle Donington, Derbyshire.

An E.P. Barrus all-terrain vehicle being demonstrated by Mark Stretton, son of agricultural engineer David Stretton of Castle Donington, Derbyshire.

Ereppi Transporter from Llanellen Farm Services at the Deer Fair in Oxfordshire in June 1997.

A Woodchester branch cutting set, for ensuring a safe line of fire and observation from high seats. Lightweight 39in (1m) alloy poles have secure fixings for complete rigidity and a saw or lopper head can be used. It is supplied with a pack-bag and is marketed by Jägersport.

fallow bucks and red deer.

For the temporary storage of deer carcases at home you will need somewhere fly-proof to hang them to cool off as quickly as possible. You may decide to adapt your garage to provide a second use as a deer larder, or even convert it for this purpose and leave your car out on the forecourt! Should you become a licensed game dealer and thus be entitled to sell venison you will need to equip yourself appropriately, with hygiene at the forefront of all arrangements you put in place – hot and cold running water, a sink, non-absorbent work surfaces and adequate freezer capacity or other cold storage facilities.

For hanging carcases you will need a suitable cross-beam and gambrils – the metal or wooden double-ended hangers from which to suspend carcases for temporary storage or for skinning. Each end of the gambril is passed through a hind leg just above the hock, thus spreading the legs. For cutting up the carcase you will need a butcher's knife and a butcher's saw, which of course should be thoroughly cleaned and sterilised after use. The highest standards of hygiene must at all times be maintained, both in your deer larder and with everything you use when preparing meat for human consumption.

You will need a jig-and-saw combination or, at the very least, an ordinary carpenter's saw for preparing trophies if your intention is to retain the upper part of the skull for mounting, discarding the remainder. For boiling out prior to cleaning the trophy for mounting a galvanised bucket will come in handy, as will a fold-away,

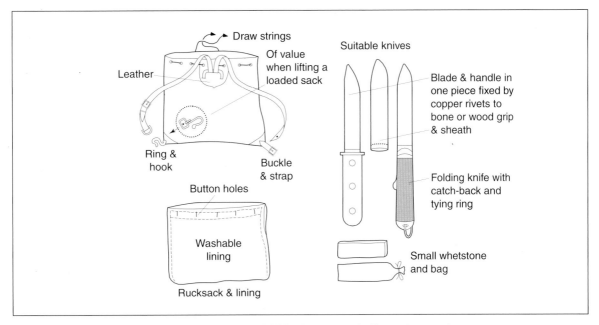

Fig. 7.1 Stalking Accessories

Stalker's belt system developed by Roger Saunders of Jägersport and Major Wally Oakman, former head stalker of Cowdray estate in West Sussex. The system does away with the need to keep important items in the pockets and avoids them being forgotten or lost. The system embodies a 1in leather belt with D-loop, a Maglite AA torch and hand-blocked pouch, torch being in plain aluminium so that it is easier to find if dropped, a Harry Boden stalking knife and gralloching knife, secateurs, Mannlicher magazine and wrist/pocket compass – all on a self-inflating cushion seat.

two-ring camp cooker with bottled gas, unless an understanding wife permits you to use kitchen facilities. As mounts for trophies you will need

suitable wooden plaques, which you can either make yourself or buy ready-made, with sizes for different species.

Other items will almost certainly suggest themselves for inclusion in your stalker's starter-kit, but you can add to your stock of accessories as and when opportunity offers and you have the cash to spare. Woodland stalkers are now catered for by specialist suppliers, who offer an almost unlimited range of clothing and general equipment on which you could easily spend a small fortune. I have in front of me a catalogue from one such supplier, Jägersport of Petersfield in Hampshire, from which I will quote some sample items. The first page features purpose-made secateurs for cutting the breast and pelvic bones of deer when gralloching or dressing, tweezers for removing ticks, larder racks for hanging carcases, fly-proof nets, saws with extendible handles for trimming branches, box-type carcase carriers, ammunition boxes, rests and clamps.

On the second page one is tempted by ammunition wallets, bags and belts of almost unimagined variety. Overleaf again are listed calls for roe and other species, curb chains for dogs, first-aid pouches, disposable latex gloves for gralloching, gun safes and hand lamps. Probing further into this Aladdin's cave of stalking

Mannlicher SSG rifle with green plastic stock, covered with self-adhesive camouflage tape. Rifle has rail fitting for Harris swivel-head bipod, allowing easy adjustment. Also in the picture are a Butler Creek padded rifle sling, a Swarovski 3-12 x 50LRS riflescope including laser for quick and accurate distance judgement, electronic ear defenders and, on ground, Mannlicher magazine, bolt and protective hold storage bag/rifle cleaning cloth.

A practising target in steel for training novices in range judgement, angle shot and accuracy on target area. An armoured steel saddle can be fitted over the head area.

goodies, one finds details of a dazzling array of knives, knife pouches, knife-sharpening equipment, map holders, tool kits, rifle-cleaning accessories, rifle sling pads, riflescope lens covers, carcase-carrying aids, portable 'low seats', seat covers, sticks, roe-sized silhouette targets, thermal gloves and much, much more. The sheer range and variety of quality optics now available is mind-blowing. As regards clothing and footwear, there is clearly no longer any excuse for going stalking dressed like a tramp or enduring physical discomfort from being inadequately attired. Profusely stocked market stalls are set out and so the choice is now yours to make.

CHAPTER 8
Deer Law

L egislation relating to deerstalking falls into two main categories: firearms and ammunition, and factors which have a direct bearing upon the humane treatment and essential control of deer. The first was dealt with in chapter 4, and the information given there need not be repeated here. What now concerns us is such matters as when, where and in what circumstances it is lawful or unlawful to shoot deer, including close times and close seasons.

In England and Wales the statutes specific to deer are The Deer Acts 1963 and 1980 and The Roe Deer (Close Seasons) Act 1977, all now consolidated in The Deer Act 1991. The Wildlife and Countryside Act 1981 and, while it remains in force, The Game Licences Act 1860 are also relevant to deer and to stalking.

Dealing with the last-mentioned item first, it is as well not to forget that, under the terms of the relevant Act, a game licence is required to kill deer except on enclosed land by the owner or occupier of such land or with his permission. Case law suggests that 'enclosed land', in this context, means land enclosed by any kind of fencing or other means and not necessarily by deerproof fencing, implying that deer may legally be shot without a game licence on farmland or in woodland enclosed by normal stock fencing, hedgerows or walls. As the current (1998) cost of a game licence is only £6 for a full year or £4 for a half-year, it is probably a wise investment while the need for such a licence in any circumstances persists. Game licences are obtainable from post offices.

In Britain the law makes it clear that living wild deer belong to no one. The right to kill or take them is held by the owner of any property on which they happen to be at any given time, or by an individual, or individuals, to whom the owner has given this right, or who otherwise has lawful authority to kill or take deer on that property. It is an offence to enter any land without lawful authority to take, kill or injure any deer or to search for or pursue deer with this intention.

Until 1977 there was no legal close season in England for roebucks like this superb gold medal specimen, shot in West Sussex by George Stefanicki.

Should you see a shootable deer just over your boundary, on the property of a neighbour where you have no permission to stalk, this means that you are likely to be in breach of the law if you enter that property, even unarmed, with a view to moving the deer to your ground for a fellow-stalker to shoot. It is also illegal to remove a deer from another person's property without lawful authority, an aspect of the law which could therefore be invoked to penalise poachers who claim to have happened to 'find' a carcase they are caught in the act of removing.

When taking on any new stalking, it is advisable to make sure there is no misunderstanding as to who actually owns the stalking rights or may have been given the right to shoot deer. The game rights may have been separately let without it being made clear whether these include the right to kill deer, or there may be some question as to whether a farming tenant or other occupier has this right on land he occupies. Make sure any such uncertainties are clarified at the outset and that the appropriate authority gives you written permission to stalk.

Except in special circumstances, such as the need for humane destruction of a sick or injured animal, it is illegal to kill deer between one hour after sunset and one hour before sunrise. This is the nightly close time, applicable to all deer species. Close seasons are as follows, all dates being inclusive:

the Republic of Ireland The Wildlife Act 1976 introduced a close season from 1 March to 31 August for the males of all three species and from 1 February to 31 October for the females of all three species. However, these seasons in the Republic are sometimes modified or extended to take account of circumstances such as an under-cull of female deer in specific areas in any one season, and the shooting of red deer of either sex is banned in County Kerry.

Shooting deer from a vehicle or from an aircraft or a helicopter, or using one of these to drive deer other than in a deer park or on a deer farm is illegal. Should you be inside a vehicle when you spot a shootable deer you should therefore have both feet on the ground before you shoot.

Species	Sex	England and Wales	Scotland
Red*	Male	1 May–31 July	21 October–30 June
	Female	1 March–31 October	16 February–20 October
Sika*	Male	1 May–31 July	21 October–30 June
	Female	1 March–31 October	16 February–20 October
Fallow	Male	1 May–31 July	1 May–31 July
	Female	1 March–31 October	16 February–20 October
Roe	Male	1 November–31 March	21 October–31 March
	Female	1 March–31 October·	1 April–20 October

*Includes hybrid red/sika deer in Scotland.

There are no legal close seasons for muntjac or Chinese water deer. In the case of muntjac, to avoid orphaning dependent fawns it is recommended that only immature and heavily pregnant does are shot. Muntjac bucks can be shot throughout the year but are most likely to be in hard antler between September and April inclusive. Chinese water deer bucks may also be shot at any season without detriment to the species but it is recommended that does should not be shot between 1 March and 31 October.

The only deer which occur in the wild state in Ireland are red deer, sika deer, hybrid red/sika deer and fallow deer. In Northern Ireland there is a close season for the males of all three species from 1 May to 31 July and for females of all three species between 1 March and 31 October, as in England and Wales, the defining measure being The Wildlife (Northern Ireland) Order 1985. In

As well as being illegal to sell venison or offer it for sale except to a licensed game dealer (unless you are a licensed game dealer yourself), it is an offence to sell or offer for sale venison from a deer which is subject to a close season more than ten days after the start of the appropriate close season. It is also illegal for a licensed game dealer to purchase venison illegally procured, or for such venison to be sold or offered for sale if it is known to have been illegally procured.

Should you wish to become a licensed game dealer so that you can retail your own venison you will need to apply to your local authority, who will advise you of any criteria you may be required to meet in order to qualify. The licence itself is obtainable from a post office. The law lays down strict standards for record-keeping by game or venison dealers in respect of every deer

Hampshire game dealer Giacomo Vignola with some of his stock-in-trade. To sell venison otherwise than to the game trade you must become a registered game dealer, as many stalkers are.

handled – date of purchase, species of deer, how it was killed, carcase details, from whom it was bought, and the registration number of the vehicle in which the venison was delivered.

It is illegal to use bows and arrows, snares or poison to kill or take deer, and only under special licence granted by English Nature, the Countryside Council for Wales or the Deer Commission for Scotland may nets or traps be employed to remove deer from one area to another or to catch them up for scientific or educational purposes. Shotguns may only be used to put down sick or injured deer or to kill deer in other circumstances where use of a rifle for the purpose is impracticable.

Aided by modern mass mobility, deer poaching is rife in many areas. Many of the perpetrators have criminal records for other offences and are dangerous men who will stop at nothing to achieve their aims. In certain circumstances you may be entitled to make a citizen's arrest but it goes without saying that firearms should never be used to assist in restraining a suspect. The law allows you to require suspects to supply their names and addresses and to order them off the ground, but if there are several of them and just one of you, have a care for your personal safety. Write down a detailed description of them and note their vehicle registration numbers for future reference, bearing in mind however that the old, clapped-out jalopies commonly used by these people may have false number plates and be

discarded or changed for other vehicles at frequent intervals. Possible penalties for poaching include heavy fines or imprisonment, or both, in respect of each deer involved, and confiscation of vehicles, dogs, weapons and anything else used in furtherance of the offence, but successful prosecutions often prove difficult due to the lack of sufficient evidence.

The Deer Acts empower police to stop and search suspects, to search and examine vehicles, animals, weapons and anything else of a suspicious nature, to arrest a suspect who fails to give his name and address, to seize and detain any item which might be used in evidence, and to enter without a warrant any property other than a dwelling house for these purposes.

Offences in general against The Deer Acts are punishable by fines up to Level 4 – the actual sum being varied periodically to take into account the effects of inflation – or by up to three months' imprisonment, or both.

The Wildlife and Countryside Act 1981 states that in England and Wales deer may be shot during the close season for their species and sex if the occupier of the land concerned is satisfied that they are causing serious damage to agricultural crops or woodland and are likely to cause further such damage unless they are killed. They may be shot by the occupier himself or by a member of his household or an employee of his, acting upon his written authority, or by a person authorised to kill deer on that land or by someone acting upon that person's written authority. If you are asked to undertake such shooting, you would be wise to obtain written authority yourself from the person complaining of the damage, and also to satisfy yourself that the damage is sufficiently serious to warrant out-of-season shooting. Should you be prosecuted for shooting deer out of season, it will be up to you to satisfy the courts that your action was justified on the grounds stated above.

Deer legislation for Scotland was initiated in 1959 with The Deer (Scotland) Act of that year, which was amended in due course by The Deer (Amendment) (Scotland) Acts 1967 and 1982. Subsidiary legislation took the form of The Deer (Close Seasons) (Scotland) Order 1984, The Licensing of Venison Dealers (Prescribed Forms etc.) (Scotland) Order 1984 and The Deer (Firearms etc.) (Scotland) Order 1985. All these measures were repealed when their various provisions were consolidated and further amended by The Deer (Scotland) Act 1996.

This all-embracing statute was designed to update deer law in Scotland in the light of experience and developments since the passing of the first Scottish Deer Act, based as this was on a prime necessity to legislate for red deer. As well as introducing close seasons and other basic protective measures, the main thrust of The Deer (Scotland) Act 1959 was directed towards the setting up of the Red Deer Commission as the central administrative body for the management of this species. Under the 1996 Act this organisation takes on a new identity as the Deer Commission for Scotland (D.C.S.) in recognition of its widened responsibilities for other deer species north of the border.

The stated aim of the D.C.S. is to 'further the conservation, control and suitable management of deer in Scotland, and keep under review all matters, including their welfare, relating to deer, and exercise such other functions as are conferred on them by or under this Act or any other enactment'. In furtherance of these purposes, the Commission is required to take appropriate account of 'the size and density of the deer population and its impact on the natural heritage, the needs of agriculture and forestry, and the interests of owners and occupiers of land'.

Responsible to the Secretary of State for Scotland, the D.C.S. consists of a Chairman and from nine to twelve members with knowledge or experience of deer management, agriculture including crofting, forestry and woodland management, and the natural heritage, or of one or more of these. Organisations representing related interests can suggest suitable persons for appointment as D.C.S. members by the Secretary of State. The D.C.S. is empowered to offer guidance and advice on all deer matters, to work in collaboration with researchers into different aspects of deer behaviour, to appoint panels to advise on specific issues, and to require appropriate standards of deer management to be met.

Having consulted such appropriate persons or bodies as he sees fit, the Secretary of State has power to fix or alter close seasons for all species and both sexes of deer. Those outlined earlier in this chapter are therefore subject to possible future variation should circumstances be judged to make this necessary or desirable.

The D.C.S. can authorise individual owners or occupiers of land, or an individual acting with the written authority of one of these, to take or kill deer which are causing serious damage to unenclosed woodland or to the natural heritage, provided that there is no alternative means of dealing with the problem. Any deer endangering public safety may also be dealt with in this way.

Where deer are causing damage to woodland, to agricultural production including crops and foodstuffs, or to the natural environment generally, or are causing injury to livestock by competing with them for pasture or for supplementary feeding, or are an actual or potential public danger, the D.C.S. may authorise control agreements with owners or occupiers of land. Depending upon the circumstances, such an agreement would require a specified reduction in the numbers of deer of any named species within a clearly defined area, or in extreme cases the complete elimination of such deer. Where no agreement can be arrived at or an agreement has not been put into effect within a predetermined time, the D.C.S. may impose a control scheme requiring a stated number of deer of a particular species or sex to be taken or killed within a specified time. If this is not done by the owner or occupier, the D.C.S. has the power to authorise an appropriate individual to carry out the culling it considers necessary, to sell or otherwise dispose of the resultant venison, and to require the owner or occupier to defray any expenses thereby incurred which cannot be met from the proceeds of venison sales.

Measures to protect the natural heritage are new to deer law in Scotland, and may be applied where a threat arises from the deer population having become unusually high in any area. In these and other circumstances where it is deemed necessary to reduce deer numbers the D.C.S. may, by agreement with owners or occupiers of land, provide equipment or assistance and charge for any expenses incurred. The D.C.S. may also enter upon any land to carry out a census of deer or to perform any other of its functions as defined by the Act.

Offences in relation to deer in Scotland are

broadly similar to those in England and Wales, with the unauthorised killing, taking, injuring or removal of deer heading the list. Deer may not be wilfully killed except by shooting with firearms, ammunition, sights and any other equipment defined by the Secretary of State as being lawful for the purpose. The use of vehicles, aircraft or helicopters for driving deer or for shooting them is illegal except as may be authorised by the D.C.S. in specific circumstances for essential management purposes. Night shooting is prohibited except under special authorisation by the D.C.S. where no alternative is available to deal with a particular problem – the short hours of daylight in winter in Scotland sometimes necessitate night shooting in individual situations. In the restricted circumstances when night shooting or the driving or shooting of deer from vehicles may be authorised, the D.C.S. issues codes of practice which it expects to be strictly observed.

For most offences against The Deer (Scotland) Act 1996 a fine of level 4 on the standard scale or a sentence of three months' imprisonment, or both, may be imposed in respect of every deer involved. Where more than one person is involved in the illegal taking, killing or injuring of a deer, the penalty may be a fine of the statutory maximum for each deer concerned, or six months' imprisonment, or both, or on conviction on indictment a fine or imprisonment for up to two years, or both.

It is not illegal to take action to prevent suffering by a diseased or injured deer, and the 1996 Act also makes it lawful to do the same thing where a calf, fawn or kid has been or is about to be deprived of its mother. In other words, if you shoot, say, a hind with a dependent stag calf or a roe doe with a dependent buck kid when males of the same species are otherwise out of season, you may shoot the youngster as well without any qualms about breaking the law.

Under Section 26 of The Deer (Scotland) Act, where an occupier has reasonable ground for believing that serious damage will be caused to crops, pasture or human or animal·foodstuffs on arable land, improved permanent pasture, 'land which has been regenerated so as to be able to make a significant contribution to the productivity of a holding which forms part of that agricultural land, or on enclosed woodland', any deer on such land may be taken, killed and disposed of by sale. This may be done by the owner in person, employees of the owner or occupier, any other person normally resident on the land in question, 'or any other person approved in writing by the Commission as a fit and competent person for the purpose', regardless of whether it might be the close season for deer of the species and sex involved. It will be noted that in these circumstances the initiative for action may come from the occupier rather than the owner or anyone else, and that the holder of any stalking rights on the land is not exclusively authorised to carry out the necessary culling, and indeed has no such right at all without direct D.C.S. approval.

Subject to any conditions imposed by order of the Secretary of State, local authorities in Scotland may license as a venison dealer any person they deem fit to pursue such a trade. Every licensed dealer is required to keep a book recording all venison purchases and receipts, noting such details as may be prescribed for the purpose. Any dealer who falsifies or fails to keep proper records, or who knowingly handles venison from a deer which has been illegally killed is guilty of an offence and is liable, among other penalties, to forfeiture of his dealer's licence.

Should muntjac or any other deer species not at present covered by this legislation become established in Scotland in the future, the Secretary of State has power to extend to such deer by order the provisions of the Act.

Deer legislation apart, those who employ professional stalkers are advised to acquaint themselves with the relevant provisions of the law governing health and safety at work, especially those which have reference to compensation for possible injury.

CHAPTER 9
Stalker Training

W hen deer legislation first reached the statute book and the way ahead for a much more extensive use of rifles for the control of deer became clear, little or no formal instruction was available for woodland stalkers in general. The Forestry Commission introduced training at an early date for those professionally employed to control and manage deer on its properties, and the St Hubert Club of Great Britain developed courses for stalker members, but the growing numbers of spare-time stalkers were at first largely self-taught. We picked up what we could along the way from kindred spirits, but for the most part the learning process was a matter of trial and error.

All this has now changed. As woodland stalking continued to grow in popularity, widely differing levels of expertise among its practitioners became ever more apparent. Those few who had learned their skills from professionals on the Continent or elsewhere began to find themselves in demand to tutor others less fortunate. *Ad hoc* weekend courses and the like started to feature among activities organised by B.D.S. branches. Support for these was such as to encourage something more ambitious in the form of residential courses, coupled with which there grew a demand for some nationally recognised standard to which trainee stalkers could aspire to demonstrate their eventual competence.

Initially there was some resistance to the concept of tests for stalkers. Older hands who had trained themselves when no alternatives were on offer were sometimes suspicious of what they saw as a threatened encroachment upon the freedom of shooting men and women to enjoy their sport without first satisfying the world at large of their credentials for doing so.

As more and more people attended courses and the balance of opinion steadily tilted in favour of tests, a training committee was set up by the B.D.S. to plan and organise all-round tuition on woodland stalking to prepare

Silhouetted broadside-on against early morning sunlight, this muntjac crossing a woodland ride in Hampshire will be out of sight in the bordering cover within seconds, so quick action is needed if it is to be culled, preferably by shooting off a stick to maximise accuracy and only against a solid background!

candidates for testing. Those who passed the ensuing test were awarded the Woodland Stalkers Competence Certificate (W.S.C.C.), later broadened in scope and changed in title to the National Stalkers Competence Certificate (N.S.C.C.) so as to embrace all aspects of stalking as pursued in Britain.

Stalker training by the B.D.S. has since been expanded to meet other needs such as specific instruction on rifles for beginners and, at the other end of the spectrum, a postgraduate course for N.S.C.C. holders on the wider implications of modern deer management.

A problem for many intending stalkers has been how to obtain legal access to the use of a suitable rifle. Such people have found themselves confronted with the chicken-and-egg situation of having no rifle of their own with which to make a start, nowhere to stalk or to learn to stalk and seemingly no acceptable grounds for being granted an F.A.C.

To help overcome this difficulty, as provided

for under Section 15 of The Firearms (Amendment) Act 1988 the B.D.S. is now registered with the Home Office as a rifle club open to probationary members who can then make use of its facilities to be trained in the safe handling and use of stalking weaponry. Training takes place on Home-Office-approved ranges, under the supervision of a qualified Range Officer and on a one-to-one basis with a B.D.S. member who has held an F.A.C. for at least two years in the role of trainer. Under these conditions a trainee can legally use his tutor's rifle and ammunition.

Trainees enrol as probationary stalkers for a minimum period of six months. Applicants are required to fill in and sign a Form of Declaration that they are not prohibited by law from possessing or handling firearms. Those who are not already B.D.S. members must pay a fee (£22 in 1997), equivalent to one year's membership, or alternatively become members. They must be sponsored by two individuals: one who knows them personally and the other a full B.D.S. member. They must be prepared to train regularly over a period of at least three months. Initial training is in the safe handling of rifles and ammunition, and not until this is completed to the trainer's satisfaction will the trainee be allowed to use a rifle on the range, again under personal supervision.

Shooting takes place on specified guest range days, which must be notified to the police at least forty-eight hours beforehand. The B.D.S. is permitted to hold up to sixty guest range days a year, organised through its various branches around the country. Training progress by each candidate is carefully recorded, with the probationary period ending when an F.A.C. is obtained. Should a trainee be considered by his tutor to be unsuitable, his status as a probationary stalker can be terminated at any time.

Costs of training are kept to a minimum but will include range charges and the trainer's expenses on such items as petrol and ammunition used, adding up to a total of, say £40 or so per training day. Factory ammunition must at all times be used for training purposes.

The core of B.D.S. training continues to be its four-day residential courses preparing candidates for the standard N.S.C.C. test at the end.

Preparatory reading for this hotel-based course is provided in the shape of the B.D.S. manual, *Basic Deer Management*, a copy of which is supplied to every course member. This covers all the prime essentials – safety, rifle maintenance, stalking equipment, the characteristics of the six different wild deer species found in Britain, law, diseases, carcase handling, ballistics and zeroing, judging distance, dogs for stalking, stalking techniques, dealing with the public, taking the shot and what to do and what to look for afterwards. Also included are a series of questions on safety and a list of 300 questions on deer and correct stalking practice, a selection from which must be answered by candidates in the final examination.

A typical course begins on the morning of the first day with lectures on ballistics and safety and rifle care. Then follows a visit to a range for zeroing and shooting practice. Back at the hotel, talks are then given on why deer need to be controlled, judging distances, deer damage and stalking accessories, with videos and informal discussions in the evening after dinner.

Much of the second day is spent on the range for the N.S.C.C. shooting and safety tests, followed by lectures on muntjac and Chinese water deer and on shot reactions and blood signs. The third day is spent at the hotel with talks on the remaining four deer species, on firearms legislation, deer law, carcase handling,

The importance of adequate camouflage is driven home in stalker training. Note how all of the stalker in this deliberately posed picture, except his hands and face, merge into a leafy background.

An important part of stalker training is knowing when, and when not, to take a shot at a target deer. In the case of deer like these two roe, the stalker should hold his fire until their heads are up, their bodies are not obscured by vegetation and one of them is not behind the other.

The doe on the right in this picture is clearly unaware of the stalker and in a suitable position for a neck or heart/lung shot.

ageing deer, stalking techniques and deer management practices on Ministry of Defence lands. Time is then allowed for revision in preparation for the N.S.C.C. written and oral tests next morning, the former consisting of fifty questions from the 300 listed in the manual. A closing address by the B.D.S. Training Officer precedes an open forum and course critique before members disperse around noon.

The cost of this course to each candidate in 1997 was £135, including the pre-course manual,

worth £27.60, but excluding hotel accommodation with full board, which is available to course members at a special all-in price. There is also a small additional charge – £9 in 1997 – to successful candidates for the N.S.C.C. certificate and badge. As well as the residential version, modular N.S.C.C. courses are organised by B.D.S. branches in response to local demand.

N.S.C.C. course participants will normally be expected to bring their own rifles and to possess an F.A.C. permitting them to use them on Home-Office-approved ranges.

N.S.C.C. holders who are also B.D.S. members can apply to take part in the Society's Practical Stalking Scheme which affords three hands-on field outings of about three hours each under the personal supervision of a stalker of experience. This facility is available at a number of locations around the country and includes the opportunity to shoot and gralloch one deer, subject to prevailing circumstances, and for the participant's performance to be assessed by his supervisor, who will complete a report accordingly. Should an intending participant's F.A.C. be area-restricted, arrangements can sometimes be made for the visiting stalker to use his stalking supervisor's rifle through the 'estate rifle' facility now available for such purposes. The cost of taking part in this scheme was £140 in 1997, £40 of which was payable as a deposit at the time of applying to be placed on an appropriate waiting-list. Those taking advantage of this scheme are responsible for their own accommodation arrangements, but supervising stalkers can often advise on available options.

Of particular value to those involved with deer as a facet of estate management as well as to individual stalkers who wish to broaden their knowledge and experience is the B.D.S. six-day Advanced Stalker Course, which is also hotel-based. As befits its wider purpose, this includes lectures on deer management policy, forestry design to facilitate deer control, deer damage prevention, censusing deer populations and cull planning as well as further, in-depth treatment of subjects covered by the N.S.C.C. syllabus, with course members working in syndicates.

Among other features of the Advanced Course are an all-day visit to a major deer park where modern management methods are demonstrated and a separate visit to a forestry location for the same purpose. Special attention is also given to rifle maintenance, to consistently accurate shooting at ranges of up to 150 metres (164 yd), and to the importance of having a suitably trained dog for following up wounded deer. There is a written examination at the end. The fee for this course, excluding board and accommodation, was £195 in 1997.

The B.D.S. also runs courses on the home reloading of ammunition. The Ministry of Defence (M.o.D.) lays down very strict standards of training and performance for members of the services and M.o.D. employees who are permitted to stalk on its lands, and the B.D.S., through its Services Branch, has been much involved with this.

Details of B.D.S. courses, with dates and venues, are obtainable from the General Manager, British Deer Society, Burgate Manor, Fording-bridge, Hampshire SP6 1EF.

Two basic stalking courses are run by the British Association for Shooting and Conservation (B.A.S.C.) for its members. Designed for newcomers to stalking it is a two-day residential course on deer identification and habitats, the why and the how of deer control, fundamental principles of stalking, firearms law and the handling of rifles, with an opportunity for range shooting and for taking the N.S.C.C. shooting and safety tests. Targeted more specifically at preparing and examining candidates for the N.S.C.C. is a four-day residential course providing instruction on deer damage and the need for deer control, the different characteristics of the six British wild deer species, ballistics and rifle maintenance, the law on deer and firearms, judging distance, safety, censusing the stalking techniques and reactions to the shot, carcase inspection, gralloching, high seats, stalking equipment and damage assessment. All four elements of the N.S.C.C. test – shooting, safety, written and visual – are included in the course, which in a typical recent programme was offered at two separate venues, Wareham in Dorset and Ludlow in Shropshire, at a cost of £250 including board and accommodation. An all-inclusive fee of £125 was charged for the two-day course, based at Farnham in Surrey and at Margam in South Wales.

The same recent B.A.S.C. programme for

Male deer with sub-standard or abnormal antlers, like this fallow buck, are obvious candidates for culling.

stalker members also included two one-day courses giving theoretical and practical instruction by a leading expert on dogs for deer, at a cost of £40 per participant. For details of all B.A.S.C. courses contact B.A.S.C. Headquarters, Marford Mill, Rossett, Wrexham LL12 0HL.

In 1997 Forest Enterprise introduced two important new courses at its Deer Training Centre at Torlundy, near Fort William in Inverness-shire. As well as roe deer, these courses give particular attention to red and sika deer management in upland woodlands. Both courses cover essentially the same ground, with a two-day appreciation course designed primarily for landowners and managers and a fuller four-day version for rangers, stalkers, keepers, foresters and any others who may benefit from hands-on instruction as well as theoretical training. Subjects covered include deer management objectives, damage to productive woodlands, impact on habitats, assessing deer densities, population dynamics, computer population modelling, forecasting forest structural change, cull setting and achievement, cohort analysis, population reconstruction and monitoring. The longer course provides practical sessions on habitat stratification, dung counting and vantage-point counting as aids to population assessment, damage assessment, age determination of deer and forest design with effective deer management in mind.

By attending these high-powered courses, private stalkers and deer managers can obtain more than a taste of the quality of training now-adays given by Forest Enterprise to its own professional rangers. The courses are non-residential, being run on a daily attendance basis for participants staying at their own overnight accommodation. A list of addresses is supplied to applicants. Presentations are given by the Chief Ranger (Deer Management) for the North Scotland Region of Forest Enterprise in his role as course leader and by other Forest Enterprise staff of long experience in their subjects. In 1997 the two-day course was held twice and the four-day one three times, with much the same pattern expected to be repeated in subsequent years. Fees for the shorter course were £200 and for the longer one £300. Further details are obtainable from Deer Management Training, Forest Enterprise, Torlundy, Fort William, Inverness-shire PH33 6SW.

The Royal Agricultural College at Cirencester runs a modular course on woodland deer management spread over several days. Aimed at landowners and agents, this combines basic stalking principles and practice with the essentials of land management, taking fully into account the presence of deer in significant numbers, leading on to the N.S.C.C. for candidates who wish to take this. Warwickshire College and Elmwood College in Scotland are among other academic establishments offering deer-related courses.

Those who contemplate a career in wild deer management or deer farming are catered for at Sparsholt College in Hampshire by a one-year full-time residential course, with the Advanced National Certificate in Deer Management as the goal. The course covers species recognition,

biology and behaviour, deer-farming systems and management techniques, wild deer and park deer management, veterinary science and practice, pasture and habitat management, legislation, and financial aspects and management. Sparsholt College also offers a three-year full-time course on the broader aspects of game and wildlife management, with deer as one of the elements, leading on to a National Diploma in these subjects. Full information about these courses is obtainable from the Principal, Sparsholt College Hampshire, Sparsholt, Winchester, Hampshire SO21 2NF.

Training and testing procedures are kept under constant review, and in 1998 the B.D.S. and other relevant organisations set up an independent body, Deer Management Qualifications Limited, to supervise and administer tests of competence in deer management, aimed at ensuring the highest possible level of proficiency. Testing takes place on a single day, successful candidates being awarded a Deer Stalking Certificate (D.S.C.) Grade One, which equates in every respect to the N.S.C.C. The N.S.C.C. remains valid and will continue to be the basis of stalker training by the B.D.S. and other national bodies.

N.S.C.C. holders can, if they wish, apply for the new Deer Stalking Certificate, Grade One, on payment of a small fee. To obtain a Grade Two Certificate, stalkers are required to demonstrate their practical skills by producing evidence, independently vouched for, of successfully shooting and preparing for onward transmission for human consumption three deer on separate occasions. Further information is obtainable from Deer Management Qualifications Limited (D.M.Q Ltd.), c/o The British Association for Shooting and Conservation (B.A.S.C.), Marford Mill, Rossett, Wrexham LL12 0HL.

Stalker training is also offered by various private individuals who advertise their services in the sporting press and elsewhere. If you are thinking of this option, you would be wise to learn all you can about the quality of instruction you are likely to receive before reaching for your chequebook.

CHAPTER 10
Obtaining Stalking

T here was a time when almost anyone who possessed a full-bore rifle could obtain free woodland stalking virtually for the asking. That was when driving deer to shotguns was still very widely practised but country people and others began to realise that there are better and far more humane ways of carrying out essential deer control. This recognition was given a fillip by long-overdue legislation restricting seasons, times and the weaponry permissible for shooting deer.

In the early days of concern for the welfare of deer, or at least for ending their maltreatment, woodland stalkers were very thin on the ground, but deer were many and often unacceptably troublesome. Since then the number of stalkers has increased a hundredfold, and property owners with deer on their land are besieged with unsolicited offers of help in reducing the numbers of these animals. So how can anyone taking up stalking for the first time get in on the act?

The first essential is to become a competent stalker and to be recognised as such. If this still sounds like a classic chicken-and-egg situation, reread chapters 4 and 9 before proceeding further with this one. If you have found an experienced mentor to see you safely through your apprenticeship, you already have at least one foot on the bottom rung of the ladder.

The importance of getting to know other stalkers cannot be overemphasised. If you have not already joined the B.D.S. or one of its two Irish equivalents, do so now and obtain a programme of current activities by your local branch, which are likely to include a mix of indoor meetings and lectures, field trips and organised range shoots. At these meets you will have the chance to form new friendships with stalkers and others, while also enlarging your knowledge of deer, their natural history and management. Do not rush your fences but let things take their natural course, and when the time is ripe ask whether you might accompany a stalker on one of his outings as a student and an observer who could also lend a hand with non-shooting aspects of the stalk.

Offer practical help with such tasks as high seat construction and erection, moving deer to rifles, censusing, or anything else that needs doing by way of back-up, support activity. The more useful you make yourself, the sooner you are likely to receive those much-desired invitations which can lead on to other things, setting you on the road towards having some stalking of your own.

Find out whether a local deer management society or group exists in your area. These organisations sometimes hold meetings to which the public are invited: go along to any such meetings and make yourself and your interests known. There may come an opportunity to be considered as a member of a panel of accredited stalkers retained by one of these societies to carry out emergency work or to undertake ongoing deer control, perhaps initially as a probationer. As with any other activity to which many are called but few are chosen, dogged persistence, patience and dedication will yield the best dividends, 'sorting out the men from the boys' among a queue of aspirants.

Free stalking may still sometimes be had, but do not count on it coming your way. If you are lucky enough to obtain some, look after it and nurture it in every possible way, or somebody else from that lengthening queue of stalking hopefuls may take your place.

So be prepared to pay for your stalking, perhaps as one of a small team sharing expenses as they arise. Where limiting damage by deer is the main reason for stalking becoming available, a peppercorn rent may be all that is asked. If part or all of the proceeds of venison sales belong to the stalkers, this can go some way towards meeting incidental costs, but never be tempted to look upon stalking as a source of significant revenue, in this way or any other, if you value it as a sport. Look upon yourself as a guardian of the countryside with its wildlife, conduct yourself accordingly and your satisfaction with what you achieve will be all the greater. The outdoor world may not be your oyster, but as a participant in its management, in no matter how small a degree, you will be in a position of privilege accorded to only a relatively few among the vast numbers of those who like to spend their leisure-time out of town.

Apart from the possibilities of renting your own regular stalking, either just for yourself and guests or as a team or syndicate member, client stalking, chargeable by the individual outing or for a predetermined number of outings within a specified period, is now fairly widely available. One source is Forest Enterprise, the commercial arm of the Forestry Commission, which offers stalking on a fee-paying basis in four of the five administrative regions into which Forestry Commission properties throughout Great Britain are currently organised; the one exception is Wales.

Forest Enterprise offers woodland stalking on many of its properties in England and Scotland but not in Wales.

Subject to some minor variation between regions, standard conditions are laid down for what Forest Enterprise defines as 'permit deerstalking'. A permit entitles a stalker to shoot specified deer in specified areas, at times convenient to the local Forest District Manager, but not on Sundays or public holidays. The permit holder will be accompanied by a Forest Ranger on all occasions and may be required to provide transport for the Ranger and himself.

The stalker must use a rifle of not less than .240 (6.1 mm) calibre (.222/5.7 mm in Scotland) and soft- or hollow-nosed bullets developing a muzzle energy of at least 1,700 ft lb or 238 metre kg (1,100 ft lb or 155 metre kg in Scotland) for roe deer and not less than 2,200 ft lb or 290 metre kg for red, sika and fallow deer. He must fire a group of sighting shots within a 10 cm (3.9 in) target area at 100 metres' (109 yd) range to the satisfaction of the Ranger or other official, for which a small charge (at least £12 in 1996) will be made. He must on request produce an F.A.C. valid for where he wishes to shoot and proof of third-party insurance cover to a value of at least £2 million, and must also indemnify the Forestry Commission against any loss, injury or damage arising from the exercise of the permit. He may use entirely at his own risk any stand or high seat provided by the Forestry Commission. Shooting from vehicles or by artificial light is not permitted, and in some forests shooting may only take place in early morning, for reasons of safety.

Priority will be given to shooting any injured deer that may be encountered. If a deer is shot and wounded, stalking will be suspended until the animal is found or otherwise accounted for, dogs being provided for this purpose as may be necessary – a stalker may not bring his own dogs into the forest. Deer carcases remain the property of the Forestry Commission but may be purchased by the stalker at the prevailing market price. The Forestry Commission reserves the right to vary the conditions and charges and to suspend or withdraw any permit, and while every reasonable effort is made to provide satisfaction, no guarantee of success is given. In cases where Forest Enterprise has obtained a Visitor's Firearms Permit on a client's behalf, and in all cases where lockable storage facilities approved by the local constabulary are not available when rifles and ammunition are not in use, these must be left on such occasions in the safe keeping of a Ranger.

For a deer shot at and missed or wounded a penalty charge will be levied – a minimum of £25 for a miss and £30 for a wounding in 1996. In the case of a badly shot deer which loses part or all of its value as venison, or one not recovered within twelve hours of being shot, the client may be required to pay what would have been the full market price of the carcase as well as for time spent by the Ranger, up to a maximum of twelve hours, searching for a lost deer. This time was charged at £12.50 per hour in 1996.

Scales of fees and the basis for charging vary between different forest regions or, in some cases, between different forest districts, and charges are of course periodically updated to take due account of inflation and other factors. But as an example, in the South and West Forest Region in 1996, a base rate of £12.50 per hour was charged for each outing, and each outing was a minimum of three hours. Subject to the agreement of the Regional Director, outings may be for the purpose of photography, sketching, or merely observing deer rather than for shooting them. Outings are charged to the nearest hour and include all time spent with the Ranger.

Shooting fees in this region are graded according to quality as well as to species and sex, medal-class trophies being retained for official assessment before being released to the client, whose property they become once the appropriate charges are paid. Trophy preparation can be carried out for the client at a cost in 1996 of £20 for roe or muntjac or £30 for red deer, fallow or sika.

For red deer stags the basic charge in 1996 in this region is graduated according to the number of points on the antlers of each trophy, rising from £70 for a head with four points or fewer to £880 as a minimum for one of over sixteen points. Heads with eleven or more points are subject to official assessment, while the charge for shooting a stag under two years old was £50. In addition to the basic scale, for heads assessed as of medal quality and scoring from 165 to 179 points on the Conseil International de la Chasse (C.I.C.) scale, that is to say a bronze medal head, there was a trophy charge of £1.80 per C.I.C.

point. (For more on the C.I.C. system of trophy evaluation, see chapter 18). The equivalent fee for a silver medal head (180 to 194 points) was £2.50 per C.I.C. point, and for a gold medal head (195 or more points) £3.50 per C.I.C. point. Hummels (stags which do not grow antlers), known as 'notts' in south-west England, and freaks, were chargeable at a minimum of £100 per stag, red deer hinds being charged at a minimum of £50 each.

Fallow bucks could cost as little as £30 at the basic rate for a beast with antlers less than 15 cm long, or as much as £300 with an antler length of 57 cm (22.4 in) or more and a palm width of at least 12 cm (4.7 in). Fallow heads longer than 52 cm (20.5 in) and with a greater palm width than 8.9 cm (3.5 in) are subject to C.I.C. assessment, with additional charges which in 1996 were £1.25 per C.I.C. point for a bronze medal head (160 to 169.99 points), £1.80 per C.I.C. point for a silver medal head (170 to 179.99 points), and £2.75 per C.I.C. point for a gold medal head (180 or more points). Freaks were charged at a minimum of £200 per buck, the minimum charge for a fallow doe being £30.

Sika stags in this region are basically charged according to the length and total number of points on the antlers, ranging in 1996 from £50 for a head with fewer than four points and less than 30 cm (11.8 in) long to £600 for a six-, seven- or eight-point head at least 50 cm (19.7 in) long, with every extra point in excess of eight being charged at £20 per point. Over and above this basic scale is an additional charge based on beam measurement, that is to say the minimum circumference of the beam of the antler between the brow and middle tines, taking the average of both antlers. The charge where the beam measures less than 8 cm (3.1 in) was £120, £160 where the beam measurement is between 8 and 9 cm (3.1 and 3.5 in) and £220 for a beam dimension of 9 cm (3.5 in) or more.

Sika trophies bearing six or more points and with a minimum beam circumference of 8 cm (3.1 in) are treated as medal heads and assessed according to a scale laid down by the Forestry Commission. Based on this reckoning, bronze medal heads are those between 45 and 49.9 cm (17.7 and 19.6 in) in length and with a beam circumference of from 8 to 8.9 cm (3 to 3.5 in), for which an additional trophy fee of £250 was charged in 1996. Silver medal heads are of similar length but with a beam circumference of 9 to 9.9 cm (3.5 to 3.9 in) for which the additional trophy charge was £350, and gold medal heads, over 50 cm (19.7 in) long and with a beam circumference of 10 cm (3.9 in) or more, rated an additional trophy fee of £550. Freak heads were charged at locally agreed and negotiated rates, and sika hinds at a minimum of £30 each.

Roe buck knobbers with antlers of fewer than four points and less than 9.9 cm (3.9 in) long were chargeable at £35 per head. Charges for roe bucks with heads of four or more points ranged from £50 for those with antlers between 10 and 15.9 cm (3.9 and 6.3 in) long to £600 for a beast with antlers 28 cm (11 in) long or more. Weights for assessment purposes are as for standard short-nose cut cleaned trophies, air-dried for twenty-four hours. Long-nose cut trophies, upper jaw excluded, have 45 g (1.6 oz) deducted and whole skulls, minus lower jaw, have 90 g (3.2 oz) deducted from actual weights in order to give comparative evaluation with short-nose cut trophies.

A surcharge of £10 per point was made for every point on a roebuck trophy in excess of six. Heads with four or more points and a length of 23 cm (9 in) or more have the average length assessed in accordance with C.I.C. criteria. For bronze medal heads (scoring 105 to 114.9 C.I.C. points), in 1996 there was a charge of £180 plus £4 per C.I.C. point. The charge for silver medal heads (115 to 129.9 C.I.C. points) was £230 plus £6 per C.I.C. point, and for gold medal heads (130 or more C.I.C. points) £400 plus £14 per C.I.C. point. Freak heads were subject to a minimum charge of £200 plus any extra sum negotiated and agreed locally, with C.I.C. assessment being made of larger heads. Charges quoted for medal heads were in addition to the basic scale. There was a minimum charge of £25 for roe does.

Muntjac bucks are charged according to antler length: in 1996 £50 if under 4 cm (1.6 in), £80 from 4 to 5.9 cm (1.6 to 2.3 in) £120 from 6 to 10 cm (2.4 to 3.9 in), or £180 over 10 cm (3.9 in). For medal heads, assessed according to the C.I.C. formula, there was an additional charge of £150 for a bronze, £200 for a silver and £300 for a gold. Freaks were charged by negotiation and agreement, the minimum being £150, and for muntjac does a minimum charge of £20 applied.

These charges were for the South and West England Region in 1996 and are taken from a brochure on permit deer stalking issued by Forest Enterprise. The region covers the whole of England south-west of a somewhat tortuous line drawn on the map from just north of Merseyside to London and the Thames estuary and taking in Staffordshire and the Chilterns. Within this region five species of deer are available for stalking: fallow, roe and muntjac in Midlands, Marches, Forest of Dean, and Downs and Chilterns Forest Districts; red, fallow and roe in Peninsula Forest District (Somerset, Devon and Cornwall); sika and roe in Dorset Forest District; and fallow and roe in Weald Forest District.

In the North and East England Forest Region, facilities and charges for client stalking vary between different forest districts. South Lakes Forest District offers some of the finest and most varied woodland stalking in northern England, with red and roe deer both available. Fees quoted here are again 1996 ones, starting with a non-returnable booking fee of £40, which also covers rifle zeroing. Stalking fees listed are £40 for an outing of up to three hours' duration and £10 per hour thereafter, or £600 for a weekly roe buck stalking package.

Shooting charges are extra. A red stag under two years of age could cost as little as £50 or a stag with fewer than five points £90. Graduated charges for stags with larger trophies range from £110 for a modest five-pointer to a hefty £1,100 for a seventeen-pointer, by no means unattainable here. These are only basic charges; all trophy heads are subject to a minimum fee of £350, although it is not made clear what constitutes such a head. Over and above this, bronze medal heads are surcharged at £1.50 per C.I.C. point, silver medal heads at £2.50 per C.I.C. point and gold medal ones at £3 per C.I.C. point. Red hinds are charged at £50 each.

Charges for roe bucks vary from £30 for a knobber with antlers less than 5 cm (2 in) long, one with three points or less and under 23 cm (9 in) long or a four-pointer under 22 cm (8.7 in) long to £200 for a five- or six-pointer over 28 cm (11 in) long, with each additional point over six being charged at £25 extra. Bronze medal heads are surcharged at £225 plus £4.50 per C.I.C. point, silver medal heads at £275 plus £6.90 per

C.I.C. point and gold medal heads £475 plus £16.00 per C.I.C. point. Part points are charged as whole points.

On the basis of these prices, a six-point roe buck of gold medal status, with antlers 26 cm (10.2 in) long and scoring, say, 140 C.I.C. points would cost the stalker £795 plus outing charges. If he had booked for a whole week and the gold medal buck was his sole success, his bill would therefore add up to £1,395, and local forest district rules require payments to be made in cash!

Roe buck stalking on a weekly package basis is also available in the 60,000 hectares of Kielder Forest District, in north Northumberland along the Scottish border. The package covers eight three-hour outings over a four-day period, accompanied by a Forest Ranger and with van transport provided. In 1997 the all-in charge for this was £600 and the stalking period was from 14 April to 26 June and from 21 July to 12 August. Roe doe stalking on a two-day package basis is sometimes available at Kielder, but this arrangement was suspended during the 1996–97 doe season. No help is available for trophy preparation.

Farther east in Northumberland, roe buck stalking is available in Rothbury Forest District, where trophies are scaled according to quality along lines broadly similar to those in South Lakes Forest District. However, charges are slightly different, and trophy weight and antler length both serve as evaluation components for all heads with five or more points. In 1997 the charge for a knobber was £10. Heads of three points or less were charged at from £20 to £60 according to length, and four-pointers at up to £70. Five- or six-pointers under 16 cm (6.3 in) or less than 160 g (5.6 oz) in weight were priced at a mere £20. Those measuring 16 cm (6.3 in) or more and weighing from 160 to 199 g (5.6 to 7 oz) attracted a £40 charge, longer and heavier ones being charged on a sliding scale of from £50 for trophies 16 cm (6.3 in) and over and weighing from 200 to 239 g (7 to 8.4 oz) to £530 for heads 28 cm (11 in) or longer and weighing 560 g (19.8 oz) or more. A standard charge of £200 was made for freak heads. The separate stalking fee was £42 per outing for up to three hours, with any additional time charged at £14 per hour. Clients must use Forestry Commission transport driven by their accompanying Ranger, a mileage charge being made for conveyance between their accommodation and where they stalk.

Planted mainly with Scots and Corsican pine in the 1920s but now much diversified, Thetford Forest brackets the Norfolk–Suffolk border in East Anglia and is England's largest lowland forest, extending to 20,000 hectares. A team of half a dozen Forest Rangers headed by a Chief Ranger is responsible for deer management, and roe and muntjac stalking is available to clients. As well as actual stalking, some shooting is also done from high seats, as is the case in forests elsewhere. Roe bucks and muntjac may be stalked between 1 April and the end of May, with bookings also being taken for the period of the roe rut, between mid-July and mid-August, while roe does and muntjac are available between 1 November and the end of February. Bookings can be made for muntjac only, although muntjac may also be shot by stalkers who are mainly concerned with roe. Muntjac does may only be shot on the instructions of an accompanying Ranger. Two-day packages are most usual, costing in 1996–7 £240 for roe bucks, £170 for roe does or £220 for muntjac. Three-, four- or five-day bookings are also sometimes available, costing respectively (1996–7 prices again) £360, £480 and £600 for roe bucks, £225, £340 and £425 for roe does and £330, £440 and £550 for muntjac. Stalking here is for sport rather than for trophies; the average quality of roe antlers in particular is only moderate. Even so, the demand for roe buck stalking in Thetford Forest is such that it tends to be fully booked well before the start of the season.

Also fully booked well ahead when I inquired was the fallow and muntjac stalking available to clients in Northants Forest District, which includes the scattered remnants of the old royal forest of Rockingham, noted for deer throughout the centuries. Stalking is organised on a daily and a weekly package basis. Prices in 1996–7 for a single three-hour outing were £15 for the stalk, plus a sliding scale for fallow bucks ranging from £20 for a beast with antlers less than 15 cm (5.9 in) long to £200 for one with antlers 57 cm (22.4 in) or more in length and 12 cm (4.7 in) or more in width across the palms. Medal category fallow bucks are not a prime feature of this area.

Muntjac bucks with antlers less than 5 cm (2 in) long were charged at £60, and £120 for those with antlers of any greater length. Muntjac and fallow does were charged at £15 per head. Weekly packages of nine stalks spread over five days cost £565 for muntjac only, £670 for fallow and muntjac bucks, £730 for fallow and muntjac bucks and does, and £500 for fallow and muntjac does. Package prices were all-inclusive, irrespective of how many deer were shot, and there was no extra charge for trophies.

At the time of writing, facilities for client stalkers were unavailable in the North Yorks Moors Forest District, Sherwood and Lincolnshire Forest District and Suffolk Forest District of the North and East England Forest Region.

The South Scotland Region covers the whole area from the English border to the southern fringes of the Highlands north of Glasgow and Edinburgh. Red deer and roe deer stalking are both available on either a daily or a weekly (Monday to Friday) basis. Red deer may be stalked in September, October and November, stags until 20 October and hinds from 21 October. Roe bucks may be stalked in May and June, and roe does from 21 October and in November. The five-day package for red deer was priced in 1997 at £755 for stags and £320 for hinds, the daily rate being £120 and £45 respectively. Equivalent charges for roe were £660 for bucks and £320 for does for five-day bookings, and for one-day clients £80 for bucks and £40 for does. These were all-in charges, exclusive of any penalties; there are no extra charge for trophies in this region. The five-day arrangement covers eight outings of at least three hours' duration when stalking red deer of either sex and nine outings for those who book to stalk either roe bucks or roe does. One-day clients for either species are entitled to one outing.

Transport is provided. Stalkers are expected to be reasonably fit and to use their own rifles, which when not in use must be stored for safe keeping by a Ranger if no suitable lockable storage is available at the client's accommodation. All stalking is Ranger-accompanied, and clients may shoot only those deer indicated by the Ranger. As with Kielder Forest, no help from forestry staff with trophy preparation is available in the region.

In South and North Scotland alike, stalking booked by the week can sometimes be shared between two stalkers, with only one operating or in the Ranger's company at any one time. Another factor common to the two regions is that trophy shooting is not a prime objective and trophy surcharges are not levied.

North Scotland Region encompasses some 300,000 hectares of actual forest, plus a further 100,000 hectares of unplanted moorland. Much of this is very rough terrain where cold, wet weather is not infrequent and a fairly high standard of physical fitness is important. All stalking is carried out under the personal supervision of a Ranger and is available on a weekly package basis at an all-in price. The package provides for twenty-seven hours of stalking spread over eight or nine outings of three or more hours' duration. It may occasionally be possible to book stalking for a shorter period than one week.

Three species are available for stalking in this region: red and sika stags from late September to 20 October, red and sika hinds and roe does between 21 October and mid-February, and roe bucks from May to mid-August. A weekly package for red or sika stags was priced in 1996 at £795 and for females of any of the three species at £420. A similar package for roe bucks was priced at two separate levels dependent upon location: £725 for 'Band A' forests, covering eleven forest districts, and £685 for 'Band B' forests, in three other forest districts.

A point worth noting by novice stalkers is that Rangers in this region are prepared to offer training in the basic principles of stalking, including the handling of firearms. They can also offer advice on trophy preparation, and some may be prepared to undertake this for a small fee on clients' behalf. Stalking takes place during the first and last hours of daylight, transport being provided. In some forests considerations of safety may restrict stalking to early morning. If bad weather or other factors cause a stalk to be cancelled, an alternative will be offered wherever possible. Firearms security arrangements are the same as in the South Scotland Region.

The North Scotland Region can advise stalking clients on where to obtain accommodation most convenient for specific forests, and on car hire facilities. For stalkers without either a rifle of their own or the necessary legal documentation permitting the use of their rifle in this region, the accompanying Ranger's rifle may be used for an extra charge.

For a small fee, Forest Enterprise is able, through its various regional offices or, in some cases, forest district headquarters, to arrange to obtain, on an overseas client's behalf, a U.K. Visitors Firearms Permit, which is essential for bringing firearms and ammunition into Britain. Residents of European Union member states must furnish their European Firearm Permit when applying for the obligatory U.K. Permit, which is valid for one year from the date of issue. Holders of U.K. F.A.C.s must ensure that their certificate permits their rifle(s) to be used for stalking in the forests of whichever region they intend to visit to pursue their sport. Holders of area-restricted F.A.C.s should therefore apply to their local constabulary for an appropriate variation – perhaps an ideal opportunity to obtain the open F.A.C. to which most stalkers aspire. Should you need further advice on this, contact the Forest Enterprise office through which you hope to arrange your stalking. It should also be borne in mind that you may have to join a waiting-list for the type of stalking you seek, which in some forest regions applies to every type of stalking offered.

Except in the case of penalty charges, which are not subject to V.A.T., all Forest Enterprise charges quoted are inclusive of V.A.T. If some of these charges seem on the high side, they reflect prevailing market conditions, largely influenced as these are by what stalkers from overseas, particularly many of those from fellow-EU countries, are prepared to pay for their sport, and it needs to be borne in mind that there is a heavy demand from Continental sportsmen for stalking in Britain. Perhaps some of us have been getting our sport too cheaply!

In conjunction with Forest Enterprise, the B.A.S.C. offers stalking to members who already have some experience, preferably having completed the Introductory Stalking or the N.S.C.C. course. Stalking is available in five forest districts and is subject to the same basic conditions as for other stalking clients of Forest Enterprise, all stalking being Ranger-accompanied. In the Wareham area of Dorset

High seats are widely used by stalking clients of Forest Enterprise.

Forest District sika stags may be stalked in September and November, roe bucks in the whole district from 1 April to 31 October, and sika hinds and roe does between 1 November and the end of February. Mortimer Forest District, near Ludlow in Shropshire, provides opportunities for shooting both fallow and roe, either from high seats or, for more experienced stalkers, on foot. Here there is also a chance to encounter the remarkable long-haired fallow which are peculiar to this area.

Kershope Forest, on the Scottish border in north-east Cumbria, offers roe stalking on foot in 5,000 hectares of largely coniferous forest on hilly terrain. By contrast, King's Forest, near Thetford on the Suffolk–Norfolk border, is entirely flat, and the roe shooting available there may only be done from high seats. Different again are the Blackdown Hills, on the Somerset–Devon border south of Taunton, where roe may be stalked, and the fringes of Exmoor, where red and fallow deer are available to B.A.S.C. stalker-members.

Charges in 1996 were based on a certain amount for the first beast culled and a lesser amount for each subsequent beast of the same sex and species shot per outing, for example £100 and £50 respectively for a first and a second sika stag, £80 and £40 respectively for a first and second roe buck and £80 and £45 respectively for a first and second fallow buck. There was a lower scale of charges for female deer of the various species, and a small administrative surcharge. A penalty fee of £50 was imposed for a missed or wounded animal, and a charge of £40 was made if no shot was fired on any individual outing. Stalks can be booked per outing, bookings for more than one outing being particularly advised for those who had to travel long distances to reach the forest of their choice. Outings are of three to five hours' duration.

Besides imposing its own stringent tests of stalker competence, the St Hubert Club of Great Britain has for a very long time provided stalking for its members on land leased from the Forestry Commission for this purpose.

In the state-owned forests of Ireland, both North and South, there are facilities for stalkers, the principal quarry being fallow and sika deer although, in the Republic, there is also some red deer stalking available. In the case of Northern Ireland, resident stalkers are required to have passed the N.S.C.C. or an equivalent test of competence. Visiting stalkers from mainland Britain must obtain a Certificate of Approval from the Royal Ulster Constabulary to be permitted to bring firearms and ammunition into the province, certificates are readily granted to Section 1 F.A.C. holders. Those who wish to stalk in the Republic must first obtain from the Department of Justice (Firearms Section) in Dublin an Importation Licence for their rifles and ammunition. The Department also grants F.A.C.s to non-residents. In 1993 the existing emergency restrictions on the private use of rifles in excess of .22/250 calibre were relaxed, permitting rifles up to .270 calibre to be held and used by stalkers, who must also obtain a hunting licence. For stalkers from other EU member countries the same basic rules for importing and using firearms and ammunition apply in both Irish jurisdictions as in Britain.

A number of sporting agencies and private individuals offer stalking by the individual outing or for longer periods, usually on the basis of being accompanied and guided throughout by an appropriate individual. The advertisement columns of the sporting press offer tempting opportunities which are well worth investigating, but before committing yourself make sure you will be getting good value for your money. There is no harm in asking for references.

CHAPTER 11
Preparing the Ground

Once you have a piece of ground to call your own in stalking terms, a mood of euphoria may grip you. You are on the threshold of new experiences with exciting possibilities, the full extent of which only the future can determine. You also have new responsibilities, new commitments, and taking stock of these has a somewhat sobering influence, helping your expectations to assume a more balanced perspective.

As for that uncertain future, all other things being equal it is yours to make or break. Whether or not the ground has ever previously been stalked, you and your performance will be subjected to critical scrutiny, hopefully cloaked, at least at first, in the polite friendliness customarily extended to a newcomer who is also, in some sense, a guest. This honeymoon period will be brief, and while it lasts you will be on trial. It will be up to you to justify the trust which has been placed in you by doing a good job of work efficiently and being seen to do so.

Establish a good working relationship with everyone involved: the owner or lessor (obviously), the Head Forester, Farm Manager or tenant farmer and those concerned with game shooting, especially the Gamekeeper. At one time deer control was largely left in the hands of keepers, who got together teams of beaters, local farmers, farm workers and fellow keepers for organised deer drives to shotguns once the pheasant season was over. These *battues*, in the minds of participants, were no more than vermin shoots, and were treated as such. At the end of the day the keepers would usually be the ones to benefit from the proceeds of venison sales, although carcases spattered with shotgun pellets were not always readily marketable.

Many keepers still do their own deer control, albeit nowadays with a rifle. Their employers often leave them to arrange this as they think best, with venison sales as perks, and the keepers tend to keep tight-lipped about the numbers of deer thus disposed of. On properties where deer

Find somewhere suitable on your stalking ground where you can set up a target to check from time to time that your rifle is correctly zeroed.

management is carried on in this way there is clearly little scope for input by unconnected leisure-time stalkers, but it is just as well to be aware how these things operate.

However, not all keepers are stalkers. Bird men by tradition, many of the older generation have looked upon deer which have arrived on their ground as a somewhat unwelcome extra, imposing new responsibilities with which they would rather not be involved, as well as demanding expertise for which they have had no previous need and which they have consequently never acquired. Typical of the kind, I suspect, was a Head Keeper of my acquaintance whose aristocratic employer had suddenly woken up to the sporting potentiality of roe which had only just begun to colonise the area. The Head Keeper felt he was being put upon when he was instructed to manage the deer as an additional sporting resource and to familiarise himself, a little late in life perhaps, with the nuts and bolts of the undertaking.

If game is preserved on ground where you stalk, with a Keeper employed for the purpose, you will fail to make friends with him at

So keep the Keeper on your side. Find out when shoots are planned and where. If you have game shooting of your own, invite him along as a guest and he may well reciprocate next time a 'keeper's day' comes around. Listen to his problems, suggest any obvious ways in which you might help to solve them, and remember him at Christmas. Once you have overcome any lingering mistrust and misunderstanding he will become your most useful ally, updating you with information about local deer activity which you may have missed if you spend less time on the ground than the Keeper himself, as is almost bound to be the case if you are purely a leisure-time stalker.

In making yourself and your activities known to those concerned with farming and forestry on ground where you will be stalking, find out what problems the deer may be causing and what may need to be done about them. Find out what harvesting, planting and other operations are envisaged and how they may impact on your stalking plans, and agree some method of letting others know when you will be stalking – perhaps a phone call or two beforehand, or a sign placed at a prominent spot to make others aware of your presence.

As a moment's thought will make clear, the key to controlling deer numbers is to cull sufficient females. The fact that most of the open season for shooting hinds and does coincides with the pheasant shooting season can be a source of serious difficulties if stalking and game shooting interests are thought to be incompatible. They certainly need not be, and there is a case for sensible compromise. Properly conducted, woodland stalking is unobtrusive. It causes almost no disturbance, and pheasants can remain secure in their coverts while you quietly creep the rides, with an occcasional shot from your rifle the only thing to break the silence. But to help make everybody happy, agree not to stalk at all on the day preceding a covert shoot.

If, in spite of all this, those concerned with game shooting are adamant that no deerstalking should take place until after the pheasant season is over, you will simply have to live with this, while pointing out to those concerned the obvious limitations this places on your ability to effect an adequate cull in the short time available. Ways of mitigating this problem are

Thorough knowledge of the ground and of patterns of movement by the deer is a prime prerequisite to successful stalking. You cannot spend too much time reconnoitring.

your peril. Many years ago I was invited to carry out deer control on property where roe had only recently moved in. The Keeper stuck to his pheasants. Although I took steps from the outset to liaise with him completely about our separate activities, with his quite sensibly taking priority over mine if our plans clashed, the new arrangement did not please him. He was particularly uneasy about a stranger with a full-bore rifle being given the freedom of the estate. It took time for his fears on this score to subside. Then one day I shot a fox which had been fattening on his pheasants, and from that time on we worked in harmony.

discussed in chapter 19.

Before you commence any actual culling, get to know the ground concerned as thoroughly as possible. If an estate map is available, study it carefully, taking particular note of boundaries, public footpaths and other details especially relevant to your future operations. A preliminary tour of the ground with the owner or his agent will help put things in perspective. When reconnoitring on foot, note all major signs of deer activity such as fraying-stocks where roe bucks have marked their presence on wayside saplings, the principal crossing-points of rides, feeding areas, and the locations and nature of any obvious deer damage.

Follow this up by spending some time getting to know the deer on the ground. Study their habits and movements. Make a provisional estimate of their numbers and sexual breakdown, recording what you see and noting the details on a photocopy of the estate map if you have been given one. If no estate map is available, buy a copy of the local Ordnance Survey map - the 6 in to the mile one - and sketch in the relevant details. Make sure to get the boundaries right: on unfamiliar ground especially it is easy to make mistakes here, and neighbours might not look indulgently upon inadvertent armed trespass.

In the course of your reconnoitring note any obvious cull candidates among the deer you see - that is to say, old, ailing, undersized or otherwise substandard specimens. Prepare a proper cull plan, indicating how many deer of each species and sex, including immature animals, you propose shooting during the period up to the end of the next or current hind/doe season, and stick to this as closely as possible as your basis for operations. Your stalking landlord may well require this, but produce one anyway. It does not have to be inflexible. During its currency fresh deer might unexpectedly move in, requiring an extra culling effort, or

circumstances might change in other respects and you should adapt your plans accordingly.

Do not leave neighbours out of the reckoning. Where deer have been present for more than a fairly short period there are not nowadays many patches of ground, however minuscule or marginal as habitat for deer, where somebody with a stalking rifle is not already active. Try to find out who else may be stalking in the area and whether such stalkers may be agreeable to exchanging information or otherwise harmonising their plans with your own. Do not mind too much if you run up against a brick wall here. Some stalkers are almost paranoid about 'doing their own thing' and letting as few people as possible know precisely what that is. After all, being the solitary activity which, for the most part, it has to be, stalking attracts loners.

In any case, there is no harm in making yourself known to those with property next door. You may need their co-operation at some time in the future. After all, deer cross property boundaries. It could happen that one from your side, shot but not mortally wounded, runs off onto neighbouring ground where you cannot legally follow it up unless the owner permits you to do so. Alternatively one of your best deer-holding coverts may lie right on the property boundary, next to pasture or other open ground which offers attractive grazing. Deer may regularly appear there - 'your' deer, as you see it - but can do nothing abut them while they remain on the wrong side of the fence. The owner concerned might welcome help from you in culling some of these animals, which will much more easily be done on his ground than in the wood on your side. Explain the problem from your angle and see if he is willing for you to shoot what are legally his deer while on his land. A haunch or two of venison or the proceeds from the sale of a carcase or two may ease the way here.

CHAPTER 12
Strategies and Tactics

Unless you have been asked to take emergency action of some kind as your first priority, you will hopefully have taken time getting to know in every possible detail the ground where you will be stalking, learning as much as you can from others as well as from personal observations about the deer there and any problems they may be causing. Having worked out an initial culling plan and agreed this with your stalking landlord, the time arrives for your first armed foray.

Some stalkers do not trouble themselves with such niceties as cull plans. Jumping straight in at the deep end, they focus their attention on the best trophy stags or bucks and proceed to annihilate them in short order. This creaming-off process completed, most probably on ground where stalking rights have had to be paid for fairly handsomely and the stalker's prime concern is to get what value he can for his money as quickly as possible, his enthusiasm may speedily wane to the point where he will start looking around for somewhere else to exploit in a similar way. If this is an obvious example of how not to go about it if the good name of the sport is to be preserved, it is certainly not rare and should claim a high place on any stalker's list of temptations to be resisted.

Guided by those basic principles of humane, responsible management which should apply in all circumstances, how you should now proceed in detail will of course depend upon the species of deer with which you are involved. Let us first assume that they are all, or mostly, roe. It is early spring, 1 April in fact. Despite the inauspicious date, you are determined, above all else, not to make a fool of yourself on what happens also to be the first day of the open season for shooting roe bucks in England and Wales and also in Scotland. In Ireland, of course, there are no roe, but many enthusiasts from that country cross the water to stalk this species.

Early April is the ideal time to see more of what deer are about and to continue and amplify your preliminary observations while perhaps also doing some culling. Trees are still bare of leaf, dead bracken has been beaten down by the winter storms, and the early bite of fresh spring greenery on surrounding pastures and fields of young corn is attracting deer to feed in the open. Although roe are browsers for the most part, always selecting the tenderest and most nutritious parts of the shrubs and woodland herbage of their choice, at winter's end such choice is minimal, making the first flush of seasonal verdure outside the woods all the more compellingly alluring. At the same time, deer in the woods themselves are easier to see now than at any other season.

Some of the older bucks will already have rubbed off the velvet which sheaths growing antlers, although many, especially the younger ones, will still be fully in velvet. As April progresses more of the older bucks will be seen to be clean of velvet. On the other hand most if not all of the yearlings, nearly all with small, single-spike antlers although there may be exceptions to this, remain in velvet throughout April and most of May and, in some cases, well into June.

No matter that yearlings are still in velvet, April is the month in which to concentrate your culling on these youthful tearaways of the deer world. They have as yet no value as trophies and should be fairly ruthlessly pruned to help reduce later forestry damage caused by too many males disputing potential territories. When May arrives, turn your attention to some of the older bucks you may already have marked down for culling, and keep a sharp lookout for possible newcomers to your ground which may be equally worth culling. The month of May in general is when roe bucks are most mobile, sorting out new territories or redefining old ones while seeing off presumptuous rivals. At the same time, surplus yearlings which you may not yet have caught up with are roaming around like lost souls, being chivvied mercilessly by their

Be ready at all times for instant action while you are stalking. If you are caught out in the open you are likely to have only seconds to achieve a cull, preferably shooting off a stalking stick rather than free-hand for greater accuracy.

elders as they try to find somewhere to call their own.

The first half of May has the added advantage that the woods are still largely bare of undergrowth tall enough to restrict your view, while deciduous trees are still in the early stages of coming into fresh leaf unless an unusually warm spring has stimulated precocious development. Once bracken starts growing in earnest visibility under the trees becomes much reduced. As for roe feeding in the open, make the most of this while it lasts. Except where flower meadows still survive and remain ungrazed by domestic stock, as soon as new grass and young cereals grow beyond a certain height there is

much less to entice deer out of the woods, where fresh foliage and ground herbage is increasingly available as a more tempting source of food. The first cut of grass for silage is another signal for roe to seek their food elsewhere than on farmland.

Having dealt with surplus yearling bucks and turned your sights to older animals, those you have earmarked for culling should particularly include any obvious 'poor doers', those which are old, sick or injured and any identified as causing significant damage. Bucks with misshapen antlers or substandard ones for their age are obvious candidates for culling, which leads on naturally to the subject of how to assess the age of deer.

From what I have said in earlier chapters, you will have gathered that the common idea that the number of points on a stag's or buck's antlers correspond to the years of the animal's age is erroneous. The number of points does increase, but to what extent depends upon variables such as species and habitat quality. First heads of antlers are almost always single spikes, regardless of species, although other species besides roe will sometimes produce more elaborate headgear where food quality and other factors are particularly favourable. Should you shoot a yearling with such a head its true age will become apparent from the absence of fully adult dentition and the continued presence of milk teeth.

As already indicated, the normal pattern is for extra antler length and thickness and additional points to appear on second, third and subsequent heads until the animal reaches its prime. The process then begins to reverse, with the difference that whereas the developing trophies of younger males are comparatively thin and sharp-pointed, those of beasts past their best are relatively thick and blunt, with a tendency towards heavier coronets and shorter pedicles.

As with other mammals, including humans, deer of both sexes show a range of other obvious signs of age. Calves, fawns and kids during their first few months are typically baby-faced, skittish and playful. Something of this juvenile innocence is retained in the general appearance and behaviour of yearlings. Slender build, upraised necks and heads when in movement and general agility are characteristic of all young deer, becoming progressively slightly less so with each additional year of age. A healthy deer in its prime should be well proportioned in every respect. In the nature of things not many deer reach old age – say nine or ten in roe and twelve or more in most larger species – but those that do tend to put on weight around the belly and elsewhere, to hold their heads at a lower angle in relation to the body when moving at walking pace and to be somewhat slower in their reactions than their younger counterparts; this coincides with a sleepy appearance and a less alert demeanour in general. Tooth wear is another age indicator which should be checked in all deer you shoot. Patterns of slot impressions (hoofprints) also vary depending upon the age of the deer involved. Slots of deer in their prime should register when walking. In other words, the fore-hoof and the corresponding hind-hoof should make contact with the ground at the same place, imprinting one on top of the other, whereas with ageing deer the hind-hoof characteristically imprints slightly behind the fore-hoof.

Returning more specifically to roe deer and their management, it is advisable to complete most of your buck cull before May ends. From then onwards summer vegetation becomes increasingly luxuriant and concealing. The bucks, having more or less resolved their initial disputes over territories, settle down for several weeks to a quieter life and you may well see much less of them during that time. In mid-July they begin to become restless again as the rut approaches. There may be some slight variation from year to year and between different places, but in general the rut proper begins around 20 July and lasts until about mid-August, peaking midway between these dates.

As the rut gets under way, the roe bucks' normal fear of humans almost takes second place to their reproductive urges. They move about during the day almost as much as at dawn and dusk, offering you opportunities not only for casual encounters with bucks judged ripe for culling but also for calling them up, a subject discussed in chapter 21.

After the end of the rut comes another period of quiescence, with the bucks recouping their energies while remaining largely unseen. Well before the end of September normal activity is resumed, while the so-called 'false rut' in October may, or may not, bring about a brief resumption of the excitement of late July and early August.

When the roe buck open season ends the open season for does begins – 1 November in England and Wales and 21 October in Scotland – so there need be no autumn respite for roe stalking except where this is constrained by game shooting interests or other factors. In the absence of such constraints you must now decide on your culling priorities, taking very much into account what to do about does with growing kids, which means practically all of them.

By late October and early November roe kids may no longer be dependent upon their mothers' milk for survival. They remain dependent in other ways, however, in the need to follow their mothers' example in every aspect of behaviour and so be educated by them in all the essentials of life for a roe deer. Roe kids orphaned in the autumn have to face a long, motherless winter and will be at a disadvantage which may not directly jeopardise their physical survival but which may none the less be judged to be to some degree inhumane, albeit quite legal. It is certainly distasteful to many stalkers and worth making efforts to avoid.

One way around this is to cull kids only until, say, the end of November, shooting both buck and doe kids without discrimination. Although bucks as such are out of season, the culling of buck kids in late autumn is justifiable to prevent suffering by an animal made motherless if the adult doe is also culled, as perhaps you intend should happen, though not necessarily at the same time.

More often than not the adult doe is likely to run away before you can shoot her if you have previously accounted for one or both of her kids, if she has twins. If you first shoot the doe, her kids will frequently remain within shooting range and can be added to the bag, but this cannot be relied upon. Should orphaned kids make off into cover before you can deal with them, you will be likely to have a second chance if you come back a day or two later and wait for them to emerge at the same place.

As to which does to shoot and which to retain, the same basic criteria should guide you as apply to bucks – if time permits such selectivity. In practice, however, one adult doe

Above: *Chinese water deer lack antlers but the bucks use their tusks to good effect when fighting. These wetland-loving deer make only limited use of woodland and have a restricted distribution as wild animals in Britain.* (David Muttock)

Below: *There are four main colour varieties of fallow deer. The white ones are not albinos and are in fact buff-coloured rather than white when immature. The other bucks in this picture are of the so-called common variety, seen here in summer pelage.*

Above: *Fallow bucks like the mature individuals with broad-palmed antlers on the right of this picture, are best retained as breeding stock until they begin to 'go back' or deteriorate with age.*

Below: *Muntjac are the smallest of Britain's wild deer species and were introduced from south and south-east Asia by the eleventh Duke of Bedford towards the end of the nineteenth century.* (Norma Chapman)

Above: A young Reeves's muntjac buck with typically small antlers growing from elongated pedicles, a distinctive feature of these animals. Despite this modest headgear, muntjac trophies are increasingly in demand by stalkers from Britain and abroad.
(Norma Chapman)

Below: Muntjac are lovers of thick cover, where tree foliage forms an important part of their diet, especially in late spring when leaves are fresh. The prominent tail of this species is raised to display a white underside when fleeing from danger or disturbance. (Norma Chapman)

Above: *Sika deer photographed in a New Forest ride. This species was introduced to Ireland in the mid-nineteenth century and is now well established there in the wild state as well as in various parts of Scotland and England.*

Below: *A young sika stag emerging from cover. These deer are slightly smaller than fallow, which live alongside them in some places. Sika will hybridise with red deer, and this has happened on a significant scale in parts of Ireland and elsewhere.*

Above: Red deer in woodland conditions, such as these in the New Forest, can produce heavy body weights with antlers to match. High quality stags like the one in this photograph are highly vulnerable to opportunistic shooters with no thought for long-term responsible deer management.

Below: High seats are invaluable for deer observation and photography as well as safe shooting against a solid earth background. First developed in Germany, their present widespread use in Britain and Ireland dates from well after the Second World War, when woodland stalking became established as a field sport in these islands.

Above: *Red deer are a traditional hunting quarry of very long standing. If they had not been preserved for this purpose, wild red deer might have died out long ago in Britain and Ireland as well as in Continental Europe.*

Below: *Red deer are a gregarious species but individual herds dwelling in woodland tend to be smaller than their counterparts on the open hills in Scotland and elsewhere.*

Above: A young red stag with his first 'head' of antlers. All being well, this woodland specimen should develop progressively larger antlers until it reaches its prime and carries a heavy, multi-tined trophy at the age of six or seven.

Above: *Roe deer are now more widely distributed in Britain than at any time since the Middle Ages. They are a prime quarry for woodland stalkers, who render a vital service to countryside conservation by helping to keep deer numbers within reasonable limits.*

tends to look much like another in most cases. If you are under pressure to cull a substantial number, especially in limited free time, you cannot afford to be too choosy. In this case, take advantage of every fine day at your disposal and shoot as many does as possible, bearing in mind that the short hours of daylight and inclement weather as winter takes hold are bound to limit your opportunities for getting on terms with the deer.

In general, the first and last few weeks of the doe open season are best for getting results, as the deer are then most predictably visible in the woods. During February, especially in mild winters, deer also begin to show up in the open to an increasing extent, not only at dawn and dusk but during the day in quiet places. December and early January are times of reduced activity when roe tend to 'keep their heads down' and to be least easy to stalk or to still-hunt.

On a frosty early morning in winter roe will often remain inactive until the sun rises and the day warms up a little. Roe dislike windy weather and will stay under cover in such conditions. A wet day after a series of fine ones may well also keep them in hiding, but during a longer spell of wet weather their normal patterns of emergence will fairly soon reassert themselves. On the odd snowy day they may not move far, but if snow continues to lie they will quickly resume normal mobility.

So much, for the present, for roe deer. Let us now assume that the deer on your ground are one of the larger, more gregarious species – fallow, sika or red. Many of the same basic strategies apply as for roe, so let us take stock of some of the differences. Most importantly, perhaps, these social animals move about more, frequently crossing property boundaries as they circulate within defined home ranges. One day they may be with you in strength, and the next on your neighbour's property or even many miles away.

Their degree of mobility varies between sexes as well as species. Red deer travel farthest, stags being considerably more mobile than hinds. Sika traverse smaller home ranges than red deer, the stags again being greater travellers than the hinds, while fallow bucks travel a good deal more than their female counterparts.

Weeding out abnormalities like this Wiltshire roebuck, shot by the author, is one of the most satisfying aspects of selective deer control.

These factors need to be taken fully into account when assessing numbers and sexes on your ground at given times. the case for inter-property co-operation is particularly strong when it comes to determining culling policy as applied to any of these three species. All too often, regrettably, greed and jealousy prevail as expressed by the common attitude, 'If I don't shoot him, somebody else will', the effects of which can be particularly devastating to mature males with trophy heads.

If your aim is to be a responsible deer manager rather than an opportunistic head-hunter obsessed with trophies, go as easy as you can on those stags or bucks, looking upon the occasional trophy head as the gilt on the gingerbread – your just reward for your hard work in pruning out inferior stock and culling sufficient females, the acid test of a job well done in this particular sphere of activity. Unless estate policy decrees otherwise, aim for a fifty/fifty cull of males and females. The open season for males being so much longer than for females of these three species in England and Wales, and for sika and fallow in Scotland, you can take time to be selective, concentrating your male deer cull on yearlings, especially those of indifferent quality. Stags and bucks are best for venison if shot before the rut or not too long afterwards, before winter proper sets in and conditions may start to deteriorate.

When culling females of these larger species, apply the same basic rules as for roe to minimise the risk of orphaning calves or fawns in the early weeks of the hind or doe open season. At least one professional stalker I know confines his culling to fallow fawns throughout the month of November, leaving adult does to be dealt with in December, January and February, and this seems to me a sensible policy. Once females are fully eligible for culling, in your judgement, and numbers are important, if you first take out the leading hind or doe in any group you will have a better chance to cull several others before they disperse. Having once been shot at in one particular location, the females concerned may well be wary of returning there for some time, so make the most of your opportunities.

Fallow deer in the open present a considerable challenge when it comes to deciding how best to approach to within acceptable range for shooting.

A word of warning about red deer. These large and somewhat ponderous animals tend to be slower off the mark when first disturbed than their smaller cousins, which makes it easier to shoot several before they take alarm and depart. Unless a really big cull is essential, do not be tempted to shoot too many. Small populations of red deer are highly vulnerable to indiscriminate culling, and some have been wiped out completely by overenthusiastic shooting.

Remember when culling these larger species that, except calves and fawns, and perhaps sika hinds, they are all too big and heavy to handle with comfort single-handed apart from dragging

for short distances. Many a chronically bad back has been the penalty for disregarding this fact. It will need at least two of you, or preferably a winch or block and tackle, to load a sika stag or an adult red or fallow deer carcase of either sex into your vehicle.

Stalking strategies for muntjac confront a different set of problems. Chief among these is how to be sure not to shoot does with dependent fawns, bearing in mind that, alone among wild deer species in Britain, muntjac have no fixed breeding season. With pregnancies lasting seven months, and does again coming into season within two or three days of parturition, there is no time of year when some does with young fawns are not at risk of being unintentionally culled.

So how can this be avoided? The best advice that can be given is to confine your culling to does which are obviously either immature or heavily pregnant, while sparing those in which the milk bag is conspicuously developed. In checking these details you are likely to pass up the chance to cull some suitable individuals which will have moved on into cover before you can line up your 'scope sight on them, so briefly do they remain visible in the open in many instances. Perhaps this is one situation in which the otherwise sound rule about always using binoculars to identify a possible target, and never employing a riflescope for this purpose, might be disregarded, although some may repudiate such a suggestion.

With muntjac bucks there is rather more of a recognisable annual cycle, with most casting their antlers in May or June and regrowing them during the summer, when seasonal vegetation affords them so much concealment that getting on terms with them with a rifle can become extremely difficult. Perhaps the best time of year for culling muntjac is March and April, when woodland undergrowth is still minimal, green rides and fresh young meadow grass entice some of them to feed in the open and the bucks remain in hard antler. Muntjac antlers, though miniscule, are not without interest as trophies, as witness the eagerness of some Continental stalkers to acquire them. As a stalking quarry muntjac are exceptionally challenging and are all the more fascinating for that very reason. Being now numerous and widespread, and increasing year by year, the need to control them is self-evident, and full-bore rifles in the hands of experienced stalkers are the means to do this. The one thing not yet widely available is sufficient expertise to cope with a very difficult quarry on the scale now clearly necessary.

Chinese water deer are a species I have watched at various places but have never stalked with a rifle. Their distribution being so limited, opportunities for stalking them are proportionately restricted and the need for culling them slight and localised. Where market garden crops need protection, a well-placed high seat should enable culprits to be dealt with fairly promptly, confining the culling of does to the months between November and March.

Although muntjac and Chinese water deer have no legal close seasons in Britain, they are covered by the same restrictions concerning firearms and ammunition as are applicable to other deer species.

Where stalking strategies end and what might be called tactics begin is something of a grey area but, no matter how we label them, our actions on the ground where we stalk are what make all the difference between the success or failure of any outing. Much will rest on your personal judgement as to how and where to proceed. If you make a random choice it will all be down to Lady Luck. The more you rely upon her favours rather than on what you have learned the hard way, from detailed observation of deer movements and general knowledge of the area, the lower will be your success rate.

You may well have weighed up in advance the relative pros and cons of stalking as such and still-hunting, or you may still be in doubt as to the best approach to adopt. The less experienced you are, the more I recommend still-hunting as a basic ploy for your earlier outings. High seats are discussed in chapter 14, and I cannot overstress the importance of these in any and every woodland stalking situation. If high seats are already available as part of the woodland furniture, well and good. Arrive early, before the first light of dawn when you are on an early morning outing, or at least an hour before deer are likely to emerge after lying up during the day in the case of a late afternoon or evening foray, and make your way as quietly and unobtrusively as possible to your chosen still-hunting venue,

bearing in mind as you do so the importance of betraying yourself by scent as little as possible.

Having settled yourself in a high seat, be alert, repeatedly scanning the ground before you for the slightest sign of deer movement. Roe in particular have a tendency to pop up as if from nowhere in the middle of an open area one hitherto thought was deerless, making one wonder how they got there without one noticing their arrival. Have your rifle ready so that when a shootable deer presents itself you can bring your weapon into action with the minimum of movement by either yourself or your rifle.

By placing a hand between the crossbar of the high seat and your rifle you can almost eliminate hand-shake and secure a rock-steady aim. Do not let this tempt you into shooting at too great a range. In optimum conditions a red or sika stag or a fallow buck should be regarded as too distant if more than 200 metres away at the very outside, and a female or immature red, sika or fallow or a roe of either sex at a range in excess of 150 metres. Before you ever shoot a deer unaccompanied, learn to estimate distances by pacing out 50, 100, 150 and 200 metres on the ground. First of all, measure your stride, which for an average man about 6 ft tall should be about one metre, and work out the distances accordingly. When you shoot a deer, estimate the distance between yourself and where it falls; then pace it out as you approach the deer to check the accuracy of your estimate. At first it is all too easy to make mistakes but you will soon improve with practice.

In any case, hold your fire until the deer is as close as it is likely to come while presenting a clearly visible target. When it is still and standing broadside-on, unobstructed by vegetation and with no other deer in the field of fire, release the safety-catch on your rifle, squeeze the trigger and then immediately reload while carefully noting the effect of your shot on the deer, where it falls or, if it does not fall while you are watching, exactly where it enters cover. Be prepared to take a second shot should the necessity arise, and never assume a deer is dead until you are absolutely certain.

These things, and more, also apply if you are shooting on the ground. When stalking, or pitting your wits against deer in any other circumstances, you need to hide yourself from notice by every reasonable means possible – suitable camouflage, silent movement and, above all, being careful not to foul potential target areas with your scent. One whiff of your rancid human odour will put any deer on the leeward side of you well out of your reach, of that much you can always be certain!

All the time you are actually stalking, no matter how cautiously you do so, you are at a disadvantage which does not arise when still-hunting, inasmuch as movement can betray you. So long as you remain perfectly still, the deer's eyesight is such that they may not recognise you as human – unless you are very close indeed, when the intrusion into a familiar scene of what may be no more than an unfamiliar shape may suffice to ring their alarm-bells loudly.

Even at a considerable distance, however, deer are quick to detect movement. The supreme test of your skill as a stalker is how successful you are at spotting deer without them first spotting you. Some people have a natural aptitude for stealthy, leopard-like movement while blending themselves into their surroundings and having all their antennae out to respond at once to the slightest deer movement. Others tend to be heavy-footed, not quite tuned in to the world around them and insensitive to signs they ought to be heeding all the while. You can tell at once to which of these categories any stalking companion belongs, and I have known many of both kinds.

If you are stalking as an accompanied guest or with someone who is showing you the ropes in the early stages, then until or unless you are directed otherwise, you should stay behind, emulating the other's movements and stopping immediately when he does. If he is skilled at what he is doing he will walk very slowly, testing the ground as he goes with the sole of his forefoot before placing his full weight on the ground, pausing frequently to examine the scene ahead for possible deer.

When you are on your own and you see a deer, stop at once, wherever you are, and examine it through your binoculars, keeping your rifle slung over your shoulder, preferably with the sling to the rear, although some prefer to have the sling forward and the rifle to the rear as some of us used to do in the Army, with the

old Lee-Enfield .303. The deer may appear to be alone but, unless it is a muntjac, the probability is that it is with others which have yet to reveal themselves. If some eventually do, there may still be others yet undetected. Make one false move and these hitherto unseen deer may spot you, so be on your guard.

If the deer are heading your way and a shootable animal is among them, either stay where you are or wait until all their heads are down before moving discreetly if you need a better point of vantage, better concealment or a tree or some other object on which to steady your hand when the moment comes to take aim with your rifle. Should one of the deer spot you and a bark or squeal of alarm cause them all to raise their heads, it will probably be too late to prevent them all running off in panic. If one deer spots you but a general alarm does not ensue, be prepared to wait several minutes until the deer hopefully decides you are not human after all and resumes feeding. Within seconds it may raise its head again to catch you out in a premature movement, so allow a good half-minute to pass before you assume that all is well and you can resume your stealthy movements.

When stalking a deer while they are grazing, move only while all heads are down and be ready to stop at once if a head is raised, as it surely will be at frequent intervals. So long as mastication continues you will know that a deer with its head erect has not detected you, but if mastication ceases and the deer stands statuesque you will know its suspicions are aroused. You must then remain totally immobile for however long it takes until all heads are down once more.

If you are stalking a solitary deer, take advantage of intervening trees or other aids to self-concealment while you cautiously move forward, remembering, as you do so, that while you are out of sight of the deer it is also out of your sight and may well move quite unpredictably while out of your line of vision. It may then reappear unexpectedly, possibly spotting you in the process. If your target is well out from cover, crawl if you must to get within range, but you will be lucky to complete such a manoeuvre unobserved. When aiming from the prone position, do not lean too far into the rifle or you may become an involuntary member of the not too exclusive 'cut eyebrow club' from a whack by your 'scope when the rifle recoils from the shot.

In fact, prone shots are rare in woodland stalking. When cover is sparse but not too much so, sitting shots are a useful option, and you can sometimes get a better field of view by lying almost flat on your back with your head supported by a rucksack or something similar before taking a sitting shot. I have used this stratagem with success when no close cover has been available. Deer are used to human beings as vertical objects, not horizontal ones. When you ease yourself upright to take a shot, you can steady your aim very effectively by resting an elbow on each knee.

Until you know your capabilities, confine your shooting to fairly short ranges, say, 50 to 60 metres or so. In your early days as a stalker, also avoid shooting free-hand. Steady your aim by placing a hand against something solid like a tree. When such a hand-rest is unavailable, use a stalking-stick. A thumbstick is ideal for this if its length corresponds to your height, and it can double as a walking-aid provided you are instantly ready to use it for its primary purpose.

Always remember to place a hand between the rifle and any solid object you use to steady your aim, otherwise the recoil will cause you to shoot wide.

Once you feel sufficiently confident, increase your range to 100 metres, the maximum at which you should shoot when actually stalking. Most stalkers will be well advised to stick within that limit in all possible circumstances except to cull a crippled deer which might otherwise escape. The longer the range at which you shoot, the greater is the potential margin of error caused by inaccuracy. The effects of very minor hand-shake in directing a bullet off target are increased in proportion to distance. Some people will boast of unvarying accuracy when shooting free-hand at a target 200 metres or more away, but what they do not brag about are the occasions when, in spite of all their assertions, things go wrong. Deerstalking, conducted properly, is a serious and responsible job of work in which the lives of sentient creatures are at all times intimately involved, not a contest in machismo and near superhuman performance by people armed with lethal weapons, and this should always be borne in mind.

Load your rifle at the start of the stalk, with a full magazine and a round in the breech, and apply the safety catch immediately. Wait until your target deer is in clear view, standing broadside-on to you, before preparing to take a shot. Aim at a point on the deer directly behind the shoulder, just over halfway up the body between the base of the chest and the top of the back, and release the safety-catch. Do not 'pull' the trigger but squeeze it gently or you may unwittingly pull slightly off your point of aim. If you have done everything correctly and the deer has not been alerted to possible danger, causing adrenalin to flow, it is likely to drop on the spot, having suffered fatal heart/lung damage. Immediately reload and be ready to squeeze off a second round if it does not drop at once or, having dropped, attempts to struggle to its feet. When no further rifle action is needed, reapply the safety-catch without further delay.

Carefully note where the deer is standing at the moment you take a shot in case it makes off into cover and you may need to follow a blood-trail. Even heart-shot deer are capable of running for 100 metres or more before collapsing and expiring. Unless daylight is fading fast and a prompt follow-up is essential, wait at least fifteen minutes before retrieving a shot deer or seeking a lost one. If the animal is down but not quite dead, this will allow time for it to stiffen up, so that it is much less likely to galvanise itself into renewed activity and flight when you eventually approach it.

Be prepared for 'buck fever' with its inconvenient symptoms of accelerated pulse, heavy breathing and nervous tension which result in trembling of the extremities. This is most liable to strike when you are just on the point of shooting. If it does so, hold your fire until you have regained normal control, and if this means passing up the chance of a shot, so be it. Never risk a badly misplaced bullet resulting in a lost deer, severely wounded but perhaps not mortally so, and impossible to find. You will hate yourself if this happens and the memory of it will haunt you for a very long time indeed, perhaps for the rest of your stalking career.

The only acceptable alternative to the heart-lung area as a target for which to aim for lethal effect is the neck. But only use this option when you are close enough to your quarry to select a critical point of aim, midway between the base and the top of the neck close to its junction with the rest of the animal's body. This will sever the main arteries as well as shattering the spine so that the shot, if correctly placed, will cause the deer to drop on the spot with minimal damage to the venison. If the bullet strikes too high or too low, however, it results in an injury that is not immediately fatal and a lost deer. Some stalkers are wary of taking neck shots but I have never known one to go wrong so long as proper precautions are taken. It has much to recommend it in circumstances where you particularly need to ensure that a deer drops dead where it was standing.

If a deer is facing you, head-on, at sufficiently close quarters, a frontal chest shot may seem tempting, but I do not recommend it. A slight aiming error left or right can miss vital organs, while a lethal impact on the lower neck, heart or lungs can also rake the abdominal cavity, resulting in spilt rumen contents and a thoroughly messy carcase.

Never, never aim at a deer's head when you are stalking. The brain cavity is too small to present a reliably accessible target area and the risk of a jaw being shattered, which is horrendously traumatic but not fatal, is far too great.

Much else can be learned from experience, simple but highly useful facts such as that a whistle or hand-clap will sometimes arrest a running deer, whether fleeing from you or something else, and so provide the chance for a shot when perhaps you had almost resigned yourself to an unsuccessful outing. Another method used by some stalkers to help maximise their cull is to put out apples, pig potatoes, split maize or other bait to attract deer to convenient target areas.

There are other ways of still-hunting than relying solely on high seats. For an infinitely varied choice of venue, use a 'low seat' in the form of a conventional shooting-stick which you can carry strapped over your shoulder ready to sit on when you need it.

By all means listen to other stalkers and study their methods when in action but also learn to differentiate their vices from their virtues. There are some who seem to be consistently able to achieve success where others fail, to take short-cuts which break all the rules and somehow to get away with it. Are there, for instance occasions when shooting running deer is acceptable? The answer is 'yes' when there is no other way of dealing with a wounded deer which might otherwise escape, but be particularly careful to shoot against a solid background. Some stalkers can demonstrate success at shooting uninjured deer while running but, as with those who scorn the good sense of not shooting at excessive ranges, one hears little about the failures which must inevitably also occur. Work it out for yourself. It may not be unduly difficult to estimate how much 'lead' to allow when shooting a running deer but, in the case of roe especially, the horizontal dimension of movement also has a vertical counterpart which can never be easy to anticipate and still less so to assess. Stick to stationary deer, broadside-on at sensible distances, and you should not go far wrong.

One final thought about acceptable angles of shot should always weigh with you. It often happens that a deer that appears to be broadside-on to you is actually standing at a slight angle, facing either towards you or away. The sharper the angle, obviously, the greater is the extent of traverse by a bullet along the length of the deer's body, and this has to be reckoned with when deciding whether or not to take a shot and, if one is to be taken, what should be the point of aim. If a deer is facing you, with its body at an angle of 45° you will need to aim at its nearest shoulder, or just inside it to the front, to minimise the possibility of abdominal penetration. If the deer is facing away, presenting its flank at a similar angle, by aiming just behind the shoulder your bullet should reach the vital parts while also avoiding a messy conclusion. If the angle is any steeper, postpone shooting until your target offers a better opportunity.

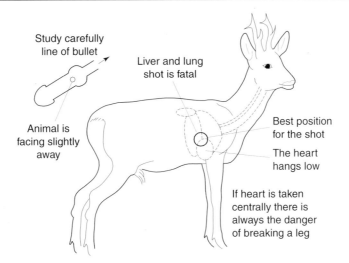

Figure 12.1 Broadside – showing most vulnerable area

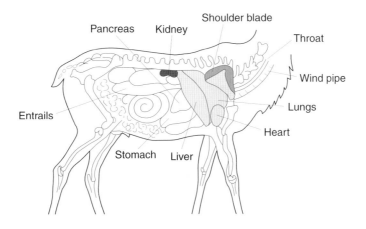

Figure 12.2 Position of bones in relation to organs

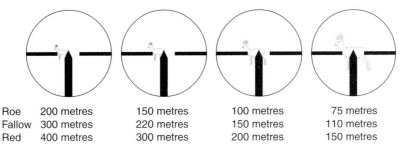

Roe	200 metres	150 metres	100 metres	75 metres
Fallow	300 metres	220 metres	150 metres	110 metres
Red	400 metres	300 metres	200 metres	150 metres

Figure 12.3 Rough method of judging distances with tel. sight.
(Space between horizontal bars = 70 cm at 100 metres)

CHAPTER 13
Record-keeping

oodland deerstalking is an ongoing process of learning. Every outing, armed or otherwise, can yield its fragments of new knowledge from which you could benefit in the future, but the value of this knowledge will be substantially diminished if you only commit it to memory. So maintain a running record of what you see and what happens on each foray, not only for your own sake but as the basis for any report you may be required to make from time to time to your stalking landlord.

Your permanent record can take the form of a sort of extended game book or a conventional diary, either handwritten or stored in the memory bank of your home computer. It should note and preserve such details as date, weather, stalking venue, times of arrival and departure and individual deer observations. Relevant particulars will be the locations and Ordnance Survey map grid references of each observation, the species, sexes and numbers of deer concerned and the nature of their activity.

The core of your record-keeping will be details of every individual cull: in what circumstances it was carried out (e.g. whether the deer was shot from a high seat or while you were stalking on foot); the rifle and ammunition used; at what range the shot was taken, the placement of the bullet and the nature of the injury inflicted; whether the deer dropped on the spot or, if not, how far it ran before dropping; and whether you had to follow up with a dog and with what result. You should also record the clean weight of each deer culled (i.e. after gralloching), and such other significant details as any physical abnormalities, previous injuries or disease signs, general bodily condition, actual or estimated age, antler dimensions or, in the case of female deer, whether pregnant and the sex of any foetuses. Useful additional information could

Fig. 13.1

DEER OBSERVATION AND CULL RECORD					
Date	Weather	Stalking venue	Time of arrival	Location and details of observation	
			Time of departure		
Time, method and location of cull			Rifle and ammunition	Range of shot	Species and sex of deer culled	Reaction to shot
Bullet placement	Previous injury and/or evidence of disease		General condition	Age (actual or approx.)	Clean weight
Antler dimensions	Sex of foetuses	Sold to	Butcher's weight and price per lb/kg	Any other comments	

include butcher's weight and the price received per pound or kilogram for any carcase sold to the game trade, and of course the name of the game dealer involved.

A useful adjunct to your diary could be a card-index system for which you complete an individual card for every cull, recording the details under separate headings for future consultation and comparison with other records you accumulate (see figure 13.1). You could have such cards specially printed, or perhaps simply draft one to suit your purpose and have it photocopied, although the result might be less satisfactory than a properly printed card.

You might also consider the possible value of marking the location of each cull on a large-scale estate map so that, as time goes on, you can note any patterns that may emerge and what lessons can be learned from them. The list could go on, but diary-keeping can be a time-consuming exercise so you may opt to strike a balance between those details that are most important and those that are less so, having regard to your own individual circumstances.

On each outing you should have with you either a notebook and ballpoint pen or a pocket tape-recorder so that key points can be noted as events unfold or at the earliest possible moment afterwards. It is safest not to rely on your fickle memory even to the extent of postponing note-making until you get home, by which time you may be too tired anyway and tempted to delay still further what you should have done at the time.

Sketches and photographs can enhance the value of your records. You need not be a skilled photographer; all that is needed for most purposes is a cheap pocket camera with built-in flash and automatic everything – the ultimate answer to the prayers of every camera-wielding duffer who just never could get it right before such marvels came onto the market.

Be methodical and consistent in your record-keeping. It is all too easy to ramble on as if you were writing your autobiography, but unless you have a genuine prospect of one day publishing your life story (and how many of us have?) you will surely come to regret adopting an inconsequential approach to so very important a series of records, and it will become well-nigh impossible to see the wood for the trees.

Sectionalise each diary entry with subheadings for each separate category of information (see figure 13.1). Decide what these subheadings should be in relation to your particular situation and then stick to them as closely as possible for all entries. If you should get it wrong at the very beginning, modify or enlarge the scope of the subheadings as necessary but only in such a way as not to make cross-reference to preceding entries unduly difficult.

If you cannot find any specific information you may be seeking without a frustratingly lengthy search, there is something fundamentally wrong with your method of record-keeping. In this case, write it off to experience as soon as you are able and reorganise your diary along lines suggested in this chapter. Should you have time to be really methodical you can index salient details so as to be able to turn up whatever you may want at a moment's notice. You will then have created something akin to a perfect record-keeping system, but do not do this at the price of biting off more than you can chew in terms of time commitment – perhaps for the rest of your stalking career!

CHAPTER 14
High Seats

For anyone managing deer in woodland, or on level terrain of any description where solid back-stops to receive spent bullets are not readily available, high seats may well be essential for reasons of public safety alone. In some situations the police may make it a condition of granting an area-restricted F.A.C. that all rifle shooting should be from high seats. Safety apart, a high seat enables the stalker using it to benefit from a very much more extended field of view than is possible from ground level. It also elevates him to sufficient height for his scent, under most conditions, to be carried above any quarry that may emerge to leeward of him, and it anchors him to one location where he will not be constantly tempted to find out what may

be lurking around the next corner, exposing himself in the process to a greatly increased chance of detection. Yet another inestimable advantage is having a firm hand-rest from which to take a rock-solid aim.

Familiar items of woodland furniture as they now are where deer are present, high seats were almost unknown in Britain prior to the mid-twentieth century. They have long been used in Germany, where the concept was first developed, and the term 'high seat' is a literal translation of the German name *hochsitz*. The colder winters of central Europe have encouraged sportsmen there to go one stage further by making extensive use of the *hochstand*, almost a miniature house on stilts, complete with sliding, double-glazed windows and an array of interior comforts.

In Britain the Forestry Commission, under the influence of its first game warden, the late H.A. ('Herbie') Fooks, was among the first to make general use of high seats for deer control. Initially these were many and varied, with different deer managers producing their own *ad hoc* designs, leading on quite soon to a degree of standardisation with the development of the Thetford high seat, a solid wooden structure built to meet stringent safety requirements as well as to embody the best from some of the earlier models.

As woodland stalking for sport and essential deer control gained pace, so too did the general use of high seats as their value came to be recognised. Many a handyman stalker constructed his own, perhaps involving quite complex carpentry or amounting to nothing more than a precarious perch in a tree, reached by a makeshift ladder or by climbing from branch to branch. At the same time, one or two manufacturers began to show an interest in catering for this new, developing market, producing a range of workmanlike models in either steel or aluminium.

Before deciding what will best suit your

A bi-sectional high seat designed to afford a measure of comfort for those who use it.

Arley two-man high seats are now manufactured in aluminium and are robust as well as lightweight.

A shooting rail, padded to obviate the clatter when the rifle is raised to the aiming position is a feature of this portable high seat marketed by Jägersport.

specific situation, reflect on the merits and demerits of the options that are available. In an ideal world you could hardly have too many high seats – apart perhaps from a problem of making your mind up which to use on any one visit! In the real world, though, other snags may arise, cost not the least of them. You could, for example, knock up several wooden seats for the price of a single metal one. Wood of course has its own disadvantages, but it is the more obvious choice of material for a permanent high seat at a fixed location, whether a lean-to or a free-standing one.

Most home-made seats are lean-tos, as these are simple to construct and economical with materials. Douglas fir timber is reckoned by many to be the very best for high seats, with larch as a close second. Beech and ash rot quickly and should on no account be used. Sawn timber is

easiest to work. The uprights should be at least 12 ft 6 in (3.8 metres) long from sections not less than 2 in x 1½ in (5 x 4 cm) in lateral dimensions, better still 2 in x 2 in (5 x 5 cm), while the treads for a single-seater will need to be about 2 ft (61 cm) long from 2 in x 1½ in (5 x 4 cm) sections. All timber should be knot-free and, if possible, pressure-creosoted, with sawn ends creosoted by hand. Pole timber, if used, should be thoroughly dry, rinded (stripped of all bark), creosoted and at least 3⅛ in (8 cm) in diameter for the uprights at their base, tapering to 2⅜in (6 cm) at the top.

A combination of uprights and struts can be used to support the all-important shooting rail which will serve as your hand-rest and which should extend along the sides of the seat as well as across the front.

Make sure to have the shooting rail at a suitable height above the seat itself for you to be able to use it in comfort, shoulder-level being just about right. A V-shaped brace behind the seat will help to support and stabilise the completed structure when it is rested against a suitable tree-trunk, with total stability being ensured by lashing the top of the seat to the tree with rot-free rope. On no account nail the seat to a tree. Galvanised nails in pre-drilled holes marginally smaller in diameter than the nails themselves should be used for the seat construction. If the seat itself is hinged, it can be up-ended when not in use, enabling water to drain straight off it and so keeping it dry for when you need it, although if you need to guard against unauthorised use you may prefer a removable seat which can be secreted somewhere near by.

A long-time friend of mine, Chris Boulton, has made many serviceable high seats along the lines I have described. He also has designed and produced a portable version in which the ladder section takes the form of two interlocking halves, with the base of the upper half's uprights slotting to a depth of two treads between the more widely spaced uprights of the lower half. The whole structure can be taken apart, easily carried in two sections to a new location, and reassembled there within minutes.

Two uprights are fine if the seat is to be rested against a tree. But a free-standing one needs four, and this of course gives a more robust construction in general. The uprights must be strongly braced for rigidity, a further aid to stability being tapered construction from bottom to top, with treads of varying lengths in proportion.

Inventively minded stalkers may well have ideas of their own as to how to adapt or improve high seat designs to suit their own circumstances and preferences. By making the ladder section

The Thetford high seat, standard issue by the Forestry Commission for Rangers and client stalkers for many years. This free-standing permanent seat is of extremely solid construction.

A bi-sectional high seat, duly assembled and ready for use.

vertical or near-vertical and allowing adequate space between the top of it and the seat you can, for example, make it possible to climb into the seat facing forward rather than backward, thus keeping a wary eye alert for possible deer while you are climbing. By padding the shooting rail with some suitable soft material you can minimise the risk of clattering the rifle against something solid while raising it into the aiming position. It also makes sense to ensure that at least one of the struts or uprights supporting the rail projects an inch or two above it to provide somewhere to hang things up – perhaps a knapsack containing a snack or a flask of coffee.

Until it is required, the rifle can be rested horizontally across a right-angled shooting rail corner, perhaps with the strap looped across a projecting strut or upright. The important point is to keep it where you can reach for it with minimal movement, either of yourself or the rifle, then ease it into your shoulder and take aim in a matter of seconds without betraying yourself to your quarry. If the rifle is hanging vertically from an upright or a strut it will not be easy to bring it into action without giving yourself away by the movement. Never imagine that you are sufficiently high above deer's eye-level for the slightest incautious movement on your part not to be noticed. This brings us to the question of camouflage. Concealing as much of yourself as possible with a hat, face-mask and mittens is obviously important. If you can get hold of some camouflage netting, drape it from the shooting rail to surround the top of the high seat or, alternatively, break up the outline of your figure with some natural woodland foliage.

If you want to wear a hair shirt, do so by all means, but there is no need to subject yourself to any unnecessary discomfort while sitting for hours at a time in a high seat. You can insulate yourself from the bottom-numbing hardness of a wooden seat by taking an inflatable air cushion, or indeed a small cushion of any sort. Then, if it is still intolerably uncomfortable there must be some serious design fault which needs to be identified and remedied next time round.

Whatever risks to your own safety you may be unwise enough to take, you would be foolish indeed to expose guest stalkers to unnecessary hazards. People have suffered serious injury by falling out of demonstrably unsafe high seats, and in today's world, with compensation being demanded on the flimsiest of grounds you could find yourself financially liable to a ruinous extent unless your insurance covers you against such contingencies or the victim had indemnified you against any responsibility for accident or injury caused while stalking as your guest or under your aegis. A further practical precaution in the interests of safety is not only to nail or screw into place the treads and other vulnerable elements of your high seats but also to wire them, using reasonably stout wire secured by staples to the timbers.

Wooden high seats require maintenance. Coat them generously with creosote or other wood preservative every four years, and protect the bases of the uprights from direct contact with damp earth by standing them on something solid such as bricks. When a high seat has not been used for a period, double-check that it is in good order before you or a guest again climb into it. Stormy weather can sometimes cause problems by dislodging and tilting structures you had thought were absolutely secure, and high seats in public access areas, or where there is no such access but people sometimes enter anyway, are all too prone to being vandalised, which is one reason why some stalkers do not favour permanent high seats.

Manufacturers of metal high seats have been at pains to produce models combining four fundamental elements: stability, durability, portability and, of course, serviceability. Among the very first in the field in Britain were Arley high seats, designed and manufactured by G. Andrews (Engineering) of Upper Arley, Bewdley, Worcestershire and widely used by the Forestry Commission as well as on private estates and by many individual stalkers, including myself. Originally constructed from mild steel, Arley seats are now all of aluminium, light in weight for ease of carrying and also virtually maintenance-free.

Three models are currently marketed. All three are 12 ft (3.7 metres) high overall and 10 ft 6 in (3.2 metres) at seat level, and are fabricated from 1 in (25 mm) and ¾ in (20 mm) outside diameter aluminium tube, flame-welded and brazed. The Arley Junior is a free-standing single-seater designed for someone up to 14 stone (89 kg)

Based on a design by Chris Boulton, of Southampton, this bi-sectional high seat is easy to carry and quick to assemble.

occupants while also providing a clear field of fire.

Where metal high seats are concerned, stalkers who are more heavily built can still opt for models of steel construction such as those marketed by Jägersport, a major supplier of stalking accessories based at Petersfield in Hampshire. Their Woodland Mark II high seat, 10 ft 6 in (3.2 m) high at seat level, weighs a basic 56 lb (25 kg) as a lean-to, plus 33 lb (15 kg) for the rear leg kit which makes it free-standing, with 1997 prices ranging from £205.62 to £352.50. Another model from Jägersport is the Parkland, supplied either as a single-seater, 11 ft 6 in (3.5 m) high at seat level, weighing 72 lb (33 kg) and priced in 1997 at £176.25, or as a double-seater, 10 ft 6 in (3.2 m) high at seat level, weighing 80 lb (36 kg) and costing in 1997 £246.75. The double-seater has an extended wooden seat whereas the Woodland and Parkland single-seat models come with moulded plastic seats. The woodland and Parkland seats are all of welded steel construction, galvanised to minimise maintenance and make painting unnecessary and matt-finished in dull grey.

An aluminium single-seater from Jägersport is the Alu Lightweight, 10 ft (3 m) high at the seat, scaling 27 lb (12 kg) and with a dismantled carrying size of 2 ft 2 in x 9 in x 4 ft 8 in (.66 x .22 x 1.42 metres). This lean-to comes with a plastic seat and back-rest, a foam-covered shooting rail and an 11 ft (3 m) stabilising strap to secure the ladder section to the tree for extra safety while the seat is being erected, and the 1997 price was £346.63. All prices quoted for Jägersport's high seats are inclusive of VAT but carriage is extra. Jägersport also supply accessories such as self-inflatable seat cushions, high seat security kits, seat clamps for rifles or optics and camouflage netting.

Variants of basic high seat design now on the market include self-elevating models such as the Miradex Portable Observation Post, consisting of two aluminium frames each of which locks onto a tree-trunk while the user raises the other one and then repeats the process until the desired height is reached. Sole UK agents for these are Sporting Services of Kent, of West Hythe, Kent.

When deciding where you would like to place high seats, first make sure your plans are acceptable to other people involved: your

plus any equipment normally needed and has been tested to support a weight of 17 stone 11 lb (113 kg). When dismantled, this seat folds down to 6 ft x 2 ft 3 in x 1 ft 3 in (1.8 x .68 x .38 metres) and was being sold in October 1996 at £248.22. A double-seater counterpart which can be erected by one man – who can also easily carry its modest 68 lb (31 kg) weight – is the Arley Professional, which folds to 6 ft x 4 ft 2 in x 1 ft 6 in (1.8 x 1.27 x .46 metres) and was priced in October 1996 at £375.48. The Arley two-man lean-to which weighs only 38 lb (17 kg), has been tested to support 28 stone 7 lb (181 kg) and when dismantled will fold down to 6 ft x 3 ft 8 in x 1 ft 6 in (1.8 x 1.1 x .46 metres), the October 1996 price being £239.30.

An optional accessory for Arley free-standing high seats is an all-weather cotton tarpaulin cover with a PVC window which can be unhooked to serve as a protective apron for the

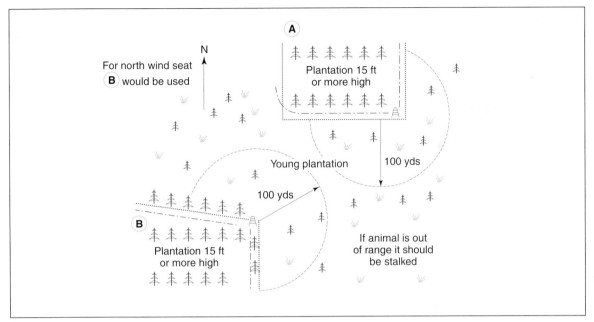

Fig 14.1 Siting of high seats

stalking landlord, the Head Forester, tenant farmers and anyone else who is likely to be affected or to have an interest in what you are doing. Find out about such things as forthcoming forestry operations which might affect where it would serve you best to site your seats. All else being equal, you will obviously want to place them where they will give you the very best opportunities for observing and shooting deer – ride crossings and overlooking clearings or vulnerable farm crops are prime choices. Study the layout of the ground and the local movements of the deer to get best value from your high seats.

The less conspicuous your high seats are the more useful they are likely to be in more ways than one. You will be all the better able to climb into them unobserved and not to be noticed once you have done so, and your seats will be that much less visible to potential thieves or vandals. A sensible balance should be struck between concealment and the ability to command a wide field of view where the two objectives may seem in conflict. A high seat well out in the open will need to be approached and used with particular circumspection if you are to avoid being detected. Overhanging branches which are likely to restrict your view can be removed with a long-handled saw, subject of course to the owner's or Head Forester's agreement. If a seat is on the edge of thick cover, a stalking path swept clear of fallen branches, leaves and other litter may offer an approach route which can be used in silence without the risk of snapping twigs underfoot – a tip well worth remembering.

CHAPTER 15
Dogs for Deer

D ogs for deer is a sensitive issue. Many stalkers of long experience appear to manage quite well without them. At various stages of our stalking careers, others among us have gone to the woods with a rifle but without a trained dog to help us out of trouble, only to find that, despite our best endeavours, a shot deer has gone away wounded, or perhaps been mortally hit but failed to drop to the shot where we could see it and retrieve it without a lengthy search in thick cover.

What do you do when that happens? If you are very inexperienced, after an instant tug of anxiety you might go charging off into the undergrowth, floundering about with increasing panic and self-doubt and, if you are a good deal luckier than you deserve to be, find the fallen deer eventually, unmistakably dead. If the fates are less kind to you, you do not find it at all but carry on searching anyway. When it is too dark to carry on further you go home in near-despair, reproaching yourself for not having handled things differently and spend a short and sleepless night before heading back at the crack of dawn to renew your search.

Still the deer may not be found. In the end you swallow your pride and seek the help of the local Forest Enterprise Ranger, or someone similar, who asks you in astonishment, and with something of an accusing look in his eye, 'Haven't you got a dog, then?'

All very embarrassing. Hopefully, however, with the Ranger's help and that of his dog, the deer will eventually be located, having fallen within feet of where you passed in the course of your search the previous evening. Hopefully, too, the experience will spur you to do something about buying and training a dog as a stalking companion and follower-up of shot deer that run away instead of collapsing on the spot.

My own faithful stalking companion for a number of happy years was a miniature wire-haired dachshund of German ancestry named Sue. As this background might suggest, Sue came from a long line of tried and tested deer dogs, and she did not disappoint.

Sue had many essential qualities: steadfastness, virtual tirelessness, unfailing enthusiasm for the job in hand and a natural aptitude which went a long way to offset any shortcomings in training. To minimise such shortcomings I took advice from professional stalker friends who had found my little bitch's close relatives well suited to their circumstances and needs and had trained them accordingly.

As soon as Sue was old enough she came with me on all my outings. Once I had taught her to walk at heel she often accompanied me on the stalk itself, but for one reason or another I sometimes left her in the car, where she liked to sit on the rear window shelf so she could watch the world go by until I returned. She exhibited no trace of gun-shyness and had a keen nose for live deer in cover: a natural-born pointer if ever there was one. After some basic tracking training, the command 'Hi, lost' brought an avid response as the search began for any shot animal which had not previously been located.

The way had been prepared for this with a series of practice follow-ups with a freshly shot deer whose whereabouts at the end I knew. When following up in earnest, if she found a fallen deer was in very thick cover, she would return with tell-tale deer hairs around her muzzle, thus helpfully narrowing down the area of search, which might well involve a lengthy belly-crawl. The hauling-out process itself, although physically more demanding, always seemed much less of a chore because at least the shot beast had been found, not only by Sue but by myself, and was in the process of being retrieved.

Although early on I tried to break Sue of her natural inclination to take off, yapping, in the wake of the odd departing rabbit or grey squirrel, there was some occasional backsliding, which earned an instant reprimand. Perversely, she would not give tongue while following a blood-trail or on finding a fallen deer – the ultimate test of a first-class deer dog but one to which many in Britain never aspire.

For all their innate gameness, miniature dachshunds like my Sue have some fairly obvious limitations as dogs for deer. In their favour, they could hardly take up less living space or room in the car or be more readily portable – they can be carried into a high seat – and, being small, they do not cost a small fortune to feed. They are also highly companionable. On the other hand they conspicuously lack the weight and strength to seize and hold down a wounded but still potentially mobile deer. Despite her willingness to have a go at almost anything, short-legged Sue was sometimes defeated by difficult ground conditions such as having to follow a trail through long, wet heather. She also shared the common dachshund proneness to back problems, and tears were shed when she had to be put down with a slipped disc at the age of nine.

The somewhat *ad hoc* approach to training with which I handled my miniature dachshund was fairly general among deer dog owners at the time, and indeed remains so. By and large, by trial and error combined with a measure of common sense, it achieves the desired result and is certainly much better than having no dog for deer at all. Even so, far more sophisticated techniques are now at our disposal. These owe a very great deal to German expertise in this field and to methods perfected on the Continent over a lengthy period of time. Knowledge of these methods was first brought to Britain by political refugees in the 1930s and strongly reinforced after the war by returning servicemen who had been exposed to prevailing sporting practices and traditions in Germany during tours of duty there.

One of the key things these teachings emphasise is the importance to every intending stalker of owning or having genuine, prompt access to a suitably trained dog for following up and finding fugitive deer after the shot. Indeed, in Germany, and also now in Sweden, it is illegal to stalk deer without such back-up. Some breeds and some mongrels have the requisite inborn qualities for this work, and some do not. Prime attributes are a good nose, biddability, responsiveness to training and an appropriate temperament.

The first choice among many leisure-time stalkers in Britain and Ireland is the Labrador, with its dual capability as a dog for game shooting and for deer. There need be no clash between the two provided that the two types of training are kept quite separate, the skills of a deer dog being mastered before gundog training proper commences. If the two are handled simultaneously, confusion is likely to result and the dog may not perform well at either.

Other potentially suitable deer dogs include the various breeds of retriever, flatcoats, Alsatians, border collies and Labrador/collie crosses. Setters and British pointer breeds are too rangey and spaniels in general too restless to be suitable for deer work.

At the other end of the scale are Continental breeds developed specifically for following up shot deer, securing wounded individuals and, when fully trained, making the whereabouts of a fallen animal known to the stalker involved. Prominent among such breeds are German hunter-pointer-retrievers (H.P.R.s), Weimaraners, large Munsterlanders, German short-haired pointers (G.S.P.s) and German wire-haired pointers. As I have said, teckels, as the Germans call wire-haired dachshunds, are excellent dogs for tracking and indeed were developed for that purpose, but they are much too small for holding down wounded deer, which of course is equally true of terriers. The Bayerischer gebirg-schweisshund (German mountain bloodhound) and the Hungarian vizsla are among other good choices for all-purpose deer work.

Continental breeds are becoming more readily available in the United Kingdom as their outstanding qualities become more widely known. An important point to remember is that whereas in the case of German H.P.R.s, the same dog may be bred for show purposes as well as for work, with British breeds it is a case of one or the other but not both. The key point here, if buying British, is to make sure to buy from a working strain and on no account from a show one. If your choice is a Labrador with deer work as its prime purpose, the best advice is to opt for a male dog as being a touch more persevering than a bitch, and having more strength.

Unless a dog comes recommended from someone you know, the advertisement columns of the sporting press will repay careful study. For a dog of the right kind with a good pedigree you are likely to have to pay hundreds of pounds, so find out all you can about it before reaching for your chequebook. If the working history and performance of the bloodline are crucial factors, so too are your gut feelings about the pup whose purchase you contemplate and how its mother impresses you. If she seems lacking in some way, the fault may well be hereditary. A second opinion is always useful if you know a suitable person, such as a long-time working dog owner, who may be prepared to go along with you for the vital interview. The best advice of all to follow when decision time comes is 'If in doubt, don't'. The vendor can always be told that you need time to think about it. If finance is a sticking-point, a visit to your local dogs' home may reveal a miracle mongrel waiting for a suitable owner!

Sound advice on all aspects of dogs for deer is lacking no longer. Training courses are available for deer dogs and their owners, with hands-on tuition by at least one recognised expert in this field – Guy Wallace, who runs a gundog training centre at Llandefalle, near Brecon in the eastern Welsh county of Powys. Guy has also written an excellent little booklet, *Training Dogs for Woodland Deer Stalking*, packed with so much good sense on its subject that I could not possibly do better than pass on some of his words of wisdom.

As a working dog rather than a household pet your puppy will need a kennel, ideally 1.2 metres (4 ft) square plus a run 2.4 metres (8 ft) by 1.2 metres (4 ft). The kennel should have a raised floor and should be positioned, if possible, so as to face the morning sun. A box or a discarded barrel can serve as a sleeping compartment and should be no larger than is necessary to accommodate one or two dogs. Two dogs can be kept in a kennel of the size described, bearing in mind that a dog is more content with another as a companion – which need not be a working dog.

The base of the run should be of concrete, or of paving slabs bonded with sand and cement, the whole being slightly sloping for drainage purposes, with a suitable drainage channel to a stone-bottomed soak-away.

The puppy should be let out for a morning and evening romp. Always remember it is a juvenile with playful inclinations, which should be allowed reasonably free rein. Allow it into the house when convenient but make it clearly understand that its home and sleeping-place is the kennel. If it cannot be housed in a kennel because of some practical limitations, adapt a suitable outhouse or perhaps a spare room indoors as a substitute, treating it as you would a kennel, as the dog's exclusive domain but one from which it may not wander at will around the house.

For food, proprietary puppy meal will serve admirably, moving up to its adult counterpart when the puppy is about four months old. A good supply of clean fresh water should always be on hand for drinking purposes and for routine cleansing of the run. Four meals a day are needed for a seven-week-old pup, but this can be scaled down to one daily feed by the time it is fifteen months of age.

At six to eight weeks old all puppies should be inoculated against four killer diseases – distemper, hardpad, hepatitis and parvo virus. If this has not been arranged by the vendor, take your puppy to the vet for it to be done as soon as possible. A yearly booster will then be needed to maintain the dog's protection. Treatment against roundworm should be given at least twice yearly. Tapeworm is also a problem, and external parasites such as ticks, fleas and deer keds should be watched out for and dealt with promptly; appropriate shampoos are available. Regular washing helps keep the dog's coat in good condition.

Accustom your puppy by easy stages to the constraints imposed by a lead. The important thing from the outside is a regular routine which it will quickly learn to recognise and accept, and built-in disciplinary measures are part and parcel of this. Begin to introduce it to the scents and sights of the countryside, always bearing in mind that scent is a far more important sense to a dog than sight or even hearing.

Training proper can begin when the pup is four to five months old. Gently but firmly teach it to obey basic commands like 'sit', an instruction reinforced by a hiss, the meaning of which will quickly become clear to your canine pupil. 'Down' and 'walk behind' are initially crisp, clear verbal commands eventually replaced by silent hand pressure on the head and nose respectively. Once the dog is used to sitting when instructed, walk away slowly with your back to it, watching it with a hand-mirror, and repeat the command as necessary until the dog learns to 'stay put' under all circumstances unless bidden otherwise. By climbing a ladder placed against a wall or tree you can take this training a stage further by teaching the dog to sit under a high seat and to stay there until told otherwise.

Whether you adopt this latter practice when stalking in earnest is a matter for individual judgement. I have been with other stalkers who do it routinely, but I have misgivings about it. One of the benefits of a high seat is that, depending on the lie of the land, your scent will often, although not always, be carried above any deer that emerge downwind of you, and this advantage is eliminated by the ground-level scent of a dog sitting under the seat.

When training the dog to walk at heel, use the word 'heel' as your command, control it with a slip-lead until it gets used to walking three-quarters of a length ahead of you, and accept no compromises with this. Guy Wallace reminds us in his booklet that this relative position of dog and stalker helps to avoid the possibility of the scent of a live but unseen deer, which the dog might point for your benefit, being overlaid by your own scent. Another piece of good advice from the same source is to walk the dog between a straight fence and yourself during training so that it learns to stay close alongside you.

When the dog has been trained to respond satisfactorily to the verbal command for walking at heel, teach it to react similarly when you pat your thigh, a substitute for verbal instruction which is invaluable at moments during the stalk when silence is critical. When at heel the dog should be trained to hold its head high to avoid being confused by ground scent, while remaining alert for the scent of deer in cover.

Once a dog becomes gun-shy it is likely to stay that way and will then only be of value if it is left in the car while you are stalking, and only brought out after the shot for blood-trailing or perhaps to follow up. This means you cannot have a stalking companion always on the spot for instant action. To accustom your dog to a rifle shot's considerable report, begin by getting it used to something much less startling, such as a .410 shotgun discharged downwind at a distance while the dog is otherwise preoccupied. Progressively reduce the distance between the gunfire and the dog, then repeat the whole process with a 12-bore, followed eventually by a full-bore rifle. The trick is to keep the dog's attention enjoyably distracted while the actual shooting is done. This is clearly a two-man operation and a vital step on the way to getting the very best out of your dog. Do not try to do it all on one day but spread it over three or four sessions. To minimise the auditory impact of the shot upon your dog, never fire except when the rifle can be pointed away from it, or you will have a deaf dog on your hands.

Serious pointer training is best undertaken with the dog on a long length of rope attached to a wide collar or harness, in mature woodland where subsequent following up can lead to a visual encounter with the quarry. As the dog strains forward, hold it back until it points as a natural process, then slacken the rope and repeat the process until the dog learns to hold point without restraint. Many dogs will point without prompting while you are walking along a ride and deer scent reaches them from one side or the other or from ahead. It is the resultant following-up which requires a further degree of careful instruction. The good scenting conditions of a moist, warm day with a slight breeze are best for this type of training.

Blood-trailing is what having a dog for deer is really all about. For some stalkers the training for this amounts to no more than dragging the carcase of a freshly shot deer for 100 metres or so and then putting the dog straight onto its scent. But real-life blood-trailing of a wounded deer, possibly shot the previous evening, makes much greater demands upon the dog.

Start, then, with cold blood-trailing training. Guy Wallace's method makes such good sense that it would be a considerable challenge to improve significantly upon it. When stalking, carry in one of your pockets two ordinary polythene freezer bags, one inside the other, containing a dessertspoonful of salt. When next you gralloch a deer, scoop up as much blood as you can and seal it in the polythene bags, where the salt will prevent coagulation. Take the blood home to store in your freezer.

When you want to start training, unfreeze the deer's blood and take it with you to an open, stock-free pasture. Lay out a trail by tying a blood-soaked rag on the end of a length of string attached to a long, thin rod or stick. Hold the lure at arm's length to your side as you walk along, out of sight of your dog, setting the scent – fairly liberally and continuously the first time, so that your own scent does not mask it. Mark out the trail with pegs for your own guidance.

This training can begin when the puppy is about four months old. It should wear a collar or harness to which a long line is attached; this enables you to hold the dog back from racing ahead and cutting corners and can also help keep it on the trail. At the start of the trail place a small amount of tripe or other offal, and a larger portion at the end. The dog will then know where its work is meant to begin, and will learn that there is something more to eat and enjoy at the finish – with all other types of training, lavish praise should be the sole reward for the dog's effort and success. All training should be made to seem fun, and none more so than blood-trailing, which requires particular perseverance. At the same time, do not overtax the dog's enthusiasm for blood-trailing by overdoing this training, especially in the early stages.

Start each blood-trailing exercise with a command reserved for this specific activity – 'Hi, lost' if your canine companion is a deer dog pure and simple and not a game-shooting dog also used for tracking deer. Otherwise, 'Seek' or 'Where's the deer?' may be better suited for this purpose.

As training progresses, make the trail steadily more difficult by changing its direction and by breaking the line at intervals. Proceed by stages to the trickier terrain afforded by woodland. Lengthen the time between laying the blood-trail and introducing your dog to it. Steadily lengthen the trail itself, always making sure that the dog is rewarded with success and a snack at the end.

Another important point to remember when training a dog for blood-trailing is to lay the trail downwind. The dog will then not be distracted by scent blowing back from the trail ahead. By placing the tripe at the trail's end on a rolled-up deerskin, the dog will be taught to associate blood-trailing directly with deer.

One way of keeping in touch with your dog while it is blood-trailing is to attach hawk bells or special dog bells to its collar – another good reason, perhaps, for using a collar in earlier training and thereby helping the dog to get used to one as well as linking it in a general way with the job of tracking deer. A much more sophisticated technique involves the use of telemetry, with a radio-collar-type transmitter worn by the dog and a special receiver carried by the stalker.

Less hi-tech but more traditional is training a dog to sit by a fallen deer as soon as it finds it and then 'bay dead', a procedure much favoured by German stalkers. Breeds which are normally mute will need special encouragement to do this. Training involves denying the dog immediate access to some desired object, perhaps its main meal of the day covered over or placed just out of its reach, or a deer carcase suspended on a gambril. The intention is to make the dog bark in sheer frustration, urging this on with the command 'bark' and even some simulated barking. Having persevered with this training and achieved the desired result, the next stage is a series of field exercises using actual shot deer for the purpose, with the dog collared and on the end of a rope holding it a little way back from the carcase. It may well take time to train the dog to repeat this process of finding and giving tongue when unrestrained, but keep on trying!

A further refinement developed by the Germans is the use of a leather device called a *bringsel* to let the stalker know his dog has found a shot deer. It is attached by a cord to the collar when the dog sets off to follow a blood-trail, and the dog returns with it in its mouth when it has located the fallen animal.

For the first lesson with this, throw the *bringsel* for the dog to retrieve as it would a normal gundog training dummy. Next, place the *bringsel* on top of a freshly shot deer carcase or, failing that, a rolled-up deerskin, command 'seek-find' and get the dog to bring back the *bringsel*. You then command 'find' for the dog to lead you back to the carcase, still with the *bringsel* in its mouth. This accomplished, take the *bringsel* from the dog while it is still by the carcase or the deerskin and let the dog know it has done well. For the third lesson lay out a blood-trail for the dog to follow before repeating the previous process. Follow on from this by doing the same thing again, but this time attach the *bringsel* to the collar by a cord about 25 cm (10 in) long and with the preliminary command 'seek-find'. The dog should then come back to you with the *bringsel* in its mouth, leading to the final lesson. This time go over the whole procedure again, but with the cord shortened so that the *bringsel* is attached directly to the collar.

It is particularly important in the early stages of training to confine the dog to its kennel on days when training is to take place until you are ready to begin. The dog will then learn to anticipate training more as a pleasure than a chore – a time of very welcome change from the long, monotonous hours preceding it and an opportunity to work off pent-up energy. Training should be enjoyable for trainer and dog alike, cementing a bond between the two which will last for the dog's lifetime and reducing the loneliness of an activity mostly carried out in solitude, away from other humans.

The dog's first few outings after formal training are an extension of the training process, so do not rush things. Correct faults as they arise, keeping the dog strictly at heel whatever temptations may present themselves to it, until the need arises for it to follow a blood-trail in earnest. When that happens, remember to wait at least fifteen minutes for the deer, if it is not already dead, to settle down and begin to stiffen up before allowing the dog to move in.

When your dog's skills become known, be prepared for stalkers without dogs who have shot a deer they cannot find to ring you up at all hours with urgent requests for assistance. You need not be shy about charging for this, on both a mileage and time basis, having let it be known beforehand that this is how you operate. You will be wise though to make sure that reports of your dog's expertise have not been exaggerated in the telling, or its reputation – and yours – may suffer accordingly!

CHAPTER 16
Deer Lost!

M any a novice stalker is disconcerted to discover how frequently it happens that a well-placed bullet does not result in the deer dropping dead on the spot. Even more dismaying is the sight of such an animal racing for cover and vanishing into it, raising the worrying possibility of a long and difficult search which might not prove to be successful.

This is something we all have experienced and have had to learn to cope with; the reassuring factor is that in most cases the deer was mortally hit, its subsequent movements being no more than a reflex action, or reaction, of very limited duration. Indeed, in a large proportion of instances, having run a few metres, it will drop within full view of the stalker, never to move again. I said in the last chapter, a shot deer can even be 'lost' by becoming instantly invisible from the moment the shot was taken, having collapsed like a pricked balloon at a spot where it is screened from view by enveloping vegetation. Such vegetation may be quite short yet still be sufficient to hide a deer, especially a small one such as a roe or a muntjac, until you almost step on it, which underlines the importance of carefully noting where a deer is standing before you take the shot.

Another important point to note is the deer's reaction to the shot before it takes flight or otherwise. The short time taken for sound to travel should make the bullet strike audible a fraction of a second after the shot itself; a hollow 'smack' indicates a strike in the chest cavity while a dull 'plop' is to be expected if the deer is hit in the abdomen. A sharp, whiplash crack could signal a shattered leg-bone or perhaps a broken spine, although in the latter case the deer will drop at once and be unable to rise again.

A heart-shot deer will commonly respond with a half-leap, rearing up momentarily on its hindquarters before plunging forward and rocketing off for anything up to 100 metres or more before dropping dead. A deer shot in the abdomen will hunch its back before running off,

often with head and neck lowered, looking distinctly sick, while one shot in the liver will briefly shiver before departing in similar fashion.

When a shot deer falls immediately, never take it for granted that it will stay down. The bullet may only have clipped the top of its spine, in which case it may quickly scramble to its feet and make off at once, probably never to be found.

Never shoot a second deer until the first has been located or you at least know it is safely down. Having waited some fifteen minutes, unless you are in a high seat, tie a white handkerchief to a tree or leave some other conspicuous object to mark the spot from which the shot was taken, and pace out the distance to where the deer was standing when you fired. By comparing what you had estimated the range to be with the actual range, you can thus test your ability to judge distance between yourself and your quarry, a useful skill to sharpen up for the future.

When you reach the spot where the deer was standing, tread with care as you examine the ground for signs of a bullet strike and where it is likely to have struck. Cut hair will often be found in profusion and its colour should give you some indication of whether it came from the flank, the underside or some other part of the deer's anatomy. Now look around for other signs, such as bone fragments, rumen contents and, particularly, blood. Frothy blood with bubbles of air is the classic sign of a lung shot, in which case the deer will not have travelled far. Blood from a liver wound is dark, and blood mixed with gut contents speaks for itself. A gut-shot deer can travel far and will be likely to die slowly, but will often settle down in some quiet place where you may later find it, still alive and ready to move on again if you approach incautiously.

If you own a deer dog, now is the time to put into practice some of the training recommended in the last chapter. In the early stages in particular, keep the dog on a long lead as it follows a blood-trail, releasing it only where the nature of the terrain makes it impracticable to restrain it in this way, as may happen if the deer has entered a young, unbrashed plantation or, say, a rhododendron shrubbery with which the lead could become thoroughly and quite hopelessly entangled.

With verbal encouragement or without it, once your dog is onto a good, fresh scent it will naturally be eager to forge ahead at a faster pace than you can comfortably keep up with, which is another excellent reason for using a lead where this is feasible. If the dog is of a breed too small to tackle and hold down a wounded deer, you will also need to keep it in view so as to be ready to deliver the *coup de grâce* with a finishing shot if the deer gets up and prepares to run off. In very thick cover this can be difficult, hence the value of a dog with adequate muscle to cope with this specific situation.

In all normal stalking situations, if the deer is still alive when you come up with it, put it down with a second shot and do not be tempted to use a knife. A kick or other sudden movement by the disabled animal at the moment when a knife is being used could all too easily make you cut yourself. If the deer is an antlered male it may also still be capable of inflicting serious injury if it is handled incautiously.

Whenever your dog has found a shot deer, praise it lavishly but do not let it maul the animal. As a preliminary to performing the actual gralloch, and once you have ensured that the deer is dead by touching an eyeball without producing any response, now is the time to use your knife by inserting the blade into the chest from the front in order to penetrate the heart and so draw off most of the blood from the carcase. Allow the dog access to the blood as a reward for its success, supplementing this with some offal from the animal once you have satisfied yourself that offal retrieved from the gralloch is free from internal parasites and is from an otherwise healthy beast.

Some stalkers, of course, do not possess a dog and cannot see their way to acquiring one, sometimes for very good reasons. Some people suggest that such people should ask themselves whether they ought to stalk at all, and unless they can genuinely call upon the help of someone who has a suitable dog and can be

If your dog can be trained to stay with the carcase and 'play dead' when it finds a 'lost' deer, its value will be greatly enhanced. Yellow labradors also have the advantage of being more readily visible in poor light, making it easier for the stalker to keep track of their movements.

available at short notice, such a question is perfectly valid. Otherwise, occasions are almost sure to arise when no amount of careful searching will lead to the recovery of a lost deer which a trained deer dog could hardly fail to locate in fairly short order.

If, for whatever reason, you are stalking without a dog and you have shot at a deer which has then made off into cover, examine the spot where the deer was standing with great care, noting the signs already indicated as giving clues as to where the bullet struck and what disablement may have resulted. Should you fail at first to find any definite signs of a hit, do not automatically assume that you missed. Remember how the deer reacted when you fired. If it immediately took flight, no matter how else it may have reacted or not reacted, the probability is that it was hit. If it remained standing perfectly still for a few seconds before departing, the likelihood that you missed is a good deal greater, but still do not take this for granted. Search with the greatest possible care – and do not shoot at another deer until you have re-zeroed your rifle and have satisfied yourself that the 'scope alignment is spot on, with bullets consistently being placed where you intend, and grouping well.

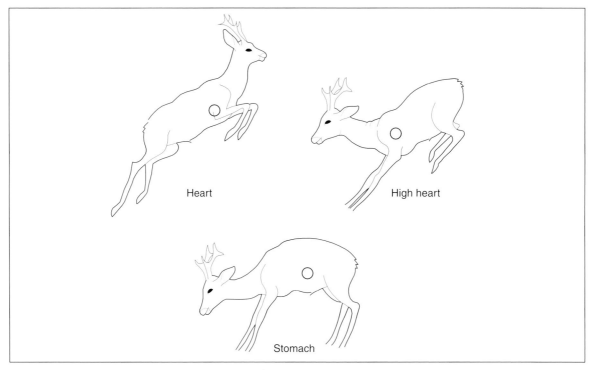

Heart

High heart

Stomach

Fig 16.1 Reaction to shot

If you fail to find any ground signs where you thought the deer was standing, you may be searching at the wrong spot. It is all too easy to do this by misjudging distance, so cast around with care until you are sure you have not missed the precise location. Blood, hair, bone fragments or body tissue, or a combination of some or all of these, can nearly always be found, although occasionally all are absent.

You will have seen which way the deer ran, so search the ground there for splashes of blood. Some stalkers have a very keen eye for blood, but those with restricted colour vision may find it difficult to detect and so should search with extra diligence before taking it as certain that there is none. Sometimes there may be little or no blood, in which case a more wide-ranging visual search may be necessary, but if you envisage having to get help from a dog later, it is better to minimise trampling which may obliterate the deer's scent by overlaying it with your own.

If blood splashes are frequent and profuse, you will probably not have far to follow the trail before you find your deer stone dead. If blood traces diminish as you follow the trail, after perhaps not having been very much in evidence from the start, be prepared for a prolonged and possibly unsuccessful search. While you are searching have your rifle ready at all times for instant action in case a wounded but still mobile deer materialises ahead of you.

If a blood trail seems to stop abruptly, the deer may have changed direction, so cast around to see if you can pick up the trail afresh in a different quarter, as in most cases you will. If you were stalking in the evening and darkness defeats you, a long-beam battery spotlight may save the day and eventually lead you to your quarry. Remember, however, that blood signs are less easy to detect and follow by artificial light, that you are more likely to disturb and move on a deer that is still mobile before you are near enough to prevent its escaping, and that even at close quarters a departing deer will be harder to intercept than in full daylight. There is also the all-important safety factor to be considered when you may have to shoot at a deer against a background which you cannot be sure is solid.

However frustrating and inconvenient it may be, if you have to go home after dark without a deer you know to have been hit, there is no humane alternative but to resume the search next day, as early as possible in the morning.

Bring canine help if possible. If this also fails, report the circumstances to the property owner, manager or tenant, or the gamekeeper or whoever else may be appropriate. Do not just slink away, saying nothing. Your reputation may suffer a little, but it will suffer very much more if you have said nothing and the victim is later discovered by somebody else, either dead or, worse still, still alive, and with the finger of accusation pointing clearly towards you as the person responsible.

If all the indications point to a clean miss as the explanation for the deer never being found, a tiny doubt will always linger in your mind and that of others who may be aware of what has happened. Chalk it up to experience and do your best to ensure that it does not happen ever again. If it does, it may be time to consider whether you should sell your rifle and stalk deer with a camera instead.

CHAPTER 17
Carcase Care

Carcase care begins at the very moment you reach a shot deer and have to set about gralloching and extracting it, although not necessarily in that order. Indeed, some would maintain that care should begin when the deer is not yet a carcase, by placing the bullet, if at all possible, where it will least damage the meat – say in the neck if your target is close enough for you to be absolutely sure of achieving an instant knock-down effect. Take no chances about this, however. The lung/heart area is always the safest aiming point, and if you smash some ribs or misjudge slightly and shatter a shoulder you will not have lost much worthwhile venison.

If your victim is a roe or is otherwise small enough and light enough for you to carry it out unaided, tie the four legs together with twine, or strap them together, a few inches above the hooves, and either hold the carcase in your hand or sling it over a shoulder, legs above and body below. Better still, stow it in a roe-sack and carry it to a point where you can gralloch it and dispose of the innards.

The recommended procedure for gralloch disposal is to bury it, so carry a spade in your car for this purpose. It has to be said, however, that many stalkers discreetly dump the gralloch inconspicuously, assuming that foxes will make short work of clearing it up or that Nature will otherwise ensure that it is not left around for long. Either way, gralloch the deer as soon as conveniently possible because, in hot weather especially, decomposition will set in very quickly, beginning in the abdominal tract and rapidly tainting the rest of the carcase, turning it green and making it useless as venison.

'Gralloch' is a Highland term which has no precise counterpart in plain English. It basically means 'eviscerate', although more than just the viscera or alimentary tract is disposed of by the post-mortem surgery involved. It is also a noun which refers to the various body parts extracted.

Different people gralloch deer in slightly

A carrying strap fastened around the legs is an ideal way of carrying-out the carcase of a muntjac. With four legs strapped or tied together, a roe carcase can be similarly carried or slung over a shoulder.

In the absence of a roe-sack with a washable plastic liner, a fellow-stalker can help make light work of carrying out a roe carcase.

A heart-shot roebuck, ready for gralloching and carrying out.

Before you begin the gralloch, examine the carcase for abnormalities of antler growth or otherwise and for external parasites such as ticks, bites from which can cause disease in humans. If you are gralloching on the ground, take particular care to keep the carcase clean once you open it.

Game dealers will sometimes accept deer carcases with head and legs still on.

different ways. Some German-trained stalkers claim to be able to complete the operation without getting a single speck of blood on themselves or their clothing, even doing so while wearing a white shirt without rolling up the sleeves. I have not personally seen this and certainly cannot do it!

The method I have always found perfectly adequate is one I learned from a professional stalker a long time ago. First, bleed the carcase by thrusting a knife blade into the heart through the base of the neck and hanging or holding the deer head down. Pumping by exerting pressure on both sides of the thorax (chest cavity) with your hands will help to maximise the blood flow.

In field conditions it is often most convenient to gralloch a deer while it is lying on the ground, belly upwards, preferably with the rear end slightly lower than the head. Wearing plastic gloves for the sake of hygiene, fully expose the throat before opening the skin at the base of the neck with your knife. Now turn the blade with

1. Begin the gralloch by cutting along the full length of the throat to loosen the windpipe and the gullet, separating these from enveloping tissues, then tie the gullet to prevent any leakage of stomach contents into the body cavity.

2. Cut carefully around the anus and rectum in preparation for clean, complete extraction of the entire digestive tract.

3. Working forward from the pelvic girdle to the rib-cage, but carefully through the belly-skin and then through the peritoneum (abdominal lining) with the knife blade upwards and a finger on either side of it to prevent the knife puncturing the paunch and spilling gut contents into the body cavity.

4. Having loosened the intestines, grasp the paunch and pull it clear of the body, maintaining a tight grip around the lower end of the gullet if you have not tied this to prevent any spillage of paunch contents.

its sharp edge uppermost and run it along the centre of the underside of the neck. Next, separate the underlying tissues to expose the windpipe and gullet. Sever these just above the larynx and then slice down both sides of them as far as the point where they enter the thorax, freeing them in the process from other neck tissue.

Having tied a knot in the gullet to prevent rumen contents leaking from it, turn to the other end of the carcase and insert your knife, cutting edge uppermost, to penetrate the abdominal skin and the underlying peritoneum – the membrane enveloping the rumen, stomach, intestines and other abdominal organs. Make this insertion just in front of the pelvis, the bony cradle containing the bladder and female reproductive tract. Now place a finger on either side of the blade to guide it and prevent it from puncturing any part of the alimentary tract as you carefully cut through the skin and peritoneum as far as the centre of the rib-cage. You reach a particularly crucial stage of this cut when you get to the rumen. If this is full or distended with gas – which can occur when food ferments due to gralloching having been delayed longer than is ideal – it is highly vulnerable to accidental rupture and the

5. Be careful not to puncture the bladder when you extract this and, if relevant, the uterus after easing out the intestines and removing the rectum and its contents.

6. If you intend to remove the heart, lungs, liver and kidneys at this stage instead of waiting until you get home or leaving these in the body for veterinary inspection, remove the liver and kidneys before opening the diaphragm and releasing blood from the chest cavity. Then grasp the heart and lungs along with the windpipe to pull these free from the body by way of the abdominal cavity.

7. Up to this point you should have a clean and bloodless gralloch.

8. Now turn the body and spread the back legs before giving it a good shake to empty out any blood. With larger species than roe, turn the body back uppermost with the fore end higher than the rear end to facilitate the draining-off process..

resultant spillage of the contents will make the rest of the gralloching a needlessly messy business.

Now grasp the base of the gullet close to where it reaches the rumen and pull the whole of it through the diaphragm, the muscular membrane separating the abdomen and its organs from the thorax. Should you have difficulty with this, sever the gullet as high up as you can reach, making sure no contents leak out as you turn the carcase on its side to pull out the rumen, stomach and intestines all in one go. Run your knife blade around the rim of the anus and rectum, grasping the rectum when you have freed it to prevent droppings from escaping as you pull it free from the abdominal cavity. Now remove the bladder, being careful not to spill its contents until it is well clear of the carcase. The female reproductive tract, if there is one, comes next, and when this is clear open the uterus to check what foetuses it may contain and their sex. In the case of a male deer, remove all interior pipework but leave the penis and testicles in situ as confirmation of its sex if the carcase is destined for sale to a game dealer.

Gralloching can be less messy if postponed until you return to where the carcase can be suspended and a drip tray and disposal bucket are available.

Fertiliser bags or feed bags can be used for stowing roe carcase in your car for the journey home or to the game dealer. Removal of lower legs and head makes a carcase easier to pack.

Your game dealer may require that the heart, lungs, liver, kidneys and spleen are left in situ for veterinary examination as required by E.U. Game Meat Regulations if the carcase is to be exported. Otherwise you can opt to remove these organs after completing the evisceration, in which case have a large freezer food bag ready to receive the liver, kidneys and heart as you free them from surrounding tissues. Cut through the diaphragm and thrust a hand deep into the thorax to grasp the windpipe and pull it through from the neck before extracting the windpipe, heart and lungs in one operation. The spleen can join the disposable gralloch. If the heart has been smashed by the bullet, keep what is left of it for your dog, or dispose of it with the other abdominal organs after you have checked both gralloch and offal alike for possible signs of disease.

If the liver is mottled in appearance, cut it open and see if the interior pipework has the characteristic thickening caused by fluke, an all too common internal parasite. Deer are also parasitised, sometimes fatally, by more than one species of lungworm, causing parasitic pneumonia which leaves its mark with whitish patches and grey areas on the lungs. Avian tuberculosis and the more serious bovine T.B. also affect deer, causing abnormalities in the lungs and other organs including, particularly, the lymph nodes.

While deer are subject to a whole range of other disorders of varying severity, including notifiable maladies such as anthrax and foot and mouth disease – and including bovine T.B. – in general they are far healthier than most domestic livestock. If pathological abnormalities of any kind are found in a deer you have shot, handle it only with plastic gloves and send suspect organs, securely wrapped and identified, to a vet for examination or to your local Ministry of Agriculture veterinary laboratory and, of course, make sure that the carcase does not end up as food for humans.

When checking the health of shot deer, do not overlook external parasites, the most common ones being ticks, keds and lice. Heavy infestations by one or more of these can result in an unhealthy animal. As I said in chapter 6, ticks can also harm humans by passing on the infective agent for Lyme disease through their bite. Warble fly and nasal bot fly parasitise red and roe deer in Scotland but are so far rare or absent in England and Wales. Warble fly eggs are laid in the hock of the host. The resultant grub travels through the deer's body to the back, from which it eventually tunnels its way out and falls to the ground before developing into a fly. Bot fly eggs are laid in the nose, where the larvae develop; as well as in the throat, sometimes causing the deer to shake its head and lick its nose repeatedly in response to the irritation to which this inevitably gives rise.

Ailing deer will usually look ill, thus forewarning you of problems to be looked for when you have shot them. Undersized or emaciated deer, whether or not they later prove to have any clinical disorder, are obvious candidates for culling.

When gralloching, whether in the field or otherwise, take off the lower half of each leg for disposal with other waste products. A frontal cut just below the hock and through the adjacent skin and sinew will do this in short order. Removing the head, in the case of a stag or buck, is not much more difficult.

If the trophy is destined for taxidermy as a full head mount, cut the skin well back and behind the neck as far back as the withers. If you have followed my method of gralloching you will already have cut along the base of the neck as far back as the lower jaw. Now skin the neck carefully with your knife, starting at the underside and rear and then working steadily up and forward as far as the base of the skull, but no

farther. To remove the head from the neck, feel for the space between the skull and the first vertebra of the spine and apply the knife there. If you have found the right spot you can sever the spinal cord with ease before cutting through the flesh of the neck and then removing the head with a twist of both hands on the antlers. Any attached neck skin will of course come off with the head. If a basic skull-and-antlers trophy is all you intend to retain to mount, the procedure is the same except that you cut through the neck skin close to the head, leaving the neck itself, with its skin, attached to the body at this stage.

Having gralloched your deer and dealt with all these other matters, allow the carcase to cool as quickly as possible, a process which is assisted by cutting through the rib-cage along its centre from base to neck with a clean butcher's hacksaw. Although this is particularly desirable in hot weather, it is not absolutely essential unless your game dealer insists upon it. If you plan to sell carcases to a dealer it makes good sense to find out from him exactly how he likes them presented. Remember too that it is illegal to sell venison except to a registered game dealer, though of course you can give it away to your friends.

These post-mortem operations may well have taught you a few things you did not know about deer anatomy. If you had the vague notion that the heart was halfway along the body instead of being tucked away under the ribs, just behind the shoulder and under the lungs, you now know why it is so important to place a shot in the latter area. You will be aware too that the kidneys are not somewhere close to the pelvis, as I myself once imagined, but a good deal farther up the back, on either side of the spinal column. Dissection will also have underlined the crucial importance of placing a neck shot in the critical spinal area.

Instructive though these anatomical revelations are, no less so is what you learn about the performance of your rifle, the placement of the bullet and its effect upon the target in terms of how the deer reacted immediately after being shot. Note all these things for your future guidance. In particular, did the bullet strike at the point of aim precisely, thus confirming that the rifle is correctly zeroed? Did it cause anatomical damage of a kind you had not intended, thus indicating, perhaps, that your point of aim was not well chosen or that the deer was not quite broadside-on at the moment when you squeezed the trigger? Did the extent of the damage suggest that a lighter bullet, or indeed a heavier one, or perhaps a rifle of different calibre, might have been rather more appropriate for the species of deer in question? The learning process is never-ending.

If you do not possess a roe-sack and the carcase is of a roe or a deer of similar size or smaller, after carrying it back to your car put it into a bin-liner, an empty feed bag or something similar and stow it where your dog cannot reach it and where it can be safely insulated from contact with the rest of the car's content. In the case of a heavier carcase you may well need help to haul it out and certainly to load it into your vehicle. Do not attempt to perform Herculean wonders single-handed, or you may well damage yourself in ways which could put stalking out of your reach for a prolonged period.

Exchanging your car for a 4WD and acquiring a winch or block-and-tackle for the vehicle-loading process could go some way towards solving this problem. Alternatives are to stalk in tandem or to make a firm arrangement with someone suitable locally, such as the Farm Manager or Gamekeeper, to help you when required. Should there be no option but to leave a carcase out overnight and collect it next day, suspend it head down if at all possible, secure from casual observation, or attach something to it which is strongly impregnated with human scent as a deterrent to prowling foxes. My own experience has been that, once gralloched and hence subjected to human handling, a deer can safely be left out overnight in heavily-foxed country where otherwise a deer not found until the following day would invariably be mauled.

Take all possible care to keep carcases where flies cannot get at them. Should this mean postponing the gralloch and head-removal until you get home, so be it. This reinforces the vital importance of having a fly-proof deer larder, or possibly making your garage fly-proof and adapting it for this purpose.

Leave your car outside and rig up a gambril over a beam to suspend the carcase by its hind legs, with an adequate drip tray underneath while you perform the gralloch. Abdominal organs in particular tend to come away more cleanly from a carcase thus suspended than from one lying on the ground.

Once the gralloch has been completed and the head and lower legs removed, if the venison is intended for home consumption – by way of a gift to your stalking landlord, distribution among friends, or for your own freezer – then the sooner you skin the carcase the easier the butchering will be. Use a good, sharp knife for the purpose, preferably one with a curved edge to the tip of the blade so as not to damage the meat – or indeed the skin – while separating one from the other.

Begin by cutting through the skin along the inside surface of the haunches, then ease the skin away from the flesh with the assistance of the knife. Next, free the skin around the rear end in similar fashion and along each side of the already opened belly and rib-cage until you can carefully fist it all away, again with some cautious knifework to assist you. If you start to tear the flesh, bringing some of it away with the skin, ease off and bring the knife once more into action. Finally, cut through the skin on the inner side of the upper forequarters just as you did with the haunches, and complete the operation by stripping the skin from the rest of the carcase much as you might remove a tight-fitting vest from a human body. If the deer has been shot at around the time when it was moulting its winter coat or was about to do so, it will be useless for preservation. If it is in sufficiently good condition to be worth curing for use as a mat or for some other purpose, roll it up carefully and put it aside for later attention.

Many stalkers can retail venison legally because they satisfy whatever conditions are laid down by their local authority for becoming registered game dealers. Minimum requirements are likely to include a fly-proof deer larder with hot and cold running water, an impervious plastered floor with an 18 in taper up the washable wall, non-wooden fitments throughout, tools of acceptable standards for butchery purposes, and basket or catch-cradle draining which permits liquid only to drain away.

Whether or not you aspire to become registered as a game dealer, if you intend to butcher carcases you will be well advised to equip yourself as above, as the hygienic handling

Above: *Hang the carcase on a gambrel to drain off before commencing skinning and butchering. This and all subsequent operations should be carried out in the open air in fly-free weather only. Flyproof conditions are at all times essential.*

Above: *You can skin a carcase while hanging, starting along the inside edge of the back legs, around the tail-bone, then around the edge of the belly cavity and along the sternum (breastbone) to the neck and along the inside edge of the forelegs, carefully easing away the skin with your knife where necessary but otherwise 'fisting' it away as you go without tearing the flesh, finally pulling it off like a tight-fitting vest.*

Left: *1. Otherwise, having removed the head and the lower legs, lay the carcase belly uppermost on a clean, flat surface and open the sternum with a butcher's saw if this has not already been done.*

Below: *2.With or without spectators, begin skinning out, starting with the forelegs.*

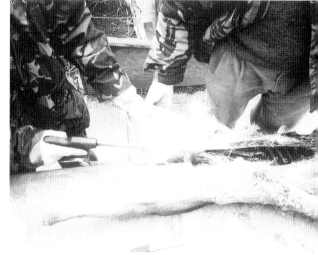

4. Now saw through the pelvis.

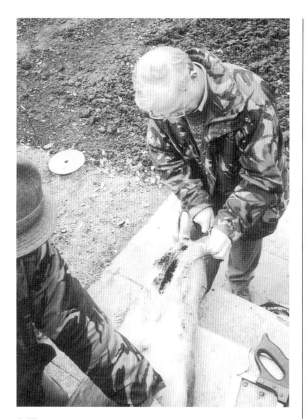

3. Then turn your attention to the rib-cage.

of deer at the processing stage is all-important. It is wise, in the course of gralloching, not to forget to remove all kidney fat and other internal bodily accretions and to mop out any spilt blood or other matter from the carcase with a clean, damp cloth kept hygienically wrapped for the purpose.

Hang the carcase if you wish for a few days to enhance its flavour, making sure to keep it fly-proof throughout this process and not to hang it for too long, or perhaps at all in really warm weather. Do not make a fetish of hanging – many people prefer their venison fresh rather than even slightly gamey!

When you are ready to begin butchery, lay the carcase belly upwards on a draining-board which should be of either metal or plastic and on no account of wood, which can absorb and retain bacteria. Start by sawing the pelvis into halves and detaching it and the haunches from the remainder of the carcase by sawing through the spine and cutting through the attendant flesh. Place the two haunches in the sink with cold running water flowing through. Next turn your attention to the saddle, the most important cut of

5. Next, skin out the hind legs.

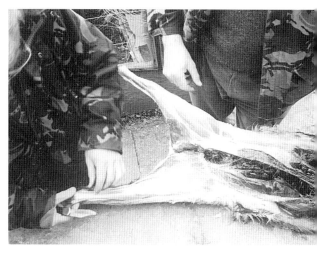

6. Finish off skinning hind legs.

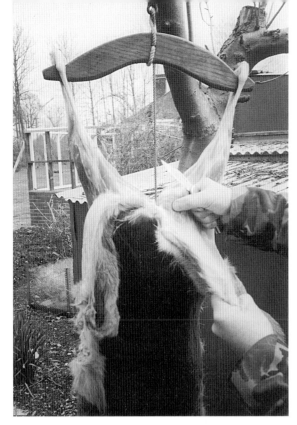

7. Hang on a gambrel to skin the back with careful knifework where necessary to expedite fisting-off.

8. Skin and flesh should separate cleanly without the flesh being torn.

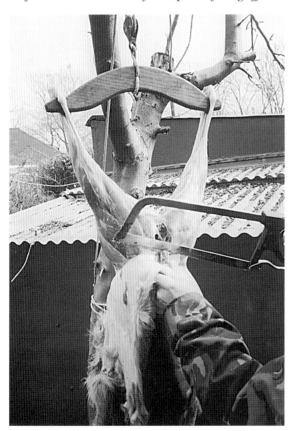

9. Saw through the tail-bone.

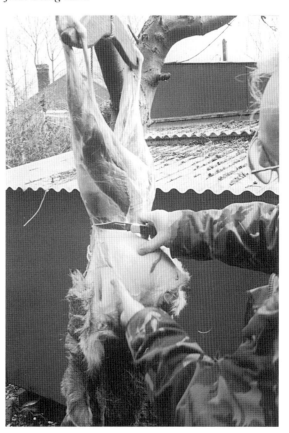

10. Ease skin down the body.

11. *Working down to the forelegs.*

12. *Skinning down the backbone as you go.*

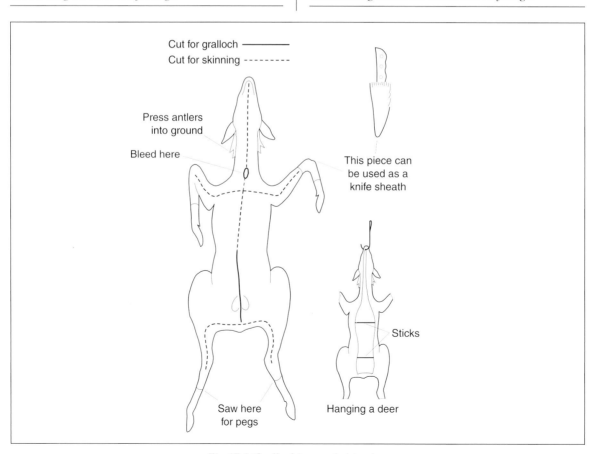

Cut for gralloch ——————
Cut for skinning ----------

Press antlers into ground

Bleed here

This piece can be used as a knife sheath

Saw here for pegs

Sticks

Hanging a deer

Fig 17.1 Gralloching and skinning

all. Damage the saddle with a misplaced bullet and your game dealer will not be a happy man should you wish to sell the carcase. Include the last two ribs on both sides and as much of the forward saddle meat as possible with the saddle proper when you cut it, using the saw again on the backbone. After you have detached the two forequarters with the knife, there will not be much left except dog meat, as there is little flesh on the ribs and nothing worth while on the neck.

Having thoroughly rinsed the various cuts in running cold water, pack them in individual freezer bags for consignment to the freezer. All that then remains is to wash all your implements thoroughly, sterilising them in boiling water, and wash down your deer larder and generally leave it in good order for the next time.

When the time comes to sample the product of your labours, at first try something simple and basic like a straightforward roast. Because venison is a very lean meat, add lard or other cooking fat before wrapping the selected cut in tin foil to contain its juices and then roasting it just as you would a joint of beef. When it reaches the table a bottle of good red wine will go down well with it.

Do not neglect the offal, which should be washed as soon as possible after the stalk. Fried deer liver and kidneys served with a rasher of bacon, fried mushrooms and tomatoes makes a breakfast fit for a king – and one which goes down particularly well after an early-morning stalk.

CHAPTER 18
Trophies

Having shot your first stag or buck, will you want to keep the antlers as a memento of that very special occasion? This may seem a strange question to ask, but the fact is that some stalkers appear to lose all interest in their quarry once they have shot it and disposed of the carcase, potential trophies being discarded with assorted detritus from the gralloch. At the other extreme are those who can never bring themselves to throw away anything, least of all something so special as the antlers of a deer they have managed to shoot themselves, no matter how unimpressive some may be as a trophy.

The jackdaw instinct to relinquish nothing one has taken some trouble to acquire may not, of course, be the only reason for retaining the antlers of every male deer shot. You may want to assemble more than a representative cross-section of all such deer, of all ages, culled over a period of time on an individual property, using this as study material for comparing, shall we say, long-term trends in antler quality resulting from a policy of selectively culling substandard animals.

The problem which then arises is where to keep all this accumulating hardware. If your house is a big one or you have suitable outbuildings, it just might be possible to collect and store unlimited numbers of trophies without jeopardising your marriage, but the odds are otherwise against this. Some spouses may be appeased if you consign your treasured, cobweb-collecting antlers to the loft, where no one can see them, although this makes hoarding them in the first place rather pointless. You will have to solve this problem in whatever way seems best for you, but do not blame me for the consequences if you make the wrong decision!

Stalkers I know mostly compromise by keeping only the better or more unusual heads they shoot over time, and manage to come to some agreement with their wives or partners as to where these should be kept – perhaps even displayed for them to reflect upon and for visitors to admire.

Only extra special trophies are nowadays normally considered for full head mounting to hang on the wall after the fashion with big game trophies from remote corners of the world in large country houses of the past. If this is intended it is of great importance to skin the head and neck very carefully. Skinning the head requires particular care, especially around the eyes. Cut along the nape of the neck, then skin to the base of the neck and back to the shoulders to form a 'cape' as you next ease the skin off the neck. Now cut off the neck itself. If you have any doubts about your ability to skin the head satisfactorily, keep the whole head, unskinned, with neck skin attached, and let the taxidermist do the rest.

Good taxidermy does not come cheap. One skilled practitioner of this craft whom I recently consulted quoted prices starting from around £120 for a roe buck, £150 for a sika stag, £180 for a fallow buck and £250 for a red stag for a full head mount.

Most of us content ourselves with skull mounts: not of the whole skull but of its upper side, including the upper half of the eye sockets. A somewhat rough-and-ready but quite effective way to do this is to steady the head with one hand, resting it on a level surface at about waist height, and with the other hand saw through the front inch (2.5 cm) of the nose, using an ordinary carpenter's saw. Detach the partially-severed nose end with the knife you use for gralloching, then turn the head, grasping it firmly with the truncated nose end uppermost. Now comes the most delicate part of the operation. Saw through the exposed bone of the upper jaw, aligning the saw with the mid-point of both eye sockets, making sure as you start sawing to get the angle exactly right to avoid ending up with an all-too-visibly uneven cut. Having sawn through the eye sockets from front to rear, carry on sawing through the brain cavity and the back of the skull before completing the operation with your

1. Trophy preparation without sophisticated aids: first saw off the tip of the nose ...

2. ...then align the saw carefully with the centre of the two eye sockets and saw off the top of the head, beginning at the exposed end of the two nose bones.

3. Scrape out with your knife the upper part of the brain and as much as you can of the honeycomb-like mass of small bones in the nose without dislodging the nose bones proper.

4. ... and then scrape away as much as you can of the skin and adherent tissue on the upper side of the skull before beginning the boiling-out process.

knife, which now comes fully into play.

Having detached the raw material for your trophy, the upper portion of the skull with antlers attached, extract the lower jaw to examine the teeth for wear as supporting evidence of the age of the deer. Teeth in pristine condition indicate a fairly young animal, but if they are worn down to the gums you have culled a veteran which was almost certainly ripe for taking out. Having said this, it should be added that tooth wear may sometimes be accentuated by dietary influences, making some deer appear older than their years. Age can sometimes be determined more precisely by subjecting a cross-section of the molar teeth to examination for annual growth by counting the number of growth rings, which should correspond to the age of the deer in years.

Some stalkers retain the lower jaw as back-up evidence of age in terms of young, middle-aged or old. If you wish to do this, run your knife around the tongue to separate it from the surrounding tissue. Next, cut around the two rear ends of the jaw to free them in turn from the enveloping tissue, then grasp the jaw behind the incisors and pull it free from the lower part of the upper jaw. If you have sufficiently freed the tissues around the rear of the lower jaw it should come away in your pulling hand while you hold the upper jaw with your other hand. Now cut or scrape away as much as you conveniently can of any flesh or tissue which is still attached to the lower jaw and lay the latter to one side – safely out of reach of your dogs!

Next, pick up the antlered portion of the skull and scrape out the upper brain cavity and eye sockets before carefully skinning the skull with your knife, starting from the front and working backwards. Free the skin and hair around the base of the antlers, then turn your attention to the mixture of fine bone and tissue filling what remains of the nasal cavity, a necessarily delicate operation if you are to avoid detaching the two separate nose bones from the skull itself, which will spoil the look of the trophy. If one or both bones accidentally come away, despite all your care, put them somewhere safe until, at the end of the whole operation, you can re-fix them with superglue, which will also require some delicacy of handling if you are not to make the damage worse!

Whether or not you retain the lower jaw, examine it and the upper jaw for tooth abnormalities. Canine teeth may sometimes be present and, in the case of roe especially, they are sufficiently unusual not to be binned or buried along with other discarded material.

Boil out the trophy and lower jaw in a galvanised iron bucket or other suitable container, keeping the water at the level of the base of the coronets so as not to risk discolouring the antlers by immersion. Boil for up to one hour, by which time any tissue still adhering should be sufficiently cooked and loosened to be easily scraped away. Some people may prefer to miss out most or all of the preliminary 'cold' cutting and scraping away of skin and tissue, and do it all after boiling. Do not boil for too long or your trophy may partly disintegrate, requiring additional supplementary treatment with superglue.

A well-finished trophy is one on which the antlers retain their full, natural colour, darkened in the process of velvet-cleaning and by exposure to the elements, and the skull portion is clean and white. Discoloration of the skull can sometimes result from the animal's untreated head being left lying around too long, exposed to the processes of decomposition. Cotton wool soaked in peroxide of hydrogen and left applied to the skull for twenty-four hours or so will help whiten it up, and even ordinary washing-up liquid can make a very worthwhile difference if it is added to warm water and the skull is gently scrubbed with it. Discoloured antlers can be doctored in a variety of ways: the application of brown boot polish and even a spell of immersion in strong, cold tea are two methods I have heard suggested. Among cosmetic treatments of other kinds which are sometimes practised are such dubious devices as substituting a whole, complete tine from one of the antlers of an entirely different deer which is less well regarded as a trophy for a tine with a broken tip on an otherwise perfect head, again with the help of superglue and a degree of subterfuge which will certainly not appeal to the purist. Before doing any of these things you will need to ask yourself what you are seeking: a trophy as nature designed it or one 'prettied up' by human artifice.

With the boiling out and cleaning process completed, air dry your trophy for at least a day before screwing it to a plaque of appropriate size for the species concerned. These plaques are obtainable from specialist suppliers such as Jägersport of Petersfield, Hampshire, who regularly advertise in journals like *Stalking Magazine* and the British Deer Society's periodical publication, *Deer*. If you are a handyman you may prefer to make your own, fashioned perhaps from stained oak retrieved from a discarded item of furniture. All that then remains is to convince your partner just how well your trophy will look at a selected spot on the wall (albeit perhaps not necessarily as the nucleus of a future collection!).

The trophies on your wall represent so many challenges met in as many different sets of circumstances, and the chief satisfaction of seeing them there is the recollections they evoke of the successful stalks involved. You may well seek nothing more; your acquisitive urges may have no competitive edge. They are your trophies, you like to be able to see them, and there is nothing more to it than that. Or you just might wonder how the best of them compare, in terms of quality, with trophies procured by other stalkers.

Some stalkers are too obsessed with shooting little but the best. Let no one deceive himself that this is 'deer management' in any true sense; quite the reverse. It is on a par with egg-collecting – self-indulgence which is bound to impoverish the wildlife species concerned by skimming the cream off the milk. As I have emphasised elsewhere in this book, responsible deer management is often a matter of self-denial involving altruistic action for the long-term benefit of the quarry and of the countryside in general. Top-quality trophies should be regarded as the jewels in a crown largely composed of lesser gems. Using a different analogy, if you were a breeder of livestock who sent your best stud males to the abbatoir but retained those of lesser calibre, the overall quality of the stock in question would rapidly deteriorate, and your income would suffer accordingly.

As an occasional reward for much hard work in other directions, or as the fruit of a substantial cash investment and some good luck as a client stalker, a proportion of quality heads can justifiably claim a place among other trophies in your collection, so to that extent at least you need have few qualms of conscience about them. And if you want to find out how they measure up to the best heads shot by others, there are set criteria for doing so.

At different times and in different countries, different systems of trophy evaluation have been employed and indeed still are: the Boone and Crockett in America, the Douglas in the Antipodes and the Rowland Ward and Safari Club International (S.C.I.) among its members worldwide. The system now most widely used throughout Europe, including Britain, and also in other parts of the world, is that operated by the Conseil International de la Chasse (C.I.C.) – the International Council of Hunting – which has developed formulae specific to individual game species. Formulae necessarily vary in detail from one species to another within the overall parameters of recognising that what is biggest

and most beautiful is best. Symmetry, as an aspect of pleasing appearance, can be measured, but in most other respects beauty can only be judged subjectively, a very considerable disadvantage when applying it as a criterion for quality assessment, as is done with several species but not all. When 'big' becomes 'gigantic' other considerations arise, as in the case of a Hampshire roe buck head of truly monstrous dimensions which was submitted as a potential world record trophy for the International Hunting Exhibition held at Plovdiv in Bulgaria in 1981. It was also monstrously ugly and was rejected as a freak.

With the C.I.C. system of trophy assessment, points are awarded according to quality as determined by measuring the length, circumference, span and, in some cases, weight and volume of the trophies. The number and length of tines or points on the antlers is also taken into account and, as already indicated, points for beauty may be added to those awarded for actual measurement, these latter being expressed in centimetres or grams sometimes multiplied or divided by a given amount. When all the points are added up, deductions are made for debit factors such as abnormalities. What then remains is the final score, heads totting up more than a given number of points being rated as gold, silver or bronze medal trophies.

Definitive C.I.C. assessments are made by panels of judges at national and international exhibitions such as the one held at Plovdiv in the early 1980s. Provisional judgements leading on to unofficial medal awards, where these are appropriate, are made by individuals recognised as specialists in this field. Many stalkers, however, like to work out their own provisional scoring before passing on their treasured trophies to someone else for a second opinion.

Roe Deer

The basic equipment for assessing the trophies of all deer species comprises a narrow and flexible steel tape which will measure centimetres and millimetres, a score sheet and a pencil or ballpoint pen. In the case of roe, more heads of which are probably measured in Britain than of all other species put together, you will

Table 18.1   C.I.C. assessment of a specimen roe buck
All linear measurements are in centimetres.

Measurements	Measurement	Total	Average	Factor	Points
Length, left antler	25.2	48.7	24.35	ˇ 0.5	12.17
Length, right antler	23.5				
Dry weight of antlers (grams)	790–90 = 700			ˇ 0.1	70.00
Volume of antlers (cubic centimetres)	315			ˇ 0.3	94.50
Inside span (0–4 points)	9.8				2.00
Beauty points					
Colour (0–4 points)					4.00
Pearling (0–4 points)					2.00
Coronets (0–4 points)					2.00
Tine ends (0–2 points)					1.00
Regularity and quality (0–5 points)					1.00
				Total	188.67
Penalty points					
Irregular and poor appearance (0–5 points)					0.00
				Score	188.67

A gold medal trophy

also need a 1,000 g spring balance and a bucket or other container for water.

Although trophies may dry out superficially overnight, they are likely to retain some moisture for a much longer period, and to obtain a true dry *weight* you should keep every individual trophy in a reasonably dry atmosphere for at least a couple of months. Weigh the trophy and if it has been cut long-nose instead of the standard short-nose cut as described earlier in this chapter, deduct 65 g or, in the case of a whole, uncut upper skull, 90 g from the total weight in order to even matters out. Note down the result in grams, then divide it by ten and you will then have a tentative C.I.C. score for the trophy's weight in points and decimals of a point.

Next, weigh the trophy suspended upside down in water with the antlers immersed to the base of the coronets but with the pedicles and skull held clear of the water. The difference between the two weights, wet and dry, should be recorded as cubic centimetres to give a reasonably accurate reading of the *volume* of the trophy. Divide this figure by ten and then multiply the resultant figure by three (i.e. multiply by a factor of 0.3) to arrive at the relevant score in C.I.C. points.

For a more precise measurement of volume, you will need to use a water container scaled in cubic centimetres, deducting the reading for the volume before immersion of the trophy from the figure after immersion.

Measure the length of each antler to the nearest millimetre, running the tape along the outside edge of the beam from the base of the coronet to the tip of the antler without indenting it around the upper edge of the coronet. Add the two measurements together and divide the result by two to obtain the average length of both antlers. Divide this figure by two to ascertain the C.I.C. score for this dimension.

Inside span is measured between the inner sides of the antlers at their widest distance apart, whether at some point along the beam or at the tip. If the span is less than 30% of the average length of the beams, no C.I.C. points are awarded for it. Points are scored for wider spans depending upon their actual width as a

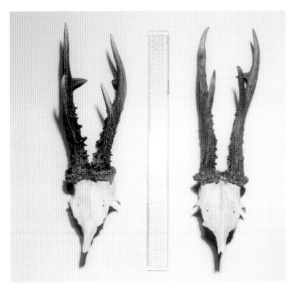

Many Continental stalkers have been attracted to West Sussex by the quality of its roe trophies, typically long and well-pearled although narrow-spanned like the two in this picture, shot by George Stefanicki.

Two trophies in one: the heads of two New Forest fallow bucks found dead with interlocked antlers and now hanging in the Verderers' Courtroom at Lyndhurst.

percentage of the beam length: one point if it is between 30% and 34.9%, two points from 35% to 39.9%, three points from 40% to 44.9%, and four points from 45% to 75%. If the percentage is more than 75 the head is regarded as abnormal and scores no points in this section.

Now we move on to points for beauty, up to sixteen of which can be awarded in this section, divided between five different categories. Pale or artificially coloured trophies receive no points for *colour*, yellow or pale brown trophies one point, light brown trophies two points, dark brown trophies three points and dark to almost black ones four points. Smooth antlers almost without *pearling* score no points in this respect, weak pearling scores one point, average pearling (small pearling sufficiently numerous) two points, good pearling (small pearling on both sides of beam) three points and very good pearling (well pearled throughout all parts of both beams) four points. *Coronets* which are feeble and weak (thin and flat) score no points, average ones in the form of a girdle with small pearling score one point, good ones sufficiently high and in the form of a crown score two points, strong ones (large and high) receive three points and very strong ones four points. Blunt or poorly developed *tine ends* rate no points, blunt ones of medium development one point and those which are pointed and white-tipped two points. The last of the beauty categories is *regularity and quality*. For regularity, or in other words symmetry of shape, up to three points can be awarded. Normal-shaped tines rate no points as such, good tines one point and very good ones two points.

Up to five *penalty points* are deductible, up to three of these being for various unspecified aberrations and up to two for the following defects to tines: absent or very short tines, two points; mediocre tines or tines emanating from one beam only, one point. No points need be deducted for tines which are normal.

Having completed all this, add up the total number of C.I.C. points you reckon your trophy has scored. If the total is between 105.00 and 114.99 the head may be assumed to be of bronze medal quality. A score of from 115.00 to 129.99 brings it to silver medal status, and any score of 130.00 or more for a roe buck trophy means you are looking at a probable gold medal head. Table

18.1 shows an example of the calculations.

The appropriate medals are obtainable for heads of roe and other deer species certified by assessors who are qualified for this purpose. In Britain the final arbiter on these matters for a very long time has been G. Kenneth Whitehead, a world authority on deer, and I am indebted to him for much of the detail in this chapter, originally published in the March, September, October, November and December 1988 issues of *Stalking Magazine*. I am also grateful to the magazine's editor, Christopher Borthen, for kindly allowing me to quote from this material.

Richard Prior, the renowned roe expert, has measured many hundreds of trophies, but has now retired after helping to set up a small team of assessors headed by Dominic Griffith, of Penwood Grange, Penwood, Newbury, Berkshire RG20 9EW. Dominic's opposite number in Scotland is Allan Allison, East Brackley Bungalow, Kinross KY13 7LU. The B.A.S.C. and the St Hubert Club of Great Britain, which holds an annual trophy exhibition, now have their own qualified assessors, and many Forest Enterprise rangers have been trained to measure trophies. It needs to be stressed, however, that all such assessments are provisional, and that official evaluations can be made only by the C.I.C. at one of the major exhibitions. There have, indeed, been instances when preliminary assessments carried out in good faith in Britain have later been found by the C.I.C. to have erred on the side of caution, and the heads concerned upgraded accordingly.

Red Deer

The C.I.C. system for measuring red deer is basically similar to that for roe, although it is necessarily more detailed because of the larger size and more complex structure of the antlers. Heads of red stags should not be assessed until at least ninety days after culling to allow time for them to dry out properly. As with roe, trophies short cut from the back of the skull through the centre of the eye sockets to the nose bones or vice versa are regarded as standard. To equalise matters for assessment purposes a deduction of 500 g from the total weight should be made for

long-nose cut trophies, or 700 g for a whole upper skull. Note down the equivalent short-cut *weight* in kilograms, then double this figure to arrive at the relevant score in C.I.C. points.

Measure the *main beam* of each antler from the lower side of the coronet up the outside edge of the beam to the tip of the longest top point. Add the two dimensions together and then divide the result by two to determine and note down the average length in centimetres and millimetres. Divide this figure by two (i.e. multiply by a factor of 0.5) and the result gives you your C.I.C. points. Now measure the length of each *brow tine* along its lower side from the point above the coronet where it leaves the main beam to its tip. Again, note the two measurements, add them together and divide the result by two to determine the average, then, in this case, divide the resultant figure by four (i.e. multiply by a factor of 0.25) to work out the appropriate C.I.C. score.

Bez tines are not always present and need not be measured at this stage. Move on up to the *trez (or normal third) tines*, measure the length of these up their outer edge, add the two together and divide by two to find out the average, then divide by four (i.e. multiply by a factor of 0.25) to obtain the C.I.C. score. Next come three measurements of circumference: of the *coronets* around their outer edge, and of the *lower beam* and the *upper beam* of each antler at its slenderest points. In each case determine the average in centimetres and millimetres, which equates precisely with the C.I.C. score (no further calculation needed here).

Measure the *inner span* of the antlers between their inside edges at their widest point apart, being careful to take this measurement at right angles to the longitudinal axis of the skull. Points are scored depending on how inside span and main beam average length relates: if the former is less than 60% of the latter, no points are awarded; if between 60% and 69.99%, one point; from 70% to 79.99%, two points; and for 80% or more, three points. The *number of tines*, which must be not less than 2 cm in length to count as such, equates to the number of C.I.C. points which may be awarded for this element: in other words, a twelve-pointer or royal would score 12.00 C.I.C. points. *Volume* is not a point-scoring element with this species.

Red deer trophies of high quality can only be produced on anything like a regular basis by long-term selective management. Head Ranger Rex Whitta, now retired, is seen here with a fine specimen from Thetford Forest in Norfolk.

Shot when its original owner strayed on to farmland, this fine New Forest red deer trophy was rescued from a pub wall and now hangs in the Verderers' Courtroom next to the Forestry Commission headquarters at Lyndhurst.

Head of an ageing roebuck killed on a busy main road in Hampshire.

Colour is the first beauty point to consider. Light or artificially coloured trophies score nothing, light brown antlers one point and dark brown or black ones two points. Smooth antlers score nothing for *pearling*, average pearling scores one point and good pearling two points. Blunt or porous *tine ends* receive no points, brown-tipped tine ends one point, and white-tipped ones two pints. *Bez tines* are next, short ones (2 to 10 cm) on one side only rating no points but scoring half a point if on both antlers. Medium-length bez tines (10.1 to 15 cm) score half a point if on one side only or one point if on both sides. Bez tines 15 cm or more long score one point if on one side or two points if on both antlers. *Crown tines* are all normal tines within the upper third of an antler's length above the trez tine, forming what may loosely be called a 'cup' at the tip of each antler. Tines close enough to the trez tine to be almost a bifurcation of it, and any which erupt below the slenderest point on the upper beam, do not count as part of the crown and bifurcations from crown tines do not count as separate tines but should be measured as part of the tine from which they sprout. Points are scored according to the total number of tines on both crowns and their length. If there are from five to seven crown tines, one or two C.I.C. points are awarded if they are short (2 to 10 cm), three to four points if they are of medium length (10.1 to 15 cm), and four to five points if they are over 15 cm long. From eight to nine tines rate four to five points if short, from five to six points if of medium length, six to seven points if long.

Long nose and short nose cut roe trophies secured on MoD land on Salisbury Plain in Wiltshire.

Two excellent fallow trophies from Hampshire, the superlative one on the left having been shot by a gamekeeper, Wally Carter, after entangling itself in wire.

Ten or more tines score six to seven points (short), seven to eight points (medium) and nine to ten points (long).

Up to three *penalty points* may be deducted for any irregularities not otherwise taken account of, such as a marked disparity between length of the two main beams, misshapen tines or abnormalities in the attachment of the antlers

Table 18.2   C.I.C. assessment of a specimen red deer stag
All linear measurements are in centimetres

Measurements	Left	Right	Total	Average	Factor	Points
Length, antler beam	96.2	95.4	191.6	95.8	ˇ 0.5	47.90
Length, brow tine	35.0	36.2	71.2	35.6	ˇ 0.25	8.90
Length, trez tine	22.6	23.2	45.8	22.9	ˇ 0.25	5.72
Circumference, coronet	20.2	18.6	38.8	19.4	ˇ 1.0	19.40
Circumference, lower beam	12.6	12.8	25.4		ˇ 1.0	25.40
Circumference, upper beam	13.2	13.8	27.0		ˇ 1.0	27.00
Weight (kilograms)			4.25		ˇ 2.0	8.50
Inside span (0–3 points)			92.00			3.00
Number of tines	6	6				12.00
Beauty points						
Colour (0–2 points)						1.00
Pearling (0–2 points)						1.00
Tine ends (0–2 points)						2.00
Bez tines (0–2 points)						1.00
Crown tines (0–10 points)						4.00
Penalty points (0–3 points)						0.00
					Score	166.82

An English bronze medal trophy

to the pedicles. Damage such as broken tines will not incur any penalties.

Medal categories for red deer vary according to the country or region of origin. For the modestly antlered stags which mostly prevail in Scotland and Norway, a C.I.C. score of 160.00 to 169.99 denotes bronze medal status, 170.00 to 179.99 is silver medal and 180.00 or more points denote a gold medal trophy. Equivalent levels for the more heavily antlered deer of western Europe, including England, are: bronze 165.00 to 179.99, silver 180.00 to 194.99 and gold 195.00 or more. To achieve medal status the even heavier red deer of the former Iron Curtain countries in eastern Europe need to score 170.00 to 189.99 for a bronze, 190.00 to 209.99 for a silver and a massive 210.00 or more for a gold. Table 18.2 gives an example of red deer scoring.

Fallow Deer

Assessment criteria for fallow buck trophies depend more upon subjective judgement than those for any other deer species present in the wild state in Britain, which inevitably exposes any overall assessment to different inter-pretations by different people examining the same trophy. Basic physical dimensions are measured and judged along lines similar to those applied to red deer, with some minor variations to take account of the distinctive characteristics of fallow deer antlers.

As with red and roe deer, deductions are made from the actual *weights* of trophies which have not been cut from the back of the skull through the centre of the eye sockets to the front end of the nose bones, or the other way round. This varies from 0.1 kg to 0.25 kg, depending upon whether the trophy is long-nose cut or consists of a whole upper skull. Weights should be recorded to the nearest 10 g, the resultant figure being doubled to obtain the C.I.C. points score: for example, a trophy with a recorded net weight of 2.5 kg will rate 5.00 points on the score sheet. Weight and other measurements should not be taken until at least ninety days after the animal has been shot.

Antler length should be measured from the base of the coronet along the outer side of the main beam and palm to the deepest point on the highest indentation on the palm, and not to the highest point on the antler, as is the case with other species. Add together the lengths of the left and right antlers, divide the total by two to determine the average, then divide the average by two (i.e. multiply by a factor of 0.5) to arrive at the C.I.C. score. Now measure the *brow tine* along its lower edge from its point of eruption from the beam above the coronet to the tip, measure the other brow tine similarly, add the two to find out the average and divide the result by four (i.e. multiply by a factor of 0.25) to obtain the C.I.C. score. Measure each *coronet* around the outer rim, omitting any abnormal outgrowths, determine the average circumference, and translate this figure unaltered to the C.I.C. score. The average circumference of the *lower beams* and the *upper beams*, measured at the slenderest points below and above the trez tines respectively, also equates in each instance to the relevant C.I.C. score. Sometimes there may be no trez tine, in which case measure the slenderest point between the

Trophy of black fallow shot in Hampshire by the author.

Table 18.3   C.I.C. assessment of a specimen fallow buck
All linear measurements are in centimetres

Measurements	Left	Right	Total	Average	Factor	Points
Length, antler	65.0	63.0	128.0	64.0	ˇ 0.5	32.00
Length, brow tine	16.0	16.0	32.0	16.0	ˇ 0.25	4.00
Length, palm	40.6	42.0	82.6	41.3	ˇ 1.0	41.30
Width, palm	14.4	13.0	27.4	13.7	ˇ 1.5	20.55
Circumference, coronet	16.3	16.7	33.0	16.5	ˇ 1.0	16.50
Circumference, lower beam	9.5	9.5	19.0		ˇ 1.0	19.00
Circumference, upper beam	10.4	10.4	20.8		ˇ 1.0	20.80
Weight (kilograms)			2.6		ˇ 2.0	5.20
Beauty points						
Colour (0–2 points)						1.00
Spellers (0–6 points)						3.00
Mass, regularity etc. (0–5points)						3.50
					Total	166.85
Penalty points						
Insufficient span (0–6 points)				–2.00 points		
Defective palm (0–10 points)				–0.00 points		–3.00
Edge of palm (0–2 points)				–1.00 points		
Irregularity etc. (0–6 points)				–0.00 points		
					Score	163.85

A bronze medal trophy

brow tine and the base of the palm and record this twice for scoring purposes.

Now comes a complicated bit. *Palm length* should be measured from the base of the palm around its outer curve to the lowest point of the highest indentation. Simple enough, you may think, but exactly where does the palm begin? Work out whether the circumference of the upper beam is more than 130% greater than that of the lower beam. If not, palm length measurement commences 1 cm above where the upper beam was measured. Otherwise, start measuring at the upper edge of where the trez tine erupts from the beam. For scoring purposes follow the standard procedure for determining the average for the two antlers, which once again equates to the C.I.C. points figure. *Palm width* is measured by ascertaining the palm's circumference between its front edge and the innermost point of the rearmost indentation,

then dividing this figure by two to determine the width. Ascertain the average width of both palms, divide the result by two and then multiply by three to obtain the C.I.C. score.

Whole or half points may be awarded for various beauty characteristics. Light or artificially coloured antlers score no points for *colour*, but if they are grey or medium brown one point is appropriate, or one to two points if brown to black. The points along the palm edge known as *spellers* must be at least 2 cm long to be taken into account. If they are short, thin and few no points should be awarded. If they are present along one-third of the edge of the palm on one side only, one point is scored, if on both antlers two points. Spellers extending along two-thirds of the palm edge rate two points for one antler, or four points for both. If spellers are well distributed along the whole palm edge and there is a rear tine at the palm's base, three points are

Not a medal head! Selective culling should concentrate on heads of lesser quality.

scored for one antler or six points for both.

Up to three points may be awarded for *mass* and up to two points for good *shape and regularity* of the trophy. Up to twenty-four penalty points can be deducted for various shortcomings, six of these being for insufficient *inside span*. This dimension should be measured at the widest point between the two antlers, identified as the spot where the measurements of antler length and width cross each other. If these locations do not precisely line up horizontally, measure from the point of intersection which gives the greatest overall width from the opposite antler, taking particular care to measure horizontally in relation to the top of the skull and not diagonally. If the span is less than 85% of average beam length deduct one penalty point, if less than 80% two points, if less than 75% three points, if less than 70% four points, if less than 65% five points, and if less

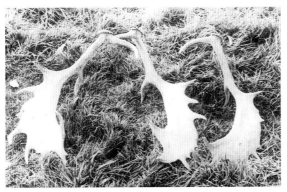

Cast fallow antlers from Petwork Park, West Sussex with the broad palmation typical of the high quality fallow there.

than 60% six points. *Defective palms* also incur penalties: if triangular or diamond-shaped deduct one to three points for one antler or two to six points for both. For split palms on one side deduct two to four points, or four to eight points if on both sides. Jagged palms warrant a deduction of three to five points for one side, or six to ten points for both sides, while spikes incur four to five penalty points for one side only or eight to ten if on both sides.

For *smooth, worn or porous palm edges* deduct up to two penalty points. Up to six points should be deducted, either as whole or half points, for *irregular and malformed antlers*, attached in some unusual way to the pedicles or with tines of very uneven length or abnormal development.

Having dealt with all these complexities, add up the total C.I.C. score. If it is from 160.00 to 169.99 you have a potential bronze medal fallow head, or a likely silver medal one if the score is from 170.00 to 179.99 points, while 180.00 or more suggests a superlative gold medal trophy: possibly that once-in-a-lifetime specimen which may make you content in the future just to weed out inferior stock. Table 18.3 shows an example of this scoring.

Sika Deer

C.I.C. criteria for assessing non-European deer were developed during the 1970s and later by a working group on trophy evaluation under the chairmanship of G. Kenneth Whitehead, who was personally responsible for recommending and instigating various changes of approach from those adopted for roe, red and fallow deer. Key elements of the system devised for sika deer were the omission of weight and beauty points as contributory factors. Weight was deemed inappropriate because some beasts may have a heavy skull and poor antlers, and others the reverse, which could give a misleading impression of the quality of a trophy which was weighty overall but modestly antlered. And as has already been demonstrated, beauty is a subjective judgement open to different interpretations by different judges, whereas features which can be measured are fixed and are therefore indisputable.

As with other Asian deer, sika trophy details are recorded under two separate headings: *Supplementary Data*, for general information only, and *Score Data*, the ones that count for evaluation purposes. Under the former heading should be noted the number of tines on each antler, and the measurement from tip to tip and of the widest spread overall. If the last two do not coincide, the widest spread is most likely to be between the tips of the two second tines.

Another important difference from the methods already described is that no averages are calculated between the corresponding dimensions of various parts of the two antlers. Instead, any difference is recorded and is deducted from the greater of the two measurements as a 'penalty'. By way of simplifying this, all measurements are recorded and totalled up under separate headings for span, left antler and right antler, with a fourth heading for differences, which are added up and subtracted from the grand total of the first three

columns to arrive at the score in C.I.C. points. Included under differences are the lengths of any abnormal tines, which are defined as any which project rearwards or which erupt from the beam at any point below the normal third tine.

Inside span should be measured at the widest point between the inside of the two main beams between the second and third tines. If the trophy is of a six-pointer with no third tine, rather than of an eight-pointer as is the case with most mature sika stags, measure inside span at the halfway point between the second tine and the antler tip.

Measure the *main beam* along its outer edge from the base of the coronet to the tip of the antler, recording left and right antlers separately for this and all other linear dimensions affecting both. *Brow tines* should be measured along their lower side from the coronet's upper edge to the tine tip in each case. If a brow tine's point of eruption is 5 cm or more above the coronet, it should be measured from where it erupts.

Table 18.4   C.I.C. assessment of a specimen sika stag
All measurements are in centimetres.

Supplementary data	Left/Right			
Number of tines	4 4			
Tip to tip	43.0			
Greatest spread	43.0			

Score data	Span credit	Left	Right	Difference
Inside span	33.3			
Length, main beam		49.2	52.2	3.0
Length, brow tine		14.6	14.0	0.6
Length, second (middle) tine		15.0	15.0	–
Length, third (inner) tine		7.4	7.0	0.4
Length, first extra crown tine		–	–	–
Length, second extra crown tine		–	–	–
Length, third extra crown tine		–	–	–
Total length, all abnormal tines		–	–	–
Circumference, lower beam		9.1	9.0	0.1
Circumference, upper beam		7.0	7.0	–
	33.3 +	102.3 +	104.2 –	4.1
	Score:	235.7		

A bronze medal trophy

Typical eight-point head of a mature Japanese sika stag shot by the author in Dorset.

Normal *second and third tines* should be measured along their outer edge from where they erupt from the main beam to their tip. The recommended method for determining exactly where to start measuring is to place the tape measure along the beam's outer curve below and above the tine in question, draw a line along the tape's upper edge where it bridges the base of the tine and use this line as your starting point. Sometimes there are *additional tines* between the normal third tine and the tip of the main beam and these are eligible for measurement, not as freaks but as credit factors which will help to bump up the score.

Lower beam circumference should be measured at the slenderest point between the brow tine and the second or middle tine. The slenderest point between the second and third tines is where *upper beam circumference* should be measured, unless there is no third tine, in which case measure at the point midway between the second tine and the antler tip. Coronet circumferences are not measured for

purposes of assessment with this species.

It will be seen that another advantage of this simplified system of assessment is that all measurements, recorded in centimetres and millimetres in common with C.I.C. linear measurements generally, are directly equivalent to the relevant points score and are subject to no supplementary arithmetic to determine the final, crucial figure.

One of the problems in establishing a uniform system of measurement for sika was the uncertain origin of many feral populations in Europe. While, on the basis of size alone, it seems safe to assume that many, if not most, of these populations consist largely, if not always entirely, of the small Japanese subspecies, some are markedly larger, notably those of the Bowland area on the Lancashire-Yorkshire border. In the past, sika of larger subspecies such as Manchurian, Formosan and Dybowski's have been imported to the West, including Britain, at various times and have not infrequently been kept in mixed groups which have freely interbred.

The detailed history of these herds, including which subspecies were introduced where, is often uncertain. It is self-evident, however, that larger stags will tend to grow larger antlers than their more diminutive brethren. Their skulls are proportionately larger. Length of nose bones has come to be recognised as a reasonably accurate method of differentiating larger from smaller subspecies, and has been adopted as the basis for two different levels of sika assessment. Measured along the suture where the left and right nose bones join, any length under 8 cm for a mature stag classifies the trophy as of the Japanese subspecies for scoring purposes, whereas any length between 8 and 11 cm categorises it as of one of the larger sika. For medal purposes Japanese sika scoring from 225.00 to 239.99 qualify as bronze, from 240.00 to 254.99 as silver and 255.00 or more as gold. Larger sika scoring from 300.00 to 349.99 rate as bronze, from 350.00 to 399.99 as silver and 400.00 or more as gold. Table 18.4 shows an example of the scoring for the Japanese sika.

A further complication arises from the tendency of sika and red deer to hybridise where the two species share the same ground. This has happened in several areas such as the Kintyre peninsula in Argyllshire, the Furness Fells in Cumbria and, most notably, County Wicklow in Ireland. Many of these hybrids are obvious for what they are from the appearance of their pelage and antlers and from their relatively large size. In cases of doubt, however, a rough rule of thumb applied by the C.I.C. for identification purposes is based once again on nose bone measurement. If the length is 12 cm or more the trophy can safely be regarded as that of a hybrid and is therefore not eligible for assessment.

Muntjac

These miniature Asian immigrants, now so widely established in central and southern England and extending their range into Wales, are a quarry species more and more stalkers are taking seriously, and a C.I.C. formula for assessing muntjac trophies is available. Simplicity is its keynote and, as with sika, it includes supplementary data, on maximum spread overall and width between antlers from tip to tip, which do not count for scoring purposes.

Score data begin with *inside span*, measured horizontally at the widest point between the inner edges of the two antlers. *Length* is measured in the usual way, from the base of the coronet along the outer edge of the beam to the tip of the antler in each instance. The length of each antler is separately recorded on the score sheet, with any difference between the two being noted down as a debit. In other words, for scoring purposes the length of each antler is assumed to be that of the shorter of the two, if there is a difference, as also applies to other differences in dimension. Next are the *brow tines*, measured from where they erupt, directly above the coronets, along their undersides to their tips, each being recorded separately. In muntjac brow tines are frequently absent, but as they are normally very short this may not reduce the score substantially. Now measure tightly around each coronet to determine the *coronet circumference* and treat in exactly the same way, deducting any difference between the two as a debit. *Beam circumference* should be similarly dealt with, measuring each halfway between base and tip.

Add up the credits, deduct any debits, and the figure you arrive at, expressed in centimetres and millimetres, should be the C.I.C. score for your trophy. Having been shot in Britain the muntjac involved will be of the small Reeves's species, native to China. Standards originally set for Reeves's muntjac were 54.00 to 54.99 for a bronze, 55.00 to 55.99 for a silver and 56.00 or more for a gold medal trophy. On the recommendation of G. Kenneth Whitehead, the C.I.C. decided at its Buenos Aires conference in March 1997 to revise these figures as follows: 56.00 to 58.49 for a bronze, 58.50 to 60.99 for a silver and 61.00 or more for a gold. Table 18.5 shows an example of scoring for muntjac.

Table 18.5   C.I.C. assessment of a specimen Reeves's muntjac buck
All measurements are in centimetres.

Supplementary data	Maximum Spread overall		Tip to tip	
	13.3		9.9	
Score data	Span	Left	Right	Difference
Inside span	11.6			
Length, main beam		10.1	9.2	0.9
Length, brow tine		1.1	1.0	0.1
Circumference, coronet		6.1	7.2	1.1
Circumference, antler at mid-distance along beam		5.5	5.6	0.1
	11.6 +	22.8 +	23.0 –	2.2

Score: 55.2 (below medal category)

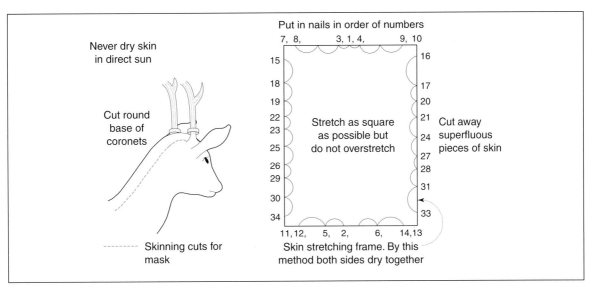

Never dry skin in direct sun

Cut round base of coronets

Put in nails in order of numbers

7, 8,   3, 1, 4,   9, 10

Stretch as square as possible but do not overstretch

Cut away superfluous pieces of skin

11, 12,   5,   2,   6,   14, 13

------- Skinning cuts for mask

Skin stretching frame. By this method both sides dry together

Fig 18.1 Preparing a skin for a full head mount and for general preservation.

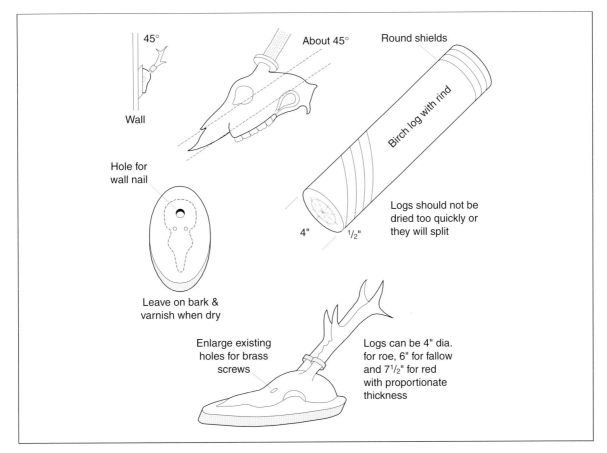

45°

Wall

About 45°

Round shields

Birch log with rind

Hole for wall nail

Leave on bark & varnish when dry

4"   1/2"

Logs should not be dried too quickly or they will split

Enlarge existing holes for brass screws

Logs can be 4" dia. for roe, 6" for fallow and 7 1/2" for red with proportionate thickness

Fig 18.2 Cutting and mounting a skull

Chinese Water Deer

Being antlerless, Chinese water deer bucks are assessed for C.I.C. purposes on the length and circumference of each of their prominent *canine teeth*, which project in the form of tusks. *Length* should be measured along the tooth's outer curve from its point of eruption from the gum to its tip, and *circumference* as closely as possible to the point of eruption. Record each dimension separately for each canine under the appropriate heading. Add the two lengths together and deduct any difference as a debit. Do the same with the two circumferences, then add up the net totals in centimetres and millimetres to obtain the C.I.C. score. A score of 150.00 to 159.99 makes the trophy a bronze, 160.00 to 179.99 a silver and 180.00 or more a gold. Table 18.6 shows an example of this scoring.

Chinese water deer in Britain being very locally distributed, comparatively few are shot and fewer still have so far been submitted for measurement.

Table 18.6   C.I.C. assessment of a specimen Chinese water deer buck
All measurements are in millimetres.

Measurements	Left		Right	Difference
Length, canine tooth	63.0		62.0	1.0
Circumference, canine tooth	33.0		32.0	1.0
	96.0	+	94.0	– 2.0
	Score: 188.00			

A gold medal trophy

CHAPTER 19
Combined Operations

Although many woodland stalkers prefer to 'go it alone' at all times, there are occasions and circumstances when teamwork can have a very important role to play. One clear example, already mentioned, is when dealing with deer which are too heavy to haul out single-handed without the facilities of a 4WD and a loading winch or something similar. Prior to the hauling-out process, each stalker in a group can operate individually, thus maximising the likelihood of overall success.

Where more than one stalker is operating on the same ground at the same time it is very important that each should know exactly where the others are, which means agreeing a detailed plan and sticking rigorously to it. For safety reasons such a plan should include clearly defined zones between individual stalkers where no shooting should take place. Where several stalkers are simultaneously operating independently it is preferable, if possible, that each should be in a high seat and that no shooting at all should take place on the ground.

By far the most effective way in which stalkers can work as a team is in moving deer to rifles. If this conjures up disagreeable images of the old-fashioned shotgun *battues* which wreaked such suffering and indiscriminate slaughter in years gone by, the truth is that, properly conducted, moving deer to rifles could hardly be more different. It does not involve a motley horde of enthusiastic but unsuitably armed country lads and others on their day off, crashing around the woods and blasting off at excessive ranges in unpredictable directions, but is a tightly controlled manoeuvre by a small team of participants well drilled in the requirements and limitations of the exercise.

This type of disciplined operation is mostly used to catch up on a shortfall in the cull of female deer, particularly roe but also, in some cases, red, fallow and sika as well as muntjac of both sexes. It helps save the day, or at least the season, for many a non-professional stalker with

limited free time in which to contend with short hours of daylight, the vagaries of winter weather and other trying circumstances such as the common desire of game shooting interests not to have the woods disturbed until after the pheasant shooting season.

Even with game shooting out of the way until the following autumn, some stalkers are not entirely out of the wood or, more precisely, have to share the wood with others whose activities may not exactly help their own. Just when they hoped that at last their hands are no longer tied by the constraints of the pheasant season, back comes the Gamekeeper with his beaters, now transformed into pigeon shooters and participants in vermin drives which make any disturbance to deer caused by game shooting insignificant by comparison. Clearly a *modus vivendi* needs to be agreed in such cases, with both the Keeper and his employer. It might be arranged, for instance, that specific coverts should be left undisturbed for deer control until lunchtime, after which the stalkers themselves

It helps to have more than one of you to haul out a heavy buck if you lack a 4WD and the facilities of a loading winch.

135

could lend a hand with vermin shooting, thus cementing good relations with the Keeper and his helpers. At all costs avoid potentially acrimonious confrontations – it is absolutely essential to keep the Keeper on your side. He has a job of work to do whereas your stalking, whatever its importance to the property in question as a wildlife management exercise, is bound to be viewed by others as more in the nature of a hobby.

Moving deer to rifles is most effective once you have gained a thorough knowledge not only of the lie of the land but of the movements of the deer. Watch and note their regular routes of departure when disturbed so that rifles can be placed at the likeliest points to intercept them. If they are to be moved across open ground, whether it be farmland or a clearing in the woods, they are most likely to pause in their flight to look around them and take stock of the situation once they have safely re-entered cover. So place your standing rifles just a few yards inside cover where they can be at just the right spot to deal with a briefly stationary target – and the emphasis here is on quick reaction. If the deer moves on before someone is quite ready to take action, he will be unlikely to have a second chance to shoot that particular animal.

Moving deer can often be done quite effectively as a two-man operation, with one walking and one standing or waiting in ambush in a high seat. Three can usually operate best as one walker-up and two standing rifles placed so as to cover alternative lines of flight by the deer.

Local topography will dictate how best to deploy a larger party. With a four-man operation it might be advisable to have two walkers-up and two rifles rather than one walker-up and three rifles, but this must always be a matter for individual judgement. Should you contemplate something like the way these operations are conducted on a grand scale on the Continent, with a small army of walkers-up working through large areas of woodland and an equally large team of standing rifles, everything must be done in strict accordance with pre-arranged rules. Each rifle must be clearly instructed to shoot only within a predetermined arc, at deer which have already passed through the waiting line of rifles after having been moved by the walkers-up. Under no circumstances whatsoever

may a shot be taken in any direction other than that prescribed for each individual rifle.

However large or small a walking-up operation of this kind may be, rifles must be clearly aware of the routes of approach of the walkers, who might do well to wear some conspicuous item of clothing as an additional safeguard. Walkers-up should proceed slowly and without excessive noise but also without any need to be furtive, tapping a treetrunk here and there as they spread their scent before them while heading downwind if possible. They may well see nothing of any deer that they disturb from start to finish, and remain unaware that they have moved any deer at all until a reassuring rifle report or two rings out from well ahead.

One way of maintaining communication which is favoured by some professionals and has obvious advantages is to make use of C.B. radio. The important thing, with or without such an aid, is thorough preliminary briefing and sustained teamwork at every stage, with nobody going off at a tangent from the agreed procedure in response to some whim of the moment. Any good ideas that suggest themselves while a walk-through is in progress should be saved for implementation another time, after full discussion by all involved. Keep your priorities in focus. Should a fox come through instead of a deer and the Keeper is keen to have foxes shot, decide in advance which is more important, to shoot it or look the other way in the hope that a doe may follow.

Moving deer to rifles is most frequently left until February, not solely out of deference to game shooting interests but because by then the scale of operations needed can be better assessed in relation to the success of the female deer cull up to that time. In the absence of other criteria as to the size of the cull to be aimed for, a minimum aim should be to cull at least as many females as males in the preceding or ongoing season for stags or bucks. Once you have got the residual population about right in terms of numbers for the area in question, you should end up in the spring of each year with much the same numbers and sexual balance of deer as in the previous spring. This is an ideal for which to aim while making adjustments along the way to cope with changes that may arise, such as in the overall deer population of the countryside around or in the requirements of estate management.

Ideals are rarely quite attainable, however. In an ideal situation, teamwork among woodland stalkers would extend to a great deal more than merely moving deer to rifles and doubling up to haul out heavy carcases. It would take almost as little account of property boundaries as the deer themselves, not in the sense of any general free-for-all on the aspect of access to stalking but by neighbouring stalkers harmonising their plans instead of maintaining the jealous apartheid which prevails so often at present.

One way of overcoming, or at least reducing, the scale of this problem is through the formation of local deer management societies and groups. The wisdom of this was seen as long ago as the 1960s when the British Deer Society, then in its early days, took the initiative in fostering a number of such bodies, in part to offer landowners a practical alternative to the shotgun drives which many still saw as the only feasible way of trimming deer numbers on their ground. The idea was to carve up deer-populated areas into manageable units for the purpose of deer control by stalkers accredited to individual local societies, membership of which was to be open to owners and occupiers of land within prescribed areas. Ground rules were promulgated to ensure that deer control was carried out safely, responsibly and humanely, and by adopting these the new local societies were affiliated to the national organisation which was their mentor and prime sponsor.

As with voluntary bodies of other kinds, deer control societies – mostly renamed deer management societies in response to later changes of emphasis – have succeeded in proportion to the quality of their management. Those consistently most successful have been landowner-orientated, with the impetus coming from those whose properties are most vulnerable to damage by deer. Societies in which the main influence comes from stalkers have been less successful, largely perhaps because of misgivings about the true motives of some of these people. One or two societies have conspicuously failed because those in charge put their desire to acquire free stalking for their members before their regard for the basic principles of sound deer management as such. The ethical basis as spelt out in earlier days has proved perfectly sound and a good recipe for success wherever it has been applied.

The trend in recent years has been towards the creation of less formally constituted deer management groups, some of which operate with considerable success. Co-ordinated management between adjacent properties within discrete geographical areas also plays an important part in the Scottish Highland scene today.

Combined operations between stalkers have considerably more potential than has hitherto been exploited. It needs a few more to give a lead in showing what might be done.

CHAPTER 20
Emergency Action

Once you gain experience and reach the stage of having been granted an open firearm certificate which does not limit you to using your rifle at specified places only, your help may be sought in dealing with one of a variety of emergency situations. You could well be called upon, as an 'expert', to deal with a deer which has become the victim of a road traffic accident or which has suffered injury from some other cause. Your stalking landlord or somebody else may request your urgent intervention against deer which are out of season for culling but which are causing serious damage to farm or forest crops. Worst of all, and perhaps most likely, someone may ask you to deal with deer causing damage in their garden or in an urban situation where any heavy-handed action could cause horrendous complications.

The chief weapons in your armoury for dealing successfully with such problems are cool judgement and sound common sense. In the case of road casualties, requests for your help are most likely to come from your local police, and

Rescuing live deer is rarely made easy by the victim, like this Hampshire roe deer, trapping itself inside a suburban garage from which it could be manhandled to safety.

will be a mark of their high expectations of professionalism on your part. Police tend to turn to a few individuals within their force area whom they have come to regard as reliable and discreet in coping effectively with animal road casualties and the like, and if they look to you in this light it will be a feather in your cap. If, on the other hand, you should be approached from some other quarter than the police for help of this nature, you would be wise to inform the police about what has happened and what you propose to do about it. They might prefer to save you the trouble by calling in their own 'tame' expert!

Many, if not most, road accidents involving deer occur around dusk at what in winter is likely to be a peak traffic period, with everyone rushing to get home or, in the half-light of early morning, to reach their place of work on time. This may not stop some of them from hanging around to watch while the accident victim is dealt with, curious as to how this will be done and perhaps with strong views of their own on how it ought to be done – or not done.

Be prepared for the well-meaning lady, possibly a vegetarian, who thinks that a hopelessly crippled deer should have a vet called out to tend it or should be sent to an animal hospital that she happens to know about. Explain as best you can that the kindest thing to do is to put the deer out of its agony as humanely and quickly as possible.

Using a knife for this purpose may be quick and silent but it can also be messy and even dangerous if the deer is an antlered male still able to lash out with his head. It is also disagreeable for people unused to the realities of Nature 'red in tooth and claw' to witness or, as in this case, people unused to coping with the victim of an unintentional human 'predator'. A smart tap on the head with a lump hammer or something similar should achieve the desired result with minimal trauma for all concerned. If you use your stalking rifle, take all obvious

Emergency action takes many forms, not least applying a brake in time to avoid colliding with jay-walking deer. If a deer is injured on the road or elsewhere you should be ready to deal with it.

precautions, especially if bystanders are present. A .22 rifle with a silencer may be illegal for use against deer in a general way, but in these special circumstances no one is likely to challenge your choice should you have recourse to such a weapon. At all costs, make sure to place the bullet in such a way that a repeat performance will not be necessary. Resolute action by a stalker who remains cool, calm and collected and clearly knows what he is about is never more important than in a situation like this.

If a deer which is known to have been hit has fled into cover and darkness has fallen, it will be best to wait until daylight and to contact the property owner concerned before taking further action. Subject to the owner's permission, you should then proceed exactly as you would when following up a lost deer in any other circumstances, remembering, however, that the deer, if found, will be the property of the owner of the land on which it died.

Remove the carcase yourself if possible, or liaise with the police for this to be done by somebody else who has the necessary facilities. If the carcase is not too badly mangled save what venison you can. The police are unlikely to say 'no thanks' if you offer them a haunch or two.

The law allows for humane destruction of deer which have suffered injury, in road accidents or otherwise, regardless of the time of day or the season of the year. Destruction, however, may not always be either necessary or desirable. Deer are tough and resilient, and can sometimes recover completely from quite serious physical injury which would be fatal to some other animals. I well remember an occasion when I chanced upon a three-legged roe doe with two very healthy youngsters plainly none the worse, in any respect, for their mother's disability. Apart from the missing member, probably resulting from a mishap with a snare, a high fence wire or some other items of countryside furniture, the doe was in excellent condition and clearly well able to cope with her maternal responsibilities. The kids being still very young and dependent, culling was clearly out of the question.

Should you be asked to cull troublesome deer out of season, ascertain the details of the damage being complained of and how serious it is so that, if you proceed with the culling and anyone questions the need for it, you can justify your action, before a court of law if necessary. While deer may legally be shot out of season if they are causing 'serious damage', whether any instances of such damage have in fact been sufficiently serious to warrant culling deer otherwise than during a relevant open season has never, to the best of my knowledge, been tested in the courts. If you agree to carry out such a cull, ask whoever is requesting it to furnish you with a letter of authorisation stating the reason for the proposed action. You can then produce this should anyone challenge the legality of the cull.

By concentrating your initial emergency cull upon male deer and juveniles you can make a significant early impact upon deer numbers while avoiding the risk of orphaning dependent youngsters. Whilst it often happens that by shooting adult females first when they have accompanying youngsters, the youngsters will stay put for long enough to be added to the cull, this cannot be relied upon and so cannot be recommended as a safe procedure to follow.

Having first dealt with male deer and youngsters, with luck you will then be able to defer action against female deer with dependent young until the appropriate open season. Should your stalking landlord's thoughts on what needs to be done differ materially from your own, try to reach a reasonable compromise or you may find yourself obliged to hand over responsibility for deer control on the property to somebody else with fewer scruples. As with so many other aspects of woodland stalking, diplomacy has a role to play here.

An even more delicate problem is how best to deal with complaints about garden damage by deer. In all likelihood the complainants will have been agreeably surprised and even delighted when they first found out that they had wild deer as near neighbours. But from desiring their total and permanent protection, the householder may well have changed his or her mind to the extent of demanding their complete eradication having discovered that garden roses are a dietary delicacy which deer find irresistible.

Here, as the 'expert' appealed to for help, you have several possible options. First of all, be concerned and sympathetic. Ask to be shown the havoc wreaked by what will almost certainly be nocturnal visitors, of unpredictable appearance in broad daylight. If the chief culprit is a roe doe, as is quite possible, and it is summer – as inevitably it will be if roses are the principal and current or most recent target for its unwelcome attentions – point out the law on deer close seasons and the obvious consequences of shooting a female deer which is also a nursing mother.

Advise the complainant about long-term protective measures such as growing flowers which are unpalatable – or at least less palatable – emphasising that there is a wide choice of these, about which garden centres should be approached for further information. Garden centres may also recommend repellents of various kinds but garden owners should be warned that their effectiveness may be no more than temporary. Homespun remedies of this nature which one sometimes hears advocated

range from human hair fairly liberally distributed and frequently renewed to strong-smelling substances such as turpentine, creosote and even lion's dung from some obliging neighbourhood zoo. Any or all could be worth trying, but satisfaction is not guaranteed! Let it be known that deerproof barriers of one sort or another are the only certain way of excluding deer from where they are not wanted, and that this usually means fencing, which can be unsightly as well as expensive.

If the householder insists on shooting and the garden is relatively small, with others adjoining, ascertain the attitude of neighbours, who are less likely to raise objections if they are suffering similar damage. In any case, put them in the picture. The deer must lie up somewhere in fairly close proximity: try to discover where this is and whether the owner of the land concerned might permit you to take the necessary action there, thus almost certainly achieving a quicker result.

If the complainant's garden is the only available place where deer can be shot, an early morning vigil in an upstairs room overlooking the scene where damage has been done may be your best option. A .22 rifle with a silencer would be ideal in these circumstances but illegal except in Scotland and if the deer concerned are roe, so warn everyone concerned to expect a fairly loud report at a thoroughly unsocial hour! Disposal of the venison will be up to you to negotiate. Above all, be prepared for the possibility of a number of blank vigils. If all the roses were eaten before you were called in you may well be wasting your time anyway.

If all this seems fraught with difficulty, with the very strong probability of ultimate frustration, a successful outcome can be a source of considerable satisfaction to yourself and to all concerned. It is one of those tasks one undertakes as a public relations exercise and in the interests of good all-round deer management, as applies with even greater force when trying to deal with problem deer in an urban situation.

Deer and towns are by no means as rare a combination as some might think. Roe deer and muntjac in particular have infiltrated many a thoroughly urban area, causing surprise and consternation among people who encounter them and, not infrequently, complaints of garden damage as well as concern about them becoming a potential traffic hazard.

In the case of a single individual, if your expertise is called upon in a situation of this kind, you may well be confronted with a ready-made 'solution' with some well-meaning person urging that the deer should be caught alive and taken to some animal sanctuary or released into the wild at some more suitable location.

Something along these lines just might be feasible if you happen to know someone who is licensed to use a narcotic dart gun for live capture purposes and is willing to lend a hand. Otherwise, forget it, and point out its impracticality to anyone who seriously suggests such a course of action.

If just one deer is involved, the probability is that its stay in town will be brief and that it will fairly soon find its way out of its own accord, having discovered for itself the unsuitability for deer of such a human-intensive environment. It is not unknown, however, for small groups of deer to establish themselves on a semi-permanent basis in some green oasis well within the confines of a town, and to sally forth from such places to wreak destruction in nearby gardens.

A fellow-stalker and I were involved in a case of this type in the heart of a southern English city not long ago. Two roe bucks were causing much mischief in several gardens which they had been visiting over a period of weeks without showing any sign of moving on elsewhere, and we found a surprising unanimity of opinion that they should be culled without further ado. After studying all the options we somewhat reluctantly agreed, if it could be done in conditions of perfect safety without attracting too much attention.

From an upper room overlooking a garden visited daily by one of the bucks we watched and awaited our opportunity. At the second attempt we were successful, and the report of a shot from the .243 caused scarcely a head to turn in the neighbourhood. With the second buck we were less successful, being obliged to pass up one otherwise good opportunity on grounds of public safety because the background was not quite suitable. Eventually this buck disappeared and so saved us further time and trouble.

In any such operation as this you will be wise to liaise with the local police before committing yourself to a cull. Misgivings about safety and unacceptable disturbance may cause objections to be raised which it will be up to you to deal with, having regard to the relevant facts.

Depending upon your circumstances, you may wish to offer your services in a general way to the police when problems arise involving deer, and to make yourself known to local authorities and other public bodies who may need assistance with deer management on properties they own or control. Any resultant intervention will give you first-class opportunities to demonstrate your professionalism while also opening the door to additional stalking possibilities.

CHAPTER 21
Calling Them Up

Much of deerstalking, woodland style, amounts less to actual stalking than to its opposite – finding somewhere suitable to wait and watch, and there staying put in the hope that a deer will come to you. While careful preliminary groundwork can do a great deal to reduce the possibility that deer may not come your way at all but contrarily head in some other direction to feed in the evening or to return to their lying-up place after an early-morning foray, there is always an element of hit-or-miss about getting on terms with them in this way.

Some stalkers try to swing fortune in their favour by spreading largesse in the form of dietary temptations such as apples, corn or pig potatoes at selected spots within range of a high seat or some other vantage point from which a shot may later be taken. To lure deer to such spots with any degree of predictability requires sustained feeding over a period of days or possibly weeks, and once deer have been shot off them those that survive may well be wary of coming back for quite some time.

To some there may also be ethical problems about such a method of culling deer, as indeed there are for some stalkers about luring deer to the rifle by means of artificial calls. Favourite subjects for this are roe deer, and indeed the calling up of roe has been developed into an art form, with growing numbers of expert practitioners and many more who are far from expert but who hope one day to perfect their performance. For those who may baulk at the notion of calling up roe to be shot, there is still the alternative of doing so for photography or for some other non-lethal purpose such as checking trophy quality or simply mastering a new skill and enjoying the fruits of it.

Roe calling works by imitating the vocal sounds used by these deer to summon each other – a buck to a doe ready for mating, or a doe to a kid in distress for some reason and needing urgent maternal intervention. If such a doe has a buck in attendance he is likely to follow her when she comes rushing to the rescue of a youngster in apparent danger.

You will need to be very close indeed to a roe at a critical moment to hear either of the two main calls uttered by one or other and so be able to learn at source just how it should be imitated. Basically, the call in either case is a soft 'pee-you' emitted three or four times in succession followed by a short spell of silence before it is repeated, and there may be further repetitions. The doe and kid calls are similar, that of a kid being thinner, higher-pitched and more plaintive.

These calls can be reproduced, with practice, by blowing on a beech leaf or on a blade of grass stretched taut between the thumbs of both hands. An altogether simpler method is to experiment with the artificial, whistle-type roe calls manufactured commercially in Britain and on the Continent and readily available nowadays from many gunshops as well as from those which specialise in the supply of stalking accessories. With some of these calls the pitch can be adjusted by the turn of a screw or something similar, while others are of a pitch predetermined to represent the call of a doe or a kid, being specific to one or the other. There is also a rubber squeeze call known as the Buttolo, which is supposed to imitate the piercing scream of a roe kid in extreme anguish, for use as a last

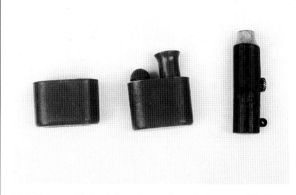

Reh-fiep and kitz-fiep calls and container and R.P. adjustable pitch roe call.

Tape

RICHARD PRIOR CASSETTE TAPE is the definitive guide to calling Roe using all types of call, with advice on their habits and habitat. Highly recommended. £7.99

Stag

The **FAULHABER STAG CALL (Hirschruf)** is a collapsible three-section instrument weighing only 100g and is 47cm long when fully extended. It has excellent acoustics and is unbreakable and weatherproof.
The detailed instruction sheet describes the various rutting calls and their proper use. £39.75

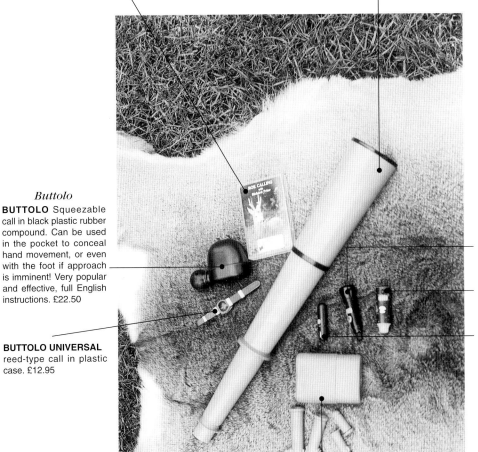

Buttolo

BUTTOLO Squeezable call in black plastic rubber compound. Can be used in the pocket to conceal hand movement, or even with the foot if approach is imminent! Very popular and effective, full English instructions. £22.50

BUTTOLO UNIVERSAL reed-type call in plastic case. £12.95

Hubertus calls

Famous Austrian calls, extremly popular. No instructions but simple to use, recommended by many professionals.

PLASTIC CALL, black, similar design to wooden. £15.00

CHERRYWOOD CALL, adjustable, with lanyard hole. £9.95

FIEP CALL, thumb-nail adjustable, plastic, in case £11.75

Faulhaber 4-call set

The complete **FAULHABER ROE DEER** Call set is the result of more than 20 years research into deer calls and consists of the following Calls in a convenient waterproof case.
THE DOE CALL (Fiep) imitates the mating call used to attract a Buck.
THE DOE'S LAMENT (Sprengfiep) is her call to attract a strong Buck.
THE CRY OF ANGUISH (Geschrei) imitates the cry of a Doe which is not yet receptive to the attentions of a rutting Buck.
THE FAWN'S DISTRESS CALL (Kitz) is used to attract a Doe and her accompanying Buck.

resort to bring the mother to the rescue.

The time to use these calls is during the rut, between about 20 July and the end of the first week in August, or slightly later. You are likely to get the best results on hot and humid days, when the air is still and thunder threatens, and during the early part of the rut when bucks are particularly responsive. You need not confine your attempts to call roe to early morning and late evening. Success is just as likely, and perhaps even more so, during the middle hours of the day. Tuck yourself away out of sight in cover, remain there quietly for a few minutes, and then blow.

In my early stalking days the classic wisdom on this subject was to blow three times on the doe call, then wait for a short time before blowing a further three calls. If this produced no reaction, after an interval of a few minutes the time would come to repeat the sequence using the *kitz* or kid call. One then waited twenty minutes before moving to some other location out of earshot of the first and going through the whole routine again.

This 'softly, softly' approach was blown wide apart some years ago when a Hungarian expert in the art, Dr Istvan Bertoti, was persuaded to come to Britain to show us how it should really be done. Armed with a battery of artificial calls, he led us in groups of half-a-dozen or more at a smart pace into the woods and there delivered a series of calls of the different kinds in rapid succession, rounding off, if all else failed, with the *geschrei* or panic scream as uttered by a kid in danger. Results, at least in most instances, were positively startling, with bucks materialising as if from nowhere like rabbits from a conjurer's hat.

Many who witnessed these demonstrations became almost instant experts in their own right, later passing on what they had learned to other stalkers in their turn. There are certainly many roe stalkers now who enjoy a high degree of success at calling up bucks. If you happen to know one of these people, your best plan by far is to ask him for some tuition, preferably in a field situation where its success can be proved.

If a buck responds to your call it is quite likely to come at a rush, so be prepared, with your rifle ready for instant action, if shooting is your intention. When it fails to find a receptive doe, it will pause for only a second or two before racing off back into cover.

However skilled you become with practice, you will not always be successful. Unseasonably cold, wet weather will dampen the ardour of many a buck, and those already attendant upon a doe in oestrus may show little interest in other apparent options. There are, however, exceptions. Hopeful of providing some entertainment for my then small son, while we were watching a rutting roe buck in the company of a doe on the far side of a fairly large forest clearing I attempted to distract it by simulating the harsh 'bough – bough' bark of a rival buck. The real-life buck reacted at once by approaching almost at a run from more than a quarter of a mile away to a point where it would have been well within easy shooting range if I had had a rifle with me. Not until it was quite satisfied that no rival was in fact present did it give up the quest and retire.

Once a buck has responded to a simulated doe call and failed to find a doe at the end of it, it will not be easily duped again, so do not spoil your future chances by indiscriminate calling. Maximise your success by getting to know your ground and its roe as thoroughly as possible well before the rutting season, and then, when the time comes, concentrate your calling within the territories of known bucks.

Having achieved success with roe, you may be tempted to experiment with calling other deer species – although here the art, if such it be, has fewer exponents to offer guidance. By using a cow horn as a sounding chamber, some have contrived to emit a sufficiently passable imitation of the rutting roar of a red deer stag to lure actual stags from the thickets to see off the apparent interloper. On one occasion I brought a fallow buck running to me from several hundred yards away by simulating the belching 'groan' of another buck in rut. There was also the time when, for the want of a better instrument, I blew on a blade of grass in lieu of a roe call and a fallow doe emerged at speed from cover to investigate. A stalker friend who annually calls up roe bucks in an area where there are also many fallow tells me that fallow does often respond, presumably out of mere curiosity – unless perhaps they believe that one of their own youngsters is calling.

Sika stags have been successfully lured into

the open by simulations of the characteristic rutting whistle of this species produced by squeakers extracted from children's toys. One eminent stalker was somewhat embarrassed when, having purchased such a toy, he had to hasten to a meeting of his local county council. The meeting was in progress when an inadvertent movement caused the squeaker in his coat pocket to give a loud and clear performance which rang out through the council chamber to the edification of all.

Will muntjac respond to calling? Until recently it was thought not, but in the March 1998 issue of *Stalking Magazine* David Barnes described how he had had some success at attracting muntjac bucks and does, and in particular at evoking a vocal response from these animals, by blowing on a variety of roe calls. He said that the best results were obtained by using the Buttolo universal call to emulate the distress cry of a roe and the not dissimilar cry of a muntjac doe in season. There is clearly plenty of scope here for extended experimentation!

If anyone has learned how to summon forth Chinese water deer by imitating their calls, the woodland stalking world at large has yet to hear how they go about this.

CHAPTER 22
Guest Stalkers

W hile it is true that many stalkers opt to 'do their own thing', on their own and without companions or assistance except under very special circumstances, few will decline an invitation to stalk as a guest on another's ground. There is also a special satisfaction in entertaining a guest stalker on one's own ground, perhaps in return for some favour given or simply to share with a kindred spirit some of the pleasure one has enjoyed there.

Any arrangement of this kind involves important responsibilities – to the property owner or tenant, to the deer and to yourself as the person with whom the buck is bound to stop should things go wrong for any reason. If you are paying for your stalking, the terms of your lease are likely to specify any restrictions concerning guest stalkers. Unless there are special circumstances which might make stalking guests unacceptable for some clearly defined reason, you will have been wise when the lease was drawn up to include provision for such guests, on a fee-paying basis or otherwise. Most leases are likely anyhow to allow for others besides yourself, under your supervision, to stalk on the ground, in effect passing responsibility to yourself for all such matters provided you and your guests operate within the parameters laid down to take full account of other interests and activities upon which stalking might impinge.

If you stalk on any ground basically to provide a service by way of controlling deer numbers; and so preventing them from becoming a local pest, and no money changes hands, obviously you should first obtain permission from the owner or occupier before you bring guest stalkers onto the property. To forestall any misunderstanding, make it clear that such a guest or guests will visit and operate solely under your personal supervision, and that they can render useful assistance in the overall objective of keeping deer numbers within bounds. Given such an assurance, no stalking landlord of my acquaintance has ever objected to my bringing a guest stalker onto his ground.

You will need to satisfy yourself that any guest with whom you have not previously stalked, and with whom you may not be fully familiar in other respects, is legally and otherwise well equipped to stalk on your ground and, hence, to shoot 'your' deer to a standard acceptable to you. Diplomatically point out that you are under an obligation to ensure that anyone stalking on the ground in question is fully insured against third party risks and has a valid firearm certificate, which he should be carrying anyway. A valid F.A.C., of course, is one which does not restrict the holder to specified properties which do not include your own ground. In short, he will need an open certificate, or one which he has had varied to include the right to stalk on ground where he will be your guest.

Express some interest in his rifle and what persuaded him to buy that particular model as well as what success he has had with it. If at all possible, make provision for him to fire a few test rounds at a target before he uses the rifle in earnest, thus satisfying both of you that the weapon is properly zeroed. It never ceases to amaze me how many stalkers of quite long experience are inclined to leave such matters to chance, taking it for granted that all is well without submitting it to the test after lengthy periods of inaction or after an accidental knock or a bumpy ride in a 4WD may have knocked the 'scope slightly askew.

On a first visit in particular, brief your guest on every detail and chaperone him throughout the stalk. If you are placing him in a high seat and it is large enough, share it with him; should it be a single-seater, tuck yourself away at the foot of it, having made it absolutely clear what may and may not be shot since you will not be alongside your guest to offer last-minute instructions. Above all, 'play it cool' and so help boost your guest's self-confidence. There are few things more unsettling to a guest stalker anxious to prove his worth than a nervy and agitated host: his mood can be all too infectious and put a guest thoroughly off his stroke.

Once you are fully satisfied that your guest needs no further shadowing and is adequately familiar with the layout of the land and with your expectations as host, by all means give him greater freedom. Unless it is clearly understood that guest stalkers may at all times be present to participate in deer culling, on every occasion make sure that the property owner or occupier, and the Gamekeeper if there is one, has prior knowledge of any visit by such stalkers, who should carry some means of identification confirming their right to be there.

Another category of guest is the trainee stalker, perhaps your son who may one day step into your shoes when you are 'past it'! This may well be a long way into the future; being subject to rather fewer physical hardships and tests of stamina than their open hill brethren in Scotland, many woodland stalkers carry on well into their eighties. However, infirmity may strike sooner, and it is especially satisfying to keep stalking in the family, being ready to hand over to the younger generation should necessity arise. It can sometimes be quite disconcerting to find how quick such pupils can be to grasp the essentials of the sport and turn the tables on their tutors in showing how to go about it!

In the case of a family member, first of all take him on a few outings to find out how keen he really is. Once you are satisfied that the desire to stalk is not just a passing whim and that your pupil is in earnest, he can apply for an F.A.C. permitting shared use of your rifle. When the time comes to have a rifle of his own he can apply for a variation of his F.A.C. to make this possible.

Close relative or otherwise, take time to guide your pupil through all the stages of stalker training, leading on to attendance at one of the courses organised by the B.D.S. and run by that body as well as by the B.A.S.C. to prepare candidates for submitting themselves to the standard test of proficiency resulting, hopefully, in the grant of the N.S.C.C.

What should paying guest stalkers be charged? In chapter 10, a breakdown is given of rates and conditions applicable to stalking clients of Forest Enterprise, and these are worth careful study as a general guide to the market in this area. Bear in mind, however, that Forest Enterprise charges are geared at least in part to the Continental market, and that stalkers from overseas have long been accustomed to paying much more for their sport than their British counterparts.

The advertisement columns of *Stalking Magazine* and the country sports press generally are also worth consulting as a guide to what others may be charging. If you accept paying guests you are clearly running a business and should keep appropriate records for tax purposes and otherwise. You should also make certain that your insurance cover is appropriate for these circumstances and that your stalking landlord incurs no additional liability. It also makes good sense that your client or clients should indemnify the property owner, tenant or other person responsible, as well as yourself as sub-lessor, against any injury, damage or loss incurred while on the property. Have a word with your legal adviser about this.

Client stalkers as well as those you may entertain on a friendly footing may well respond with invitations of their own. The grass may not always be greener but it is always a pleasure to take a peep on the other side of the fence or even, with very special good luck, on the other side of the Channel to see how the stalking scene looks there.

CHAPTER 23
Ethical Considerations

D eerstalking generates strong emotions. Success, especially in difficult circumstances or when it seems least likely, can induce a mood of euphoria which makes any earlier disappointment seem unimportant and can carry you along on the crest of a wave for some time afterwards. Recognise the mood for what it is, no more than a temporary uplift from the basic ruck of reality, and no harm need come of it. Allow it to make you over-confident by seemingly shedding a rosier light on your capabilities as a stalker, and you are liable to be brought down to earth with a bump in fairly short order.

Failure can have an equally potent effect on one's mood of the moment. After investing much time and effort, not to mention financial outlay, one would need to be superhuman not to hope for some reward in terms of ultimate satisfaction, no matter how well aware one may be that success can never be guaranteed and that the element of uncertainty is part of stalking's perennial appeal.

The same considerations apply of course in other field sports and in competitive sports of all kinds, but with stalking, or so it may seem to those of us who are bitten by the bug, they prevail with extra special force. Frustration and gloom are all the greater when something one could have influenced goes wrong. Self-criticism runs rampant and self-doubt can follow, sometimes fatally undermining one's confidence in one's own fundamental abilities.

So what has all this to do with ethics? It has everything to do with them, for the very simple reason that emotions in general, and the mood of the moment in particular, can have a devastating influence upon vital decision-making. We are all vulnerable to temptation. Equally, in our cooler moments, we recognise that decisions made under the influence of emotion are all too often bad decisions which would have been better deferred until we could bring some rational thinking to bear on whatever was under consideration at the time.

Unwise decisions can be taken in many different situations, all with ethical implications, so let us consider a few of these. So simple a matter as an ill-judged shot can create problems in several areas. Perhaps, towards the very end of a long and fruitless stalk, a tempting quarry presents itself at an awkward angle, at what you know is an excessive range, or in dense woodland where a clear, unobstructed view of the target zone on the animal is difficult to obtain. The deer is slowly moving away, the light is almost too poor for shooting and it is obvious that no better opportunity for a shot will present itself. Adrenalin is flowing freely, and the urge to take a slightly risky shot is very strong.

You let off the safety-catch and squeeze the trigger. The deer drops at once, and the gamble comes off. With your self-confidence over-inflated by this one-off chance achievement, you are likely to yield to similar temptations in the future, when the law of averages will be certain, in the end, to work against you. Whether failure comes sooner or later, the consequences are the same – an apparent miss about which you may never be quite convinced or, at worst, a crippled beast you may never recover. Someone to whom you may later have to give an account of the stalk may have heard the shot and will want to know what the result was, and if the answer is unsatisfactory your reputation will take a tumble. If no one else was within earshot you may think nobody need know, but the error will niggle at your conscience if you have any pretensions to being a responsible deer manager. Should you have lost a crippled deer, there is always the chance that others will find it, possibly still alive and in agony, so that the finger of suspicion will point unerringly at you.

'Bending the law' is another temptation to which some woodland stalkers are prone, perhaps by shooting out of season by a day or two, or by shooting from inside a vehicle when a cull has proved difficult to complete by other means. Accepting occasional invitations to use your rifle other than where an area-restricted F.A.C. permits may not seem, in itself, an unduly heinous breach of ethics, but is a foolish risk to take and is all too plainly irresponsible. As already mentioned in chapter 20 there may be special circumstances when, for example, a .22 rifle might be justifiably employed to put down an accident victim, but these must be judged with exceptional care.

Particularly hard to resist may be an offer of free or inexpensive stalking under the guise of essential deer control when common sense dictates that you already have as much as you can cope with in the time at your disposal. You may persuade yourself that somehow you will manage. In any case the offer, you feel, is far too good to turn down and so you bite off more than you can comfortably chew. All may seem to go well for a time, with some very enjoyable and successful stalks on new ground to your credit, but in the end something is bound to suffer – not least your good name as a deer manager. Once you take on responsibility for controlling the deer population on any specific piece of property, doing a satisfactory job of work there should be your prime consideration, no matter

what else you may have to sacrifice. Should you find it all too much because of competing claims on your time or for any other reason, do yourself and the deer a service by seeking help from another stalker or by handing over to somebody else.

Greed can be a besetting sin for some stalkers in other areas and negates the basic principles of responsible deer management. Chief among these, without much doubt, is the temptation to shoot quality heads to the total neglect of proper selective control. It is by no means unknown for a stalker to lease a tract of woodland for his purposes on a relatively short-term basis, shoot all the best heads himself or sub-let them to client stalkers, and then move on to repeat the process on another property. Hopefully, landowners eventually get wise to such individuals, put their name on a blacklist and pass the word around among their brethren.

Working mainly alone as they do, woodland stalkers are in a position of trust and any who fall short besmirch not only their own good name but that of stalking as a whole. Theirs is a sport which at all times demands the very highest standards of discipline, and this plainly means self-discipline in all possible circumstances.

CHAPTER 24
Public Relations

In an age when the lives of so many people are remoter than at any previous time from the realities of the countryside it should not be surprising that countryside sports in general are nowadays misunderstood by so many. While hound sports head the list of those which excite much public opposition, shooting sports too are in the firing line in more senses than one, and it can be only a matter of time before angling is subjected to the full force of condemnation orchestrated by the 'antis'.

As a shooting sport, stalking finds itself in a curious position from the standpoint of public opinion. Deerstalking conjures up archaic images of plutocratic participants lording it over the Scottish Highlands and over the lives of those who live there, manifesting itself as a more than vaguely distasteful activity for which there is no very clear justification, in economic terms or otherwise. The fact that the livelihood of significant numbers of people depends upon it escapes the notice of most strangers, while even less well understood is the need to cull Highland

Live capture of deer for translocation under licence can be excellent PR. Here netting is being unrolled for such an exercise around a cover to be driven.

red deer for their own sake as well as for that of the environment which supports them.

Most people are probably still unaware that woodland stalking takes place at all, still less that it is nowadays a sport attracting several thousand enthusiasts from literally all walks of life. Meeting somebody in the woods who is armed with a rifle instead of a shotgun, the average townsman enjoying a country ramble with his family might not at first recognise the difference. Should he do so, his reaction might be more than mere incomprehension – perhaps mild disquiet or incipient repugnance for what he may suppose to be gratuitous blood-letting. He may be horrified to realise that private citizens armed with such lethal weapons are still permitted to be at large in the British countryside. Dunblane and Hungerford are names which have impressed themselves indelibly upon the memory of the public as synonymous with the misuse of guns on a truly horrific scale, making some question whether anyone should be allowed to own such weapons.

In this climate of gross misunderstanding, woodland stalkers have the advantage that their activities go unnoticed by the world at large for

As part of good public relations the public need to be educated into keeping their dogs under proper control when being exercised in deer country. These twin roe kids were killed by a walker's dog in a West Sussex nature reserve.

When a deer runs into a net it is gently restrained, tied and masked to help minimise stress during subsequent movement.

In the bag! Dr Oliver Dansie, an expert on humane live capture, with a roe deer about to be removed to a safer haven following public anxiety about the wellbeing of deer in an area being encroached upon by development. In this case shooting as a solution would have caused much local offence.

most of the time. Even so, they are sometimes reminded that at least some members of the public are not entirely unaware of what goes on when a few of these people vent their hostility by vandalising high seats.

All this highlights the importance of maintaining good public relations. 'Least said, soonest mended' is a common attitude among stalkers who think it best to distance themselves from any debate about the subject, thus avoiding unwanted publicity and potential antagonism which can only damage their sport and their personal vested interest in it.

While there is much to be said for keeping a low profile and for carrying on one's stalking activities as unobtrusively as possible, there are occasions when one needs to meet misunderstanding head-on by explaining unequivocally what woodland stalking is all about. This need cause no embarrassment because no outdoor activity involving the use of firearms could be easier to justify. Point out that deer, like rabbits and many others, including the antelopes of Africa are natural prey species which, in the absence of predators such as the brown bear, wolf and lynx to keep their numbers within bounds would increase by as much as one-third each year, soon eating themselves out of house and home and causing serious crop damage.

Explain how this necessitates man taking the place of extinct predators by culling a predetermined number of deer of both sexes each year. What many non-shooters find particularly hard to accept is that female deer, especially pregnant ones, need to be shot under any circumstances. It therefore needs to be made clear that by culling male deer only and leaving the females, an unbalanced and ever-increasing deer population would be the result, and that culling of females is carefully timed so as not to orphan dependent youngsters. Stress, moreover, that the object of all deer culling is a clean and instant death, causing no suffering to the animal, and invite your audience to compare this with what happens where natural predation is the main determinant of prey numbers, as they are likely to have witnessed on their television screens.

When discussing the public safety angle, highlight the supreme importance placed upon

Roe quickly become quiescent when immobilised and masked.

this in all stalker training, explain that you have undergone such training either formally or otherwise, and point out the specific steps you take to ensure that human life is never in danger from what you do.

It has to be borne in mind that the thought processes of humans tend to be governed by a fine balance between reason and emotion. Emotion is dominant in some to the extent that no amount of carefully reasoned explanation will overcome an instinctive aversion to killing in any shape or form. 'What right have you to play God to these creatures?' I was asked by one such person, a country-dweller whose ire had been roused by deer culling on the property of a neighbour near his home. In the end you can only agree to differ in your respective views on the matter and do your reasonable best to avoid any future confrontation with an individual like this.

At another level are those non-shooters who reluctantly accept the rationale of deer management as explained by someone like yourself, but whose distaste for any personal involvement in taking the life of a wild animal will keep them at a distance from the nuts and bolts of so disagreeable a business.

So at all times be discreet, taking great care not to offend the sensitivities of others either by your attitude or by any other aspect of your activities. Do your best to keep on good terms with everyone on the properties where you stalk, with stalking neighbours (if at all possible!) and with anyone whose goodwill might prove an asset in the future, either to yourself or to woodland stalking as a whole. None of us needs enemies; woodland stalkers least of all, in the hypersensitive world of today.

Glossary

This is a selective checklist of terms relating to deer and to woodland stalking. Archaic terms which are rarely used now have for the most part been omitted but some which may be worth reviving are included. Other terms and their meanings are listed which have no direct bearing on stalking as such but may help to present a broader picture of deer in Britain and their environment. No apology is made for including some terms which may be familiar to most readers but less so to some others, especially complete newcomers.

Albino. An organism lacking the pigmentation which produces normal external body colour, resulting in white hair and pink eyes among other characteristics in deer and other animals thus affected

Anal tush. A common misnomer for the tail-like tuft of white or whitish hair below the vaginal orifice of roe does, which is prominently visible when these deer are in winter pelage and readily distinguishes them from bucks which have cast their antlers

Antlers. Bony appendages regrown annually on the heads of male deer of most species. Female reindeer and caribou and sometimes, abnormally, female deer of other species, especially roe, also grow antlers. The deciduous character of antlers is what primarily distinguishes them from horns such as those grown by antelopes, cattle, goats and sheep, which are retained throughout life

Ballistics. The interaction of firearms, explosives and ammunition and its study

Bare buck. A four-year-old fallow buck

Bark. The alarm or challenge call uttered in mutually distinctive forms by deer of many species

Barrel. The part of a gun or rifle through which projectiles are discharged and set on course to reach a target

Bay tine. See *bez tine*

Beam. The stem or trunk of an antler

Beat. An area of ground for which an individual gamekeeper or forester is responsible

Beating up. In forestry, replacing young trees in a plantation which have failed in a previous planting

Bell. Poetic term for the rutting call of a red deer stag

Bez (bay) tine. Branch of a red deer's antler between the first (brow) tine and the third (trez or tray) tine; bez tines are sometimes absent

Bifurcation. Abnormal dividing of a branch or tine of an antler, producing one or more subsidiary tines

Bipod. A two-legged support enabling a rifle to be aimed and fired with greater steadiness and accuracy from the prone position

Bole-scoring. Forestry damage sometimes caused by sika stags gouging the boles of trees with the brow tines of their antlers, usually as part of their rutting activity

Bolt. A sliding lever by means of which rounds of ammunition are loaded into the firing chamber of a rifle and are subsequently extracted, live or spent

Bolt-action rifle. A rifle in which rounds of ammunition are manually loaded with a bolt rather than being automatically fed into an empty firing chamber; bolt-action, single shot and 'Blaser' or double-barrelled rifles are the only ones now legally permissible for shooting deer in the United Kingdom and the Republic of Ireland

Bore. The interior of a gun or rifle barrel

Brashing. Removing side branches ('brash') as the first stage of thinning young trees in a forestry plantation

Brocket. A one-year-old red or sika stag, sometimes also called a pricket

Brow tine. The first branch of a deer's antler, immediately above the coronet

Browsing. The action by a herbivorous animal of eating buds, leaves or other parts of a tree or shrub, as distinct from grazing (feeding on ground herbage); where deer are numerous a distinct 'browse line' at deer's head height is often visible in plantations

Buck. Among British wild deer, the male of Chinese water deer, fallow deer, muntjac or roe deer. In ancient forest nomenclature the term was applied more specifically to a five-year-old fallow buck

Bull's eye. A black circular area at the centre of a range shooting target, often abbreviated to 'the bull'

Burnishing. The action by a male deer of cleaning velvet from newly grown antlers

Burr. The base of an antler beneath the coronet

Butt. The part of a rifle held against the shoulder when taking aim and firing

Butts. Rifle range area where targets are placed

Calf. Among British wild deer, a young red or sika deer in its first year

Calibre. The diameter of the firing chamber and inside bore of a rifle barrel which determines the size of ammunition to be used

Call. An implement for simulating vocal emissions by a deer for the purpose of luring it to a human observer

Canopy. The merging crowns of mature trees in a forestry plantation

Cartridge. The cylindrical envelope housing a bullet or other projectile(s) and the components for firing these

Cast.   To shed an antler prior to growing a replacement; a cast antler

Catch-up.   The live capture of deer, usually by narcotic-darting or driving them into nets

Chamber.   The area directly to the rear of a rifle barrel into which a round of ammunition (cartridge) is introduced ready for firing

Cleaning rod.   An implement for introducing brushes and other cleaning materials into the bore of a rifle

Cleaning.   See *Burnishing*

Clear felling.   Removal of all standing timber from an area of woodland

Close season.   A designated period of time during which deer of a specified species and/or sex may not legally be shot

Close time.   The nocturnal period (in the United Kingdom, between one hour after sunset and one hour before sunrise) when deer may not legally be shot

Compartment.   A section of woodland, usually bounded by rides or other conspicuous features setting it visually apart from other compartments, separately identified for purposes of forest management

Conservation.   The management of habitat and wildlife on a sustained, ongoing basis by means of human intervention

Coppice.   An area of woodland in which underwood such as hazel or chestnut is harvested in rotation (i.e. coppiced), leaving the stools in place for natural regrowth to follow

Coronet.   The raised rim of an antler immediately above its base

Couch.   An area of flattened herbage or bare ground where a deer has rested

Coupe.   In forestry, a basic unit of management such as an even-aged stand of trees of a particular species within a compartment; usually a sub-compartment although sometimes a coupe may extend to a whole compartment

Cover.   Trees, shrubs or other growth providing concealment, shelter and seclusion for wildlife

Covert.   An area of woodland or other cover providing harbourage for game or, sometimes, foxes

Creep.   A worn area where deer have passed under a fence or other obstacle

Crotties.   Heaps of fewmets (deer droppings)

Crown.   The cluster of points around the tip of a fully developed red deer antler; also called a cup

Cull.   The killing of deer or other animals in order to reduce numbers, to eliminate undesirable elements or to achieve some other predetermined objective

Cup.   See *Crown*

Deer drive.   The unselective mass-destruction of deer by being driven by beaters to individuals armed with shotguns, often resulting in many animals being wounded but not recovered; an inhumane and largely outmoded method of deer control once almost universally practised in the United Kingdom in woodland areas

Deer forest.   A term applied, particularly in Scotland, to an area of uncultivated ground, usually hilly or mountainous and often sparsely wooded or even treeless, set aside primarily for deer and for deerstalking 'open hill' style

Deer larder.   Enclosed accommodation for the storage and butchering of deer carcases

Deer lawn.   An open area, usually in woodland, where deer are encouraged to graze and where they are thus made more accessible for observation and culling

Dew claws.   The two rear cleaves or 'toes' of the hoof of a deer or other cloven-hoofed mammal, often imprinted only on soft ground by a deer in motion

Doe.   Among British wild deer, the female of Chinese water deer, fallow deer, muntjac or roe deer

Entry.   A gap made by deer when passing through close cover or when circumventing an obstacle

Fawn.   Among British wild deer, the young of a Chinese water deer, fallow deer or muntjac under one year old

Fewmets.   Individual deer droppings

Final crop.   In forestry, mature trees harvested at the final felling of a particular forest crop

Firearm certificate.   A document issued by police to authorise ownership and use of a specified firearm or firearms by a specified individual or individuals in specified circumstances

Foil.   The track of a deer through grass or other herbage

Fore end.   The front portion of the stock of a rifle

Fraying.   Tree damage resulting from a deer using the tree concerned to rub off the dead velvet from its newly grown antlers

Fraying-stock.   Sapling, branch or other object against which a male deer rubs its newly matured antlers to remove dead velvet and set scent

Gait.   A mammal's style of locomotion, e.g. walking, cantering, running or galloping

Going back.   Used to describe a male deer past its prime, with antlers of declining quality

Gorget.   An area of pale coloration around the throat, apparent in some roe in winter pelage

Gralloch.   To eviscerate a deer; the viscera of a deer once removed

Grass.   To 'render a deer into possession' by shooting it; the term is mainly used in connection with red deer stalking in Scotland

Grazing.   Feeding on grass or other ground herbage, as opposed to browsing, which is feeding on the buds, foliage or other parts of trees or shrubs

Great buck.   In ancient forest terminology, a fallow buck six years old or more and at its pinnacle of development

Groan.   The characteristic, belch-like call uttered by a fallow buck during the rut

Gutters.   Linear indentations in the main beam of an antler

Harbouring.   The traditional method by which a 'harbourer' locates a suitable deer for hunting with hounds prior to a meet of the pack concerned

Hart. Alternative term for a red deer stag, now little used except on the Atholl estates in the Scottish Highlands. As anciently employed, the term usually applied to a stag of particularly high quality

Havier. A castrated male deer

Head. An alternative name for a potential or actual trophy of a deer, i.e. 'a head of antlers'

Heel trail. The trail of a deer followed in a reverse direction from that in which the deer moved

High forest. Mature woodland with a closed canopy

High seat. An elevated seat from which to observe or shoot deer; a development of the *hochsitz* and *hochstand* originated in Germany for shooting deer and boar in woodland

Hind. Among British wild deer, the female of red or sika deer

Home range. The area within which an individual deer normally lives and travels but which it does not defend, often coinciding with or overlapping the range of other deer of the same species

Horn. A bony outgrowth from the skull of e.g. a cow, goat, sheep or antelope, not deciduous like an antler but lasting a lifetime; not an acceptable alternative term for 'antler'

Hummel. A male red deer which fails to grow antlers but is otherwise normal; half-hummels with an antler on one side only also occur

Inner. In range shooting, the innermost of three white rings encircling the bull's eye on a target

Jag. The ribbed metal attachment to a rifle cleaning rod around which a cleaning patch ('four-by-two' in military parlance) is wrapped for insertion into the bore

Keyholing. The abnormal action of a bullet in striking its target sideways after a tumbling, irregular flight, due either to faulty ammunition or to having been fired through a badly worn rifle barrel

Kid. Young roe deer under one year old

Knobber. Young male deer with short, single-spike antlers

Lands. Divisions between rifling grooves in the bore of a rifle barrel

Lair. Where a deer lies down. (A red deer 'harbours' and is 'unharboured', a fallow deer 'lodges' and is 'roused', and a roe deer 'beds' and is 'dislodged', according to the traditional terms for identifying these activities)

Ligging. See *lair*

Magazine. The part of a stalking rifle in which ammunition is stored before being fed by bolt action into the firing chamber

Magpie. In range shooting, the middle one of three white rings encircling the bull's eye on a target

Management. The control and care of deer and their habitat along systematic lines

Mean point of impact (M.P.I.). In range shooting, the median point on a target between the positions of impact of three individual rounds of ammunition fired in succession for rifle zeroing purposes

Melanistic. Predominantly black or very dark in coloration as in the case of the black variety of fallow deer. Black roe also occur, but are extremely rare in Britain

Menil. Colour variety of fallow deer characterised by light overall coloration, with white dappling on the flanks especially prominent and a feature of both summer and winter pelage

Misprint. Hoofmarks of a deer in which the imprints of a hind hoof fail to be superimposed precisely over the imprints of the fore hoof on the same side of the animal; a hind hoof consistently misprinting to the rear of a fore hoof is characteristic of an ageing animal

Monopod. A single-legged support

Moving deer to rifles. A co-ordinated means of enhancing a cull, especially of female deer in winter, whereby one, two or possibly more 'rifles' (stalkers) wait in ambush while a similarly small number of individuals quietly walk through cover where deer are likely to be present, with a view to disturbing them sufficiently to move them past the rifles, who are thus provided with opportunities for selective shooting. This type of operation is in no way comparable to the random mass slaughter and wounding so often inflicted by the drives to shotguns so often practised in the past

Murderer. A mature roe buck with single-spike antlers bereft of tines and therefore easily capable of inflicting mortal injury on a rival buck when fighting

Muzzle energy (M.E.). The force exerted by a bullet at the moment of leaving a rifle, measured in foot/pounds or joules

Muzzle velocity (M.V.). The speed of a bullet at the moment of leaving a rifle, measured in feet or metres per second

Natural regeneration. The natural regrowth of trees from seed dropped by adjacent parent trees following the felling of mature timber in a forestry plantation

Nott. A traditional term used in south-west England for what in Scotland is called a hummel – an otherwise normal red deer stag which fails to grow antlers

Nurse trees. Fast-growing trees, usually conifers, interplanted with slower-growing ones (especially broadleaved trees such as oak and beech) to help provide initial shelter and a subsequent earlier timber crop as the slower-growing trees approach maturity

Offer. A bony projection from the beam of an antler too small to rate as a tine; traditionally, if binoculars could not be hung by their strap from such a projection, it was not a tine

Outer. In range shooting, the outer one of three white rings encircling the bull's eye on a target

Pace. The speed of movement by a deer as indicated by the length of step or stride as the trail of an unseen animal is followed

Paint. A local term for blood splashes from a wounded deer on the ground or vegetation

Palm. The broad, flattened upper portion of a mature fallow buck's antler

Parallax. The optical distortion of an image viewed through a telescopic sight

Parcel. A Scottish Highland term for a group of red deer, e.g. 'a parcel of hinds'

Pass. A point where deer regularly cross a river or surmount some other obstacle

Pattern. The relative placement of hoofprints in a trail, indicative of changes of gait, if any

Pearling. Knobbly extrusions along the antlers of a roe buck or other male deer, on the main beam in particular; heavy pearling is characteristic of the trophy of a mature, top-quality buck

Pedicle. The stem erupting from the skull from which an antler develops and grows

Pelage. The coat of a deer, which varies seasonally in colour and texture

Peruque. The grotesquely abnormal development of antlers into the semblance of the type of wig known as a 'peruque', usually as a consequence of injury to the reproductive organs

Pizzle. The penis of a deer; one of a number of deer by-products used in Oriental medicine

Pollarding. A local term for antler casting

Pole crop. A forestry plantation in the early stages of thinning

Pricket. A one-year-old fallow buck, usually with short, single-spike antlers. See also *Brocket*

Pullthrough. A length of cord with a weighted end and a loop or loops at the other end for the attachment of cleaning materials to pull through the bore of a rifle

Rack. A track made by deer when passing through vegetation. In forestry, a track cut through a young plantation to facilitate extraction

Range. In stalking, the distance between the person firing a rifle and the target, now usually measured in metres

Register. The action of a moving deer in placing a hind hoof precisely on the spot vacated by the fore hoof on the same side, thus leaving a single imprint

Ride. A route of access through a forestry plantation, originally mainly for equestrian use and timber extraction by horses as well as to serve as a firebreak

Rifle. A gun with a rifled bore designed to fire a single projectile to which the rifling gives a spin for the purpose of stabilising its flight. In stalking, the term is also used to denote an appropriately armed participant, as in 'two rifles will be on the ground today'

Riflescope. See *Telescopic sight*

Rifling. The spiralling grooves within the bore of a rifle barrel

Ring. 'Roe rings' are circular tracks in woodland vegetation, field crops or other herbage made by roe deer during the rut, when a buck commonly circles in the wake of a doe in season prior to

mating; these rings sometimes develop into figures of eight. 'Play rings' also occur, especially where fallow deer congregate and fawns may be present in the group

Roar. The characteristic challenge call of a rutting red deer stag. In New Zealand the red deer rutting season is commonly known as 'the roar'

Royal. A red deer stag with a total of twelve points on its antlers, preferably six on each antler. Subsidiary tines within the crown or cup of such antlers are traditionally known as 'sur-royals'

Rubbing. The action of a deer in marking its territory by rubbing its antlers and the scent glands on its forehead against a sapling or other vegetation. The term is also applied to the action of shedding its winter coat by rubbing it off against a tree or other object

Rut. The mating season of deer, varying in time and length between individual species

Rutting stand. The location where a stag or buck takes up its stand for rutting purposes

Safety-catch. A thumb-operated safety control on a rifle which, when applied to the 'safe' position, prevents accidental discharge of a round of ammunition

Sanctuary. Designated area(s) within deer-populated ground where no shooting ever takes place

Scrape. A patch of ground scraped bare by deer for territorial marking purposes by setting scent from interdigital glands and sometimes, additionally, by urinating

'Scope mounts. Accessories fitted to a rifle as points of attachment for a telescopic sight

Selective shooting. A policy of culling specific deer or categories of deer to the exclusion of others in pursuance of a predetermined plan

Shooting-stick. A combined walking-stick and seat, designed basically for the covert shooting of driven pheasants and other winged game but useful also as a readily portable 'low seat' for a woodland stalker waiting in ambush wherever the need of the moment suggests as a likely place to intercept deer as they emerge from cover

Signs. Ground evidence and other visual indications in general as to the identity and activities of deer as they have moved around their habitat

Single. A traditional term for the tail of a deer

Sling. A carrying strap for a rifle

Slot. The hoofmark of a deer in soft ground; also sometimes applied to the foot of a deer

Snag. A miniscule bony projection from the beam of an antler, smaller than an offer

Sore. A three-year-old fallow buck

Sorel. A two-year-old fallow buck

Speculum. The white or light-coloured rump patch of a deer, also called a target

Spellers. Spiky projections along the rear edge of the palm of a fallow antler

Splay. The spread of the cleaves of a slot, especially apparent in very soft ground and where deer have been moving at speed

Stag. Among British wild deer, a male red or sika deer

Stalk. To track a deer stealthily, moving on foot; an outing for this purpose. By common consent, the term 'stalking' also applies to still-hunting (shooting from a predetermined location), especially in woodland situations

Stalking-stick. A long stick, ideally almost head-high to the stalker, for steadying the rifle when shooting while standing upright with no alternative means of support for the purpose

Step. The distance between one hoofprint and the next imprinted by hooves on opposite sides

Stock. The wooden or plastic frame of a rifle or shotgun on to which the metal action elements are fixed when the weapon is assembled

Stool. The remaining stump of a tree or shrub after felling

Stride. the distance between successive imprints of the same hoof

Stripping. Forestry damage caused by deer stripping off tree bark with their teeth, exposing the tree to disease and jeopardising its future value as timber

Sway. A conspicuous lateral deviation between the imprints of left and right hooves in the trail of a deer, usually indicative of an ageing beast or a heavily pregnant female

Target. See *speculum*

Taxidermy. The craft of preparing, stuffing and mounting the skins of animals, or of parts of animals, to simulate attitudes when alive

Telescopic sight. A magnifying optic for attachment to a rifle to enhance the visual image of a target and to help in aligning the rifle accurately with that target. These sights are 'telescopic' only in the sense of being monocular, and are perhaps better termed 'riflescopes', the term generally used in this book

Territory. An area of ground dominated by one mature male deer and defended by that male against incursions by rival males, as commonly happens with roe bucks when in hard antler

Thicket. In forestry, a young plantation which has grown to the stage of forming dense cover which has still to undergo any thinning

Tine. Any one of the various branches from the main beam of an antler

Tops. The tines of a red deer antler above the trez tine and forming the crown or cup of the antler

Trade. The ground signs of deer activity in general

Trail. Hoofmarks and associated signs of a deer's passage

Trajectory. The path followed by a bullet after leaving the rifle and before reaching a target

Tray tine. See *trez tine*

Trez (tray) tine. The third tine above the coronet on a fully developed red deer antler; the bez tine is sometimes absent, making the trez tine the second tine

Trigger. The spring-loaded control on a rifle to which a forefinger is applied and squeezed to fire a round of ammunition when the safety-catch is released

Trigger guard. A protective metal surround beneath the trigger

Trophy. The head, skull or part of a skull of a male deer with antlers attached. Trophy-hunting as a prime objective is counter-productive to sound deer management

Tufters. Specially trained hounds employed in stag- and buck-hunting to locate and separate from its companions a deer selected for hunting before the main pack is 'laid on'

Underplanting. In forestry, the practice of planting young trees under older ones in a plantation to provide an eventual successor crop

Variety. A distinctive type of plant or animal within a given species; for example, black, common, menil and white fallow deer are all varieties of one species

Velvet. The combination of skin, hair, blood vessels and other elements which nourishes and protects growing antlers and which dies and is rubbed off when antler growth is complete

Venison. Muscle tissue and other elements forming the edible flesh of deer

Wallow. A patch of moist and muddy ground where red or sika stags 'go to soil', wallowing and rolling, especially during the rut

Waster. A deer in poor physical condition which looks unlikely to improve

Whistle. The characteristic rutting call of a sika stag, most often uttered in a succession of three whistles followed by an interval of silence

White fallow deer. A colour variety of fallow which looks superficially white but has a buffish tinge to the pelage which is most pronounced in fawns; such fallow are not albinos and retain full pigmentation in the eyes

Yeld. An adult female deer (especially a red deer) which fails to produce a calf, fawn or kid in any one year but may well do so the following year

Zeroing. The process of correctly aligning the line of sight (L.O.S.) of a riflescope or telescopic sight with the point at which a bullet can be expected to strike a target at a predetermined range

Useful Addresses

England, Wales and Scotland

British Association for Shooting and Conservation (B.A.S.C.), Marford Mill, Rossett, Wrexham LL12 0HL. Tel: 01244 573000.

British Deer Society (B.D.S.), Burgate Manor, Fordingbridge, Hants. SP6 1EF. Tel: 01425 655434.

Countryside Alliance, The Old Town Hall, 367 Kennington Road, London SE11 4PT. Tel: 0171 5825432.

Countryside Council for Wales (C.C.W.), Plas Penrhos, Ffordd Penrhos, Bangor, Gwynedd LL57 2LQ. Tel: 01248 385500.

Deer Commission for Scotland (D.C.S.) (formerly Red Deer Commission), 82 Fairfield Road, Inverness IV3 5LH. Tel: 01463 231751.

English Nature, Northminster House, Peterborough, Cambs. PE1 1UA. Tel: 01733 455000.

Forest Enterprise, North and East England Regional Office, 1A Grosvenor Terrace, York YO3 7BD. Tel: 01904 620221.

Forest Enterprise, North Scotland Regional Office, 21 Church Street, Inverness IV1 1EL. Tel: 01463 232811.

Forest Enterprise, South and West England Regional Office, Avon Fields House, Somerdale, Keynsham, Bristol BS18 2BD. Tel: 01272 869481.

Forest Enterprise, South Scotland Regional Office, 55/57 Moffat Road, Dumfries DG1 1NP. Tel: 01387 272440.

Forestry Commission, 231 Corstorphine Road, Edinburgh EH12 7AT. Tel: 0131 3340303.

Institute for Terrestrial Ecology (I.T.E.), National Environmental Research Council (N.E.R.C.), Monks Wood, Abbot's Ripton, Huntingdon, Cambs. PE17 2LS. Tel: 01487 773381.

Scottish Natural Heritage (S.N.H.), 12 Hope Terrace, Edinburgh EH9 2AS. Tel: 0131 4474784.

Stationery Office (formerly Her Majesty's Stationery Office), Publications Centre, P.O. Box 276, London SW8 5DQ. Tel: 0171 8739090.

Northern Ireland

Northern Ireland Deer Society. Hon. Secretary: John Hetherington, Camgart, Clabby, Fivemiletown, Co. Tyrone BT75 0RL. Tel: 013 655 21752.

Northern Ireland Department of Agriculture (Forestry Division), Dundonald House, Newtownards Road, Belfast BT4 3SB. Tel: 01232 520100.

Royal Ulster Constabulary (Firearms Licensing Branch), Lisnasharagh, 42 Montgomery Road, Belfast BT6 9LD. Tel: 01232 650222.

Republic of Ireland

Department of Justice (Firearms Section), 72/76 St Stephen's Green, Dublin 2. Tel: 01 6028202.

Office of Public Works (O.P.W.), National Parks and Wildlife Service, 51 St Stephen's Green, Dublin 2. Tel: 01 6613111.

Wicklow Deer Group. Chairman: L.M. Nolan, 14 Sefton Park, Rochestown Avenue, Dun Laoghaire, Co. Dublin. Tel: 01 2350598.

Note: The initials shown in brackets after names of organisations listed above are commonly used abbreviations for those names.

Further Reading

M any books on deer and related matters have been published in recent decades and any or all of the following are recommended for further reading.

Alcock, Ian (1993) *Stalking Deer in Great Britain*. Shrewsbury: Swan Hill Press.

Alcock, Ian (1996) *Deer: A Personal View*. Shrewsbury: Swan Hill Press.

Bradley Taylor, Michael (ed.) (1996) *Wildlife Crime: A Guide to Wildlife Law Enforcement in the U.K.* London: The Stationery Office.

British Deer Society (1996) *Basic Deer Management*. Fordingbridge: British Deer Society.

Chapman, Norma and Stephen Harris (1996) *Muntjac*. Fordingbridge: British Deer Society.

Dalton, Diane and Nicholas (1991) *The Venison Cook.*: Crowood Press.

Dansie, Oliver, Arnold Cooke and Lynne Farrell (1983) *Muntjac and Chinese Water Deer*. Fordingbridge: British Deer Society.

Delap, Peter (1970) *Fallow Deer*. Fordingbridge: British Deer Society.

Delap, Peter (1970) *Red Deer*. Fordingbridge: British Deer Society.

Delap, Peter (1970) *Roe Deer*. Fordingbridge: British Deer Society.

De Nahlik, A.J. (1992) *Management of Deer and Their Habitat: Principles and Methods*. Gillingham, Dorset: Wilson Hunt.

Eicke, Ernst, Robert Konig and John A. Willett (eds) (1995) *Sika*: Cervus Nippon *Temminck, 1838* (two volumes). Mohnesee: International Sika Society. Available from Ernst Eicke, Internationale Arbeitsgemeinschaft Sikawild, Kurkolner Strasse 13, 4173 Mohnesee 1, Germany.

Fawcett, John K. (1997) *Roe Deer*. Fordingbridge: British Deer Society.

Frost, David (1995) *Sporting Firearms and the Law*. London: British Field Sports Society.

Garbutt, Jane (1993) *Cooking with Venison*. Devizes: Hillworth Publications.

Horwood, M.T. and E.H. Masters (1970) *Sika Deer*. Fordingbridge: British Deer Society.

Prior, Richard (1993) *Deer Watch*. Shrewsbury: Swan Hill Press.

Prior, Richard (1994) *Trees and Deer*. Shrewsbury: Swan Hill Press.

Prior, Richard (1995) *The Roe Deer: Conservation of a Native Species*. Shrewsbury: Swan Hill Press.

Ratcliffe, P.R. and B.A. Mayle (1992) *Roe Deer Biology and Management: Forestry Commission Bulletin 105*. London: The Stationery Office.

Springthorpe, G. and N.G. Myhill (eds.) (1994) *Wildlife Ranger's Handbook*. London: Forestry Commission/The Stationery Office.

Taylor Page, F.J. (ed.) (1982) *Field Guide to British Deer*. Oxford: Blackwell Scientific Publications for the British Deer Society.

Wallace, Guy (1994) *Training Dogs for Woodland Deer Stalking*. Brecon: Fawley Publications.

Wallace, Guy (1995) *The Versatile Gun Dog: Handling HPRs for Gun, Rifle and Hawk*. (1995): The Sportsman's Press.

Whitehead, G. Kenneth (1993) *The Whitehead Encyclopedia of Deer*. Shrewsbury: Swan Hill Press.

Whitehead, G. Kenneth (1996) *Half a Century of Scottish Deer Stalking*. Shrewsbury: Swan Hill Press.

Regulations governing the handling and preparation of wild game for human consumption have been tightened considerably in recent years and the following advise on what is expected of those involved with deer and venison.

The Culling and Processing of Wild Deer (1989) John Adams and Norman Dannatt. Arun District Council/Forestry Commission. Arun District Council Directorate of Environment, Tourism and Leisure, Maltravers Road, Littlehampton, West Sussex BN17 5LF.

The Food Safety (General Food Hygiene) Regulations 1995. The Stationery Office.

The Food Safety (General Food Hygiene) Regulations (Northern Ireland) 1995. The Stationery Office.

LACOTS 1997 Food Safety Hazard Analysis. Guidance on securing compliance with the hazard analysis requirement, Regulation 4(3). LACOTS Croydon.

The Wild Game Meat (Hygiene and Inspection) Regulations 1995). The Stationery Office.

Index